TABLE OF CONTENTS.

Please note that these subject headings are approximate. Books dealing with multiple subjects are repeated under each appropriate heading.

GLYPTIC ARTS: From Page:

Cylinder Seals - Stamp Seals 3
Eastern - Phoenician Gems 14
Egyptian Scarabs 19
Minoan - Mycenaean Gems and Vessels 21
Greek Gems, incl. Graeco-Persian and Cypriot 26
Etruscan Gems 33
Roman Gems, incl. "Gnostic" Gems 37
Sasanian Gems 46
Byzantine Gems and Mediaeval Seals 49
Renaissance and Later Gems 51

JEWELRY - OBJECTS - TECHNOLOGY - TEXTS - VARIA:

Egyptian Jewelry... 55
Near Eastern - Phoenician Jewelry 57
Greek Jewelry 62
Etruscan Jewelry 69
Roman Jewelry 72
Finger Rings, all periods 80
Byzantine Jewelry and Silver Objects 85
Prehistoric European Jewelry 90
Mediaeval, Anglo Saxon and Dark Ages Jewelry 94
Sasanian Jewelry - Silver Vessels 101
Islamic Gems and Jewelry 102
Ethnic Jewelry 106
Amber 112
Beads 113
Ancient "Kleinkunst" - Metal Vessels - Objects 118
Renaissance and Later Jewelry 128
Technology - Ancient Texts - Varia 139

Please note:

INDEX OF AUTHORS on pages 150-155.

INDEX OF MUSEUMS AND INSTITUTIONS on pages 156-158

INTRODUCTION

This list, our seventh, offers another selection of our stock of both out-of-print and recently published titles dealing with most aspects of the glyptic arts and goldsmithing.

Substantially, all books listed are either in stock - though some in single copies - or are known to be in print at the time this list is issued. In order to increase the usefulness of this bibliography, a few out-of-print books sold just before press time are still listed. Because we reasonably expect to obtain additional copies in the future, orders for these books will be accepted and a quote will be sent once another copy is secured. Requests will be filled on a first order basis.

Also, many of our regular clients know that we are able to obtain single copies of most of the more obscure books dealing with our subjects. Therefore, do not hesitate to request titles not listed or to send us your "want-list".

We frequently get requests for specific title- and bibliographic information about specialized topics; therefore, if you are publishing in any one of our fields and would like to increase your intended audience, we are willing to include such information in a targeted advance mailing to interested parties, or on our next regular list.

The recent computerizing of our inventory, as well as of our personal library of more than 3000 titles dealing with engraved gems and jewelry, allows us to provide precisely tailored bibliographies on these subjects. Because this is an ongoing project, we welcome any information on obscure publications that should be entered into this databank. Likewise, we are always willing to print a specialized bibliography for research projects for a nominal fee. Photocopies of specific sections of non-copyrighted books can also be provided. Please write for details.

Librarians please note, whenever known we have entered ISBN numbers into our databank; titles may be requested by ISBN number or by using other generally accepted cataloguing data. Details available upon request.

If this bibliography is of no interest to you, please notify us so that we may delete your name from our mailing list. Additional copies of this list will gladly be provided upon request.

We are always looking for books to buy, single copies or entire libraries are always welcome, please write for additional information.

Finally, in addition to books describing gems and jewelry, we also carry an inventory of the objects themselves; we are always pleased to send photographs and gem-impressions to institutions and serious collectors interested in the purchase of ancient preciosa.

Cylinder Seals - Stamp Seals

703.682 Amiet, P. Musée Lavigerie
Les Intailles Orientales de la Collection Henri de Genouillac conservées au Musée Departemental des Antiquités de Seine-Maritime à Rouen. (Cahiers de Byrsa, vol. VII, 1957). Carthage, 1957. 21.5 x 27. 38 pp., 22 pls. Paper. $12.50
Publishes and illustrates 120 cylinder seals, the personal collection of this scholar of early glyptics.

20.1 Amiet, P.
Notes sur le Répertoire Iconographique de Mari à l'Époque du Palais. (Syria, vol. XXXVII, 1960). 28 x 22.5. 17 pp., 13 figs. Paper. $7.50

21.2 Amiet, P.
La Glyptique de Mari à l'Époque du Palais, note additionelle. (Syria, vol.XXXVIII, 1961). 28 x 22.5. 6 pp., 8 figs. Paper. $3.50

22.3 Amiet, P.
La Glyptique Syrienne Archaïque. (Syria, vol. XL, 1963). 28 x 22.5. 26 pp., 2 pls., 31 figs. Paper. $16.00
Describes Mesopotamian influence on Syrian seals.

23.4 Amiet, P.
Cylindres Syriens Présargoniques. (Syria, vol. XLI, 1964). 28 x 22.5. 55 pp., 1 pl., 4 figs. Paper. $4.00

24.5 Amiet, P.
Les Intailles Orientales de la Collection Chavanne à Tunis. (Mélanges de Carthage, 1964-65). 26 x 21. 10 pp., 2 pls. Paper. $4.00
Second Part only.

25.6 Amiet, P.
Éléments Émailles du Décor Architectural Néo-Élamite. (Syria, vol. XLIV, 1967). 28 x 22.5. 24 pp., 2 pls., 15 figs. Paper. $7.50
Bound together with: Lambert, M. **Shutruk-Nahunte et Shutur-Nahunte.**

26.7 Amiet, P.
Glyptique Susienne des origines à l'époque des Perses Achéménides; Cachets, sceaux-cylindres et empreintes antiques decouverts à Suse de 1913 à 1967. Paris, 1972. 27.5 x 35. 2 vols.: xi, 316 pp., num. figs.; and 196 pls. $120.00
Major survey of early Iranian glyptics, describes 2,332 seals.

27.8 Amiet, P.
L'Iconographie Archaïque de l'Iran. (Syria, vol. LVI, 1979). 28 x 22.5. 19 pp., 23 illus. Paper. $7.50
Stamp and cylinder seals illustrating Iranian iconography.

28.9 Amiet, P.
La Glyptique Mesopotamienne archaïque. Paris, 1980. 24 x 31. 530 pp., num. illus. 2nd ed. $87.50
Important study of early seals, recommended!

456.416 Arthaud, G.
Étude sur les Sceaux Hétéens. Paris, 1920. 16.5 x 25. 200 pp., 43 figs. Paper. $31.50
Challenging attempt to link Hittite script to Archaic Chinese scripts. Uncut copy.

29.10 Barnett, R.D.
Homme Masqué ou Dieux-Ibex? (Syria, vol. XLIII, 1966). 28 x 22.5. 17 pp., 6 pls., 7 figs. Paper. $10.00
Mysterious representation on a group of seals.

622.571 Barrelet, M.-T.
Les Déesses Armées et Ailées. (Syria, vol. XXXII, 1955.). Paris, 1955. 27 x 22. 37 pp., 1 pl., 25 figs. Paper. $6.50
Iconographical study of Inanna-Ishtar, illustrated with details from cylinder seals.

30.11 Beran, T.
Die Hethitische Glyptik von Bogazköy. vol. I: Die Siegel und Siegelabdrücke der vor- und althethitische Perioden und die Siegel der hethitische Grosskönige. Berlin, 1967. 92 pp., 27 pls., 6 maps. $97.50

31.12 Billiet, J.
Cachets et Cylindres-Sceaux de Style Sumérien Archaïque et de Styles dérivés du Musée de Cannes, (Collection Lycklama). Paris, 1931. 24.5 x 16. 35 pp., 6 pls. Paper. $11.50
An obscure collection of 57 cylinders is catalogued and illustrated.

32.13 Bittel, K.
Die Kleinfunde der Grabungen 1906-1912. I: Funde heth. Zeit. 72 pp., 43 pls., 30 figs. Paper. $115.00
Reprint of the 1937 ed.

33.14 Boehmer, R.M.
Die Entwicklung der Glyptik während der Akkad-Zeit. Berlin, 1965. 21 x 30. xv, 194 pp., 63 pls. $68.00
A corpus of Akkadian seals with thorough discussion of iconography and stylistic development.

34.15 Bossier, A.
Mélanges d'Archéologie Orientale. 25 x 16. 8 pp., 4 figs. Paper. $3.50
Contains descriptions of 5 Near Eastern seals and scaraboids.

35.16 Brandes, M.A.
Siegelabrollungen aus den archaischen Bauschichten in Uruk-Warka. (FAOS, vol. III). Wiesbaden, 1979. 17 x 24. 2 vols.: xi, 233 pp.; and 20 pp., 32 pls. Paper. $48.50
Includes many careful line drawings and photographs illustrating iconographical details. Two Vols.

667.632 Brentjes, B.
Alte Siegelkunst des vorderen Orients. Leipzig, 1983. 223 pp., num. pls. and figs. $22.50
Excellent survey of glyptic arts in the ancient Near East.

41.22 Buchanan, B.
Catalogue of Ancient Near Eastern Seals in the Ashmolean Museum. I: Cylinder Seals. Oxford, 1966. 28.5 x 22. xxv, 242 pp., 67 pls., num. figs. $60.00
Major collection of seals, expertly catalogued! See also our no. 67.47.

42.23 Buchanan, B.
Early Near Eastern Seals in the Yale Babylonian Collection. New Haven, 1981. 498 pp., 1286 illus. $75.00
Important publication of a major collection.

457.417 Buchanan, B. and Moorey, P.R.S.
Catalogue of Ancient Near Eastern Seals in the Ashmolean Museum. II: The Prehistoric Stamp Seals. Oxford, 1984. 28 x 22. xviii, 43 pp., 16 pls. $45.00
First major study dealing with Pre-Historic Stamp Seals; all of the 246 seals are illustrated several times, illustrating the front and back and classifying both shapes and designs in one comprehensive system.

603.552 Buchanan, B.
A Cypriote Cylinder at Yale (Newell Collection 358). (BCH, vol. XCII, 1968.). Paris, 1968. 5 pp., 2 figs. Paper. $18.00
Also contains: Lévy, E., **Nouveaux bijoux à Délos.**

459.419 Buhl, M.-L.
Un Sceau de Zimrilim. (Syria, vol. LIX, 1982). 27.5 x 22. 7 pp., 8 figs. Paper. $4.50
Publishes a Syrian cylinder seal and compares its iconography to other similar seals.

43.24 Collon, D.
The Seal Impressions from Tell Atchana/Alalakh. (A.O.A.T., 27). Neukirchen, 1975. 30 x 21. 217 pp., 75 pls. $77.50
Shows many, clearly illustrated deities and other iconographical details, all taken from the sealings.

44.25 Collon, D.
The Alalakh Cylinder Seals: A new catalogue of the actual seals excavated by Sir Leonard Wooley at Tell Atchana, and from neighbouring sites on the Syrian-Turkish border. (BAR-I.S., 132). Oxford, 1982. 29.5 x 21. 132 pp., 27 pls., 120 figs. Paper. $22.50
Companion volume to the above, now out of print.

45.26 Collon, D.
Catalogue of the Western Asiatic Seals in the British Museum. Cylinder Seals II: Akkadian - Post Akkadian, Ur III Periods. London, 1982. 22 x 28. 172 pp., 52 pls., num. figs. $75.00

460.420 Contenau, G.
Cylindres Anépigraphes de la collection Lycklama, Musée de Cannes. (Revue d'Assyriologie, vol. XIII, 1916). 4 pp., 10 figs. Paper. $4.50
Publishes and illustrates 10 cylinder seals.

461.421 Contenau, G.
Les Cylindres Syro-Hittites. (Revue d'Assyriologie, vol. XIV, 1917). 13 pp., 18 figs. Paper. $5.50
Early attempt to distinguish Syro-Hittite seals as a distinct class.

462.422 Contenau, G.
La Question des Origines Comparées les Cylindres Chypriotes. (Revue d'Assyriologie, vol. XV, 1918). 11 pp., 15 figs. Paper. $4.50
Attempt to link Cypriote and Elamite seals.

46.27 Delaporte, L.
Catalogue des Cylindres Orientaux et des Cachets Assyro-Babyloniens, Perses et Syro-Cappadociens de la Bibliothèque Nationale. Paris, 1910. 19.5 x 29.5. Ii, 384 pp. Paper. $65.00
Text, (only), of this scarce catalogue of the French National Collection. The extremely scarce portfolio of 86 plates, which was issued separately, is available in photocopy for an additional $45.00.

47.28 Delaporte, L.
Intailles Orientales au Palais des Arts de la Ville de Lyon. n.d. 6 pp., 5 pls. Paper. $6.00
Presents 43 cylinder- and stamp seals.

48.29 Deshayes, J.
Cachets Susiens et Chronologie Iranienne. (Syria, vol. LI, 1974). 11 pp., 2 figs. Paper. $3.50

49.30 Digard, F., (et al.).
Répertoire analytique des cylindres orientaux publiés dans des sources bibliographiques éparses. Paris, 1976. vol. I: 320 pp., vol. 2: 349 pp., num. figs., maps., vol. 3: 217 pp., num. figs. $175.00
        vol. 1: **Principes et resultats.**
3 vols.: vol. 2: **Code.**
        vol. 3: **Commentaire.**
2 boxes incl. 4719 separate cards; each illustrates and describes one seal with its published history. Many iconographical details. Recommended!

50.31 Frankfort, H.
Cylinder Seals, A Documentary Essay on the Art and Religion of the Ancient Near East. London, 1939. 19.5 x 25.5. xlvii, 328 pp., 47 pls., 116 figs. $425.00
Basic text, long out-of-print and quite scarce!

51.32 Furlani, G.
Tre Sigilli Neoassiri. (Mélanges Syriens, n.d.). 28 x 22. 5 pp., 3 figs. Paper. $3.50

588. 540 Genouillac, H., (et al.).
Fouilles de Telloh. I: Époques Présargoniques. II: Époques d'Ur IIIe Dynastie et de Larsa. Paris, 1934-1936. 29.5 x 23. xii, 106 pp., 96 pls., incl. 2 color, figs; and 70 pp., 103 pls., incl. 2 color. 2 portfolios. $550.00
Two very scarce portfolios publishing the finds from Telloh; shows many cylinder seals, beads and other small finds as well as the pottery and idols.

52.33 Gibson, M. and Biggs, R.D., (Eds.).
Seals and Sealing in the Ancient Near East. Malibu, 1977. 28 x 21. 158 pp., num. figs., microfiche. Paper. $27.50
Various aspects of ancient glyptics as discussed at a symposium.

464.424 Gorelick, L. and Williams-Forte, E.
Ancient Seals and the Bible. Malibu, 1983. 21 x 27.5. 63 pp., 12 pls., 20 figs. Paper. $18.50
Six lengthy articles by six different authors dealing with Hebrew seals, seal manufacture, seal lore and iconography.

465.425 Gorelick, L. and Gwinnett, A.J.
Close work without Magnifying Lenses? (Expedition, vol. 23, 1981). 8 pp., 10 illus. Paper. $7.50
Fascinating account of gem-cutters lack of need for magnifying glasses; myopia, increased through hereditary factors, may have sufficed. See also our no. 467.427

466.426 Gorelick, L. and Gwinnett, A.J.
Ancient Seals and Modern Science. (Expedition, vol. 20, 1978). 9 pp., 12 illus. Paper. $5.50
Using the scanning electron microscope as an aid in the study of ancient seals.

467.427 Gorelick, L. and Gwinnett, A.J.
Close work without Magnifying Lenses? (Expedition, vol. 23, 1981). 2 pp., 2 illus. Paper. $5.50
Follow-up article to our no. 465.425, above. This issue of **Expedition** contains five related articles.

468.427 Gorelick, L.
The Origin and Development of the Ancient Near Eastern Cylinder Seal. (Expedition, vol. 23, 1981). 14 pp., 15 illus. Paper. $5.50
Plausible speculation on the development of cylinder seals out of early bead-shapes and technologies.

574.527 Gorelick. L. and Gwinnett, A.J.
Beadmaking in Iran in the Early Bronze Age. (**Expedition,** vol. 24, 1981). 14 pp., 29 illus. Paper. $5.50
Fascinating study of the earliest technologies employed to create stone beads; includes many detailed scanning electron microscope photographs showing actual processes used. Equally applicable to the manufacture of early seals.

53.34 Gueterbock, H.G.
Siegel aus Bogazkoey. vol. I: Die Koenigssiegel der Grabungen bis 1938. 30 x 21. (Reprint of the 1940 ed.). 60 pp., 48 pls. Paper. $45.00

54.35 Gueterbock, H.G.
Siegel aus Bogazkoey. vol. II: Koenigssiegel von 1937 und die uebrigen Hieroglyphensiegel. 30 x 21. (Reprint of the 1942 ed.). 64 pp., 48 pls. Paper. $47.50
Two quality reprints of a scarce cylinder seal "classic".

469.428 Gwinnett, A.J. and Gorelick, L.
Ancient Lapidary. (**Expedition**, vol. 22, 1979). 15 pp., 30 illus. Paper. $5.50
Most interesting article describes, and illustrates with scanning micrographs, ancient drilling techniques and materials.

470.429 Heuzey, L.
Sceaux inédits des Rois d'Agadé. (**Revue d'Assyriologie et d'archéologie orientale**, vol. IV, 1897). 12 pp., 6 figs. Paper. $4.50

40.21 Homès-Fredericq, D., (et al.) Musées Royaux d'Art et d'Histoire.
Sceaux-Cylindres de Syrie/Rolzegels uit Syrie. Brussels, 1982. 20.5 x 29.5. 74 pp., num. illus., maps. Paper. $18.50
Exhibition catalogue of, mostly, unpublished cylinder seals from Syria.

55.36 Homès-Fredericq, D.
Les Cachets mésopotamiens proto-historiques. Leiden, 1970. 29.5 x 22.5. xii, 199 pp., 51 pls., 30 figs., 4 maps. $95.00
Survey of the earliest known seal types, well illustrated.

56.37 Houston-Smith, R.
Un Cylindre Syrien Représentant Baal. (**Syria**, vol.XLII, 1965). 28 x 22. 6 pp., 2 figs. Paper. $3.50

57.38 Hrozny, B.
Sur un cachet "Hittite"-Hiéroglyphique de Ras Shamra. (**Mélanges Syriens**, n.d.). 3 pp., 1 fig. Paper. $2.50

153.113 Karageorghis, G.
Un Cylindre de Chypre.(**Syria**, vol.XXXVI, 1959). 8 pp., 1 fig. Paper. $3.50

614.563 Karg, N.
Untersuchungen zur aelteren fruehdynastischen Glyptik Babyloniens: Aspekte regionaler Entwicklungen in der ersten Haelfte des 3. Jahrtausends. (**Baghdader Forschungen**, 8). Mainz, 1985. xiv, 85 pp., 16 pls., containing 166 illus., 12 figs. $48.50

76.56 Kuehne, H. Eberhard-Karls-Universitaet.
Das Rollsiegel in Syrien, zur Steinschneidekunst in Syrien zwischen 3300 und 330 vor Christus. Tuebingen, 1980. 21 x 14. 175 pp., 95 illus., 14 figs. Paper.
$13.50
First publication of cylinder seals from Syrian museums.

58.6 Lambert, M.
Shutruk-Nahunte et Shutur-Nahunte.(Syria, vol. XLIV, 1967). 24 pp., 2 pls., 15 figs. Paper. $7.50
Bound together with: Amiet, P. **Éléments Émaillés du Décor Architectural Néo-Élamite.**

37.18 Le Brun, A.
La Glyptique du Niveau 17B de l'Acropole (Campagne de 1972). (D.A.F.I., vol. VIII, 1978). 27 x 21. 18 pp., 2 pls., 10 figs. Paper. $4.50
Cylinder Seals from Susa, Iran.

59.39 Legrain, L.
Ur Excavations, III: Archaic Seal-Impressions. Philadelphia, 1936. 24 x 33. 51 pp., 58 pls. $180.00
Scarce catalogue describing and illustrating 560 cylinder seals.

471.430 Legrain, L.
Five Royal Seal Cylinders. (**The Museum Journal**, 1922). 17 x 25.5. 18 pp., 5 illus. Paper. $8.50

472.431 Legrain, L.
Gem Cutters in Ancient Ur. (**The Museum Journal**, 1922). 17 x 25.5. 48 pp., 3 pls., illustrates 120 seals. Paper. $5.50
120 seals are catalogued and illustrated. This issue of **The Museum Journal** contains two related articles.

557.510 Legrain. L.
Nippur's Gold Treasure. (**The Museum Journal**, 1920). 17 x 25.5. 7 pp., 1 fig. Paper. $5.50
Translation and background of an inscribed cuneiform tablet which contains a catalogue of 125 jewels and seals dating from the 14th c. BC.

666.431 Legrain, L.
The Boudoir of Queen Shubad. (**The Museum Journal**, 1929). 17 x 27.5. 34 pp., 12 pls., 4 illus. Paper. $5.50
Precious metal and stone regalia from early Ur, 3500 BC, are shown and discussed. Cylinder seals show the fashions that complemented the metal and bead jewelry.

474.432 Lemaire, A.
Cinq Sceaux Araméens Inscrits Inédits. (**Syria**, vol. LIX, 1982). 7 pp., 5 illus. Paper. $3.50

475.427 Loding, D.
Lapidaries in the Ur III Period, Written Sources Concerning Stoneworkers, (ca. 2000 B.C.). (**Expedition**, vol. 23, 1981). 9 pp., 9 illus. Paper. $5.50
Textual information about ancient Near Eastern Lapidaries. This issue of **Expedition** contains five related articles.

646.614 Markoe, G., (Ed.).
Ancient Bronzes, Ceramics and Seals: The Nasli M. Heeramaneck Collection of Ancient Near Eastern, Central Asiatic, and European Art. Los Angeles, 1981. 25 x 23.5. 271 pp., 360 illus., incl. 13 color. Paper. $18.50
A catalogue showing 1349 objects ranging from cylinder seals to small Luristan bronzes. Much unusual material from various Steppe Cultures and an extensive series of early stampseals is also included.

60.40 Masson, E.
Quelques Sceaux Hittites Hiéroglyphes. (Syria, vol. LII, 1975). 26 pp., 3 pls., 49 figs. Paper. $13.50
Well illustrated Hittite seals, with inscriptions.

590.542 Matous, L. and Matousova-Rajmova, M.
Kappadokische Keilschrifttafeln mit Siegeln aus den Sammlungen der Karlsuniversität in Prag. Prague, 1984. 29.5 x 21. 186 pp., 130 illus., num. figs. $48.00
Hitherto unpublished collection of the Karls University in Prague. 140 seals are classified, transliterated and illustrated.

589.541 Matousova, M.
Quelques Remarques sur la Danse en Mésopotamie. (Archiv Orientalni, vol. XXXVIII, 1970). 24 x 17. 5 pp., 12 illus. Paper. $4.50
Dancing as shown on ancient cylinder seals.

61.41 Matousova-Rajmova, M.
Einige Siegelabdruecke aus dem Diyala-Gebiet. (AO, 1972). 14 pp., 9 pls. Paper.
$6.50

62.42 Matthiae, P.
Empreintes d'un cylindre Paléosyrien de Tell Mardikh. (Syria, vol. XLVI, 1969). 43 pp., 2 pls. 3 figs. Paper. $9.50

63.43 De Mecquenem, R.
Cylindres-Cachets de la Collection G. Schlumberger. Paris, 1924. 4 pp., 6 figs. Paper. $4.50

67.47 Moorey, R.S. and Gurney, O.R. Ashmolean Museum.
Ancient Near-Eastern Cylinder Seals Acquired by the Ashmolean Museum, Oxford, 1963-1973. (Iraq, vol. XL, 1978). 28 x 19. 19 pp., 2 pls., 6 figs. Paper. $6.50
Supplement to : Buchanan, B. **Catalogue of Ancient Near Eastern Seals in the Ashmolean Museum. I: Cylinder Seals.** (Our no. 41.22).

539.493 National Palace Museum.
Masterpieces of Chinese Seals in the National Palace Museum. Taipei, 1974. 27.5 x 22. 111 pp., 100 color pls. Slipcase. $36.00
One hundred Chinese seals are shown, in color, in three views: top, sealing surface and impression. A history of Chinese seals is included.

64.44 Nougayrol, J.
Cylindres-Sceaux et Empreintes de Cylindres trouvés en Palestine. Paris, 1939. 28.5 x 22.5. xxiv, 71 pp., 12 pls. Paper. $18.50
150 seals, all from known sites and all illustrated in careful line drawings.

36.17 Noveck, M. The Brooklyn Museum.
The Mark of Ancient Man, Ancient Near Eastern Stamp Seals and Cylinder Seals: The Gorelick Collection. Brooklyn, 1975. 19.5 x 13.5. 96 pp., 90 illus. Paper. $11.50

68.48 Parrot, A.
Cylindre Hittite Nouvellement Acquis (AO-20138). (Syria, vol. XXVII, 1951). 28.5 x 22.5. 10 figs., 2 pls., 6 figs. Paper. $4.50

477.434 Parrot, A.
Glyptique Mésopotamienne, Fouilles de Lagash (Tello) et de Larsa (Senkereh) (1931 - 1934). Paris, 1954. 21 x 27. 95 pp., 16 pls., 284 figs. Paper. $42.50
Publishes 325 cylinder seals from controlled excavations at Larsa and Lagash in the Thirties. Included are translations and transliterations of the inscriptions by Professor M. Lambert. Indispensable for the study of early glyptics.

478.435 Parrot, A.
Le "Trésor" d'Ur. (Mission Archéologique de Mari, vol. IV). Paris, 1968. 21.5 x 27.5. 67 pp., 3 color pls., 22 pls., 42 figs. $45.00
Illustrates jewelry, many seals and small precious objects from Ur.

69.49 Porada, E.
Les Cylindres de la Jarre Montet. (Syria, vol. XLIII, 1966). 16 pp., 2 pls. Paper. $5.50
See also: Tufnell, O. and Ward, W.A. **Relations between Byblos, Egypt and Mesopotamia at the end of the third Millenium BC, a study of the Montet Jar.,** our no. 8.69

70.50 Porada, E.
Tchoga Zanbil (Dur-Untash).IV: La Glyptique. Paris, 1970. 35 x 28. 149 pp., 15 pls., num. figs. $58.00
An important group of Elamite cylinders from this famous site is carefully described and fitted into its 13th c. context.

71.51 Porada, E., (Ed.).
Ancient Art in Seals. Princeton, 1980. 24 x 16. 131 pp., 27 pls., 2 maps. $28.50
Essays by P. Amiet, N. Ozguec and J. Boardman with a lengthy introduction by Dr. Porada on various aspects of ancient glyptics.

604.553 Ravn, O.E.
A Catalogue of Oriental Cylinder Seals and Seal Impressions in the Danish National Museum. Copenhagen, 1960. 30 x 21.5. 135 pp., 29 pls. Paper. $175.00
Publishes the national collection of Denmark. All 175 seals are shown in good photographs of the casts.

458.418 Jacob-Rost, L. Staatliche Museen zu Berlin.
Die Stempelsiegel im Vorderasiatischen Museum. Berlin, 1975. 24 x 17. 102 pp., 17 pls., num. figs. Paper. $87.50
Catalogues, illustrates and dates 482 stamp seals, most for the first time.

72.52 Rutten, M.
Les Sceaux de la Mésopotamie au IVe millénaire. (R.E.S., 1937). 25 x 16.5. 12 pp., 15 figs. Paper. $4.50

73.53 Rutten, M.
Les Origines de la Glyptique en Mésopotamie et en Iran. (Babylonica, vol. XVI, 1936). 25.5 x 16.5. 14 pp., 4 pls. Paper. $4.50

479.436 Schaeffer-Forrer, C.F.A.
Corpus des Cylindres-Sceaux de Ras Shamra-Ugarit et d'Enkomi-Alasia. I. Paris, 1983. 21 x 29.5. 209 pp., 41 pls., num. illus. Paper. $29.50
Includes an extensive section of enlarged iconographical details taken from the seals which show the manifold influences that shaped these Western Syrian and Cypriot seals.

74.54 Six, J.
De la Glyptique Syro-Hittite jusqu'a Praxitèle. (Syria, 1925). 28 x 22. 10 pp., 15 figs. Paper. $5.50
East meets West in art on cylinder seals.

38.19 Speleers, L. Musées Royaux du Cinquantenaire.
Catalogue des Intailles et Empreintes Orientales. Brussels, 1917. 24 x 18. 211 pp., num. illus. Paper. $125.00
Only publication of Belgium's premier collection, long out-of-print. Uncut copy.

39.20 Speleers, L. Musées Royaux d'Art et d'Histoire.
Catalogue des Intailles et Empreintes Orientales. Brussels, 1943. 18 x 24. 211 pp., num. illus. Paper. $125.00
Supplement to the above. Uncut copy.

453.251 Teissier, B.
Ancient Near Eastern Cylinder Seals from the Marcopoli Collection. Berkeley, 1984. 28.5 x 22.5. xxviii, 407 pp., 114 pls. illustrating 719 seals., 1 chart. $75.00
Very well laid out and illustrated new catalogue of a large private collection, hitherto unpublished, of mostly Syrian cylinder seals.

75.55 Thaplyal, K.K.
Studies in Ancient Indian Seals. Lucknow, 1972. 25 x 18. 437 pp., 36 pls. $48.50
Lengthy study of seals and their history in India from ca. 3rd century B.C. to 7th century A.D. A thorough presentation.

577.529 Tosi, M. and Piperno, M.
Lithic Technology behind the Ancient Lapis Lazuli Trade. (Expedition, vol. 16, 1973). 9 pp., 14 illus., map. Paper. $6.50
Discusses finds from Shahr-i Sokta, Afghanistan, dating to 3000-2000 B.C., which illustrates the techniques and tools used to make beads and seals.

77.408 Tunca, Ö.
Catalogue des sceaux-cylindres du Musée régional d'Adana. (Syro-Mesopotamian Studies, vol. 3). Malibu. 1979. 27.5 x 21. 34 pp., 15 pls. Paper. $11.50

463.423 Vollenweider, M.-L. Musée d'Art et d'Histoire.
Catalogue raisonné des sceaux, cylindres, intailles et camées. III: La Collection du Révérend Dr. V.E.G. Kenna et d'autres acquisitions et dons récents.
Mainz, 1983. 22 x 30. xx, 242 pp., 115 pls. $85.00
Third volume of the Geneva Collections; especially strong in Near Eastern material of all periods.

65.45 Von der Osten, H.H.
Ancient Oriental Seals in the Collection of Mr. Edward T. Newell. Chicago, 1934. xiii, 204 pp., 41 pls., 28 figs. $87.50
Major collection of 695 seals, carefully catalogued with emphasis on iconographical details.

66.46 Von der Osten, H.H.
Altorientalische Siegelsteine der Sammlung Hans Silvius von Aulock. Uppsala, 1957. 32 x 24. 235 pp., 14 pls. Paper. $120.00
Presents 365 seals; with very extensive bibliography on glyptic arts generally. Uncut copy.

78.57 Ward, W.
Un Cylindre Syrien Inscrit de la Deuxième Période Intermédiaire. (Syria, vol. XLII, 1965). 28 x 22. 10 pp., 1 pl., 13 figs. Paper. $4.50

606.555 Weber, O.
Altorientalische Siegelbilder. Leipzig, 1920. 22.5 x 14. v, 133 pp.; and viii, 117 pp., 596 illus. $148.00
Two volumes bound together. The plate section shows all 596 seals discussed in the text.

Eastern - Phoenician Gems

79.58 Acquaro, E.
Amuletti Egiziani ed Egittizanti del Museo Nazionale di Cagliari. Rome, 1977. 20 x 28. 158 pp., 61 pls. Paper. $32.50
Catalogues 1271 amulets and illustrates these mostly Egyptian and Aegypto-Phoenician amulets from Sardina.

80.59 Amiet, P.
Bactriane Proto-Historique. (**Syria**, vol. LIV, 1977). 28 x 22. 32 pp., 4 pls., 22 figs. Paper. $9.50
Important article on recent finds of beads, jewelry, seals and other 3rd Millenium objects in the Iranian-Afghani plateau.

81.60 Amiet, P.
Antiquités de Serpentine. (**Iranica Antiqua**, vol. XV, 1980). 27.5 x 19. xv, 314 pp., 36 pls., 41 figs. $77.50
This volume also contains, among others: Gignoux, P. **Sceaux chrétiens d'époque sasanide.**; Pottier, M.-H. **Un cachet en argent de Bactriane**; Porada, E. **A Lapis Lazuli Figurine from Hierakonpolis in Egypt.**

456.416 Arthaud, G.
Étude sur les Sceaux Hétéens. Paris, 1920. 16.5 x 25. 200 pp., 43 figs. Paper. $31.50
Challenging attempt to link Hittite script to Archaic Chinese scripts. Uncut copy.

82.61 Avigad, N.
Bullae and Seals from a post-Exilic Judean Archive. (**Qedem**, 4). Jerusalem, 1976. 28 x 19. 36 pp., 15 pls. $20.00
Describes and illustrates a large find of Jewish seals and seal impressions.

641.608 Boardman, J. Museo Arqueologico Nacional.
Escarabeos de Piedra Procedentes de Ibiza. Madrid, 1984. 25 x 20. 103 pp., 41 pls. $18.00
Long awaited book on the Phoenician and Graeco-Phoenician scarabs from the Western Mediterranean.

83.62 Bordreuil. P.
Inscriptions Sigillaires Ouest-Semitiques. I: Épigraphie Ammonite. (**Syria**, vol. L, 1973). 14 pp., 4 illus. Paper. $5.50

586.538 Bordreuil, P.
Inscriptions Sigillaires Ouest-Semitiques. II: Un Cachet Hébreu Récement acquis par le Cabinet des Médailles de la Bibliothèque Nationale. (**Syria**, vol. LII, 1975). 11 pp., 2 figs. Paper. $4.50

34.15 Bossier, A.
Mélanges d'Archéologie Orientale. 25 x 16. 8 pp., 4 figs. Paper. $3.50
Contains descriptions of 5 Near Eastern seals and scaraboids.

667.632 Brentjes, B.
Alte Siegelkunst des Vorderen Orients. Leipzig, 1983. 223 pp., num. pls. and figs. $22.50
Excellent survey of glyptic arts in the ancient Near East.

457.417 Buchanan, B. and Moorey, P.R.S.
Catalogue of Ancient Near Eastern Seals in the Ashmolean Museum. II: The Prehistoric Stamp Seals. Oxford, 1984. 28 x 22. xviii, 43 pp., 16 pls. $45.00
First major study dealing with Pre-Historic Stamp Seals; all of the 246 seals are illustrated several times, illustrating the front and back, and classifying both shapes and designs in one comprehensive system.

603.552 Buchanan, B.
A Cypriote Cylinder at Yale (Newell Collection 358). (BCH, vol. XCII, 1968.). Paris, 1968. 5 pp., 2 figs. Paper. $18.00
Also contains: Lévy, E., **Nouveaux bijoux à Délos.**

495.450 Cintas, P.
Amulettes Puniques. Tunis, 1946. 21.5 x 28. 171 pp., 19 pls., num. illus., tables. Paper. $87.50
Scarce publication describes and shows many amulets, scarabs and jewelry from Carthaginian sites.

617.566 Cintas, P.
Carthage, sa Naissance, sa Grandeur: Les Collections Puniques des Musées du Bardo, de Carthage et d'Utique. (Archéologie Vivante, vol. I. No. 2.). Paris, 1968-1969. 28.5 x 21.5. 155 pp., 181 illus. incl. 45 color., 36 figs., 3 maps. Paper. $28.50
This issue of the short lived quarterly **Archaeologia Viva** contains 15 separate articles by different scholars each describing a different aspect of Carthaginian culture. Phoenician gems and jewelry are discussed and well illustrated.

462.422 Contenau, G.
La Question des Origines Comparées les Cylindres Chypriotes. (Revue d'Assyriologie, vol. XV, 1918). 11 pp., 15 figs. Paper. $4.50
Attempt to link Cypriote and Elamite seals.

87.66 De Ridder, A.
Collection de Clercq. VII: Les Bijoux et les Pierres Gravées. Paris, 1911. 28 x 36.5. Paper. $190.00
Part II: **Les Pierres Gravées.** 438 pp., 15 pls. Catalogues 1135 ancient gems. Scarce!

84.63 Densmore Curtis, C.
Sardis. XIII: Jewelry and Goldwork. Rome, 1925. 28 x 34.5. 48 pp., 11 pls. $115.00
Scarce publication showing all the gems and jewelry from this important East Greek site.

642.610 Furtwaengler, A.
Die Antiken Gemmen. Geschichte der Steinschneidekunst im klassischen Altertum. 3 vols.: xvi, 67 pls.; and viii, 330 pp.; and xii, 464 pp., 3 pls. $650.00
Three volume reprint of the original 1900 edition, now out-of-print. Contains the full text and all plates of the original edition at a fraction of the cost. A classic!

464.424 Gorelick, L. and Williams-Forte, E.
Ancient Seals and the Bible. Malibu, 1983. 21 x 27.5. 63 pp., 12 pls., 20 figs. Paper. $18.50
Six lengthy articles by six different authors dealing with Hebrew seals, seal manufacture, seal lore and iconography.

468.427 Gorelick, L.
The Origin and development of the Ancient Near Eastern Cylinder Seal. (**Expedition**, vol. 23, 1981). 14 pp., 15 illus. Paper. $5.50
Plausible speculation on the development of cylinder seals out of early bead-shapes and technologies.

574.527 Gorelick, L. and Gwinnett, A.J.
Beadmaking in Iran in the Early Bronze Age. (**Expedition**, vol. 24, 1981). 14 pp., 29 illus. Paper. $5.50
Fascinating study of the earliest technologies employed to create stone beads; includes many detailed scanning electron microscope photographs showing actual processes used. Equally applicable to the manufacture of early seals.

86.65 Hestrin, R. and Dayagi-Mendels, M. Israel Museum.
Inscribed Seals. Jerusalem, 1979. 21 x 15. 179 pp., 1 color pl., 136 illus. Paper. $18.50
136 Seals with Hebrew inscriptions, all illustrated, transliterated and translated.

599.551 Kenna, V.E.G.
The seal use of Cyprus in the Bronze Age, III. (**BCH**, vol. XCII, 1968.). Paris, 1968, 14 pp., 6 figs. Paper. $11.50
Also contains: Kenna, V.E.G., **The Kouklia ring from Evreti** and Catling, H.W., **Kouklia: Evreti Tomb 8.**

476.433 Margain, J.
Une Nouvelle Amulette Samaritaine portant le texte d'Exode 38.8. (**Syria**, vol. LIX, 1982). 4 pp., 2 figs. Paper. $2.50

646.614 Markoe, G., (Ed.).
Ancient Bronzes Ceramics and Seals: The Nasli M. Heeramaneck Collection of Ancient Near Eastern, Central Asiatic, and European Art. Los Angeles, 1981. 25 x 23.5. 271 pp., 360 illus., incl. 13 color. Paper. $18.50
A catalogue showing 1349 objects ranging from cylinder seals to small Luristan bronzes. Much unusual material from various Steppe Cultures and an extensive series of early stampseals is also included.

539.493 National Palace Museum.
Masterpieces of Chinese Seals in the National Palace Museum. Taipei, 1974. 27.5 x 22. 111 pp., 100 color pls. Slipcase. $36.00
One hundred Chinese seals are shown, in color, in three views: top, sealing surface and impression. A history of Chinese seals is included.

531.485 Nicholls, R.
The Wellcome Gems: A Fitzwilliam Museum Catalogue. Cambridge, 1983. 15 x 21. 57 pp., num. illus. Paper. $12.50
Supplementary catalogue of 250 Ancient and Later gems to the soon to be published **Classical Gems: Ancient and Modern Intaglios and Cameos in the Fitzwilliam Museum, Cambridge.**, most are illustrated.

69.49 Porada, E.
Les Cylindres de la Jarre Montet. (**Syria**, vol. XLIII, 1966). 16 pp., 2 pls. Paper. $5.50
See also: Tufnell, O. and Ward, W.A. **Relations between Byblos, Egypt and Mesopotamia at the end of the third Millenium B.C., a study of the Montet Jar.**, our no. 8.69.

458.418 Jacob-Rost, L. Staatliche Museen zu Berlin.
Die Stempelsiegel im Vorderasiatischen Museum. Berlin, 1975. 24 x 17. 102 pp., 17 pls., num. figs. Paper. $87.50
Catalogues, illustrates and dates 482 stamp seals, most for the first time.

88.67 Scandone, G.M.
Scarabei e Scaraboidi Egiziani ed Egittizanti del Museo Nazionale di Cagliari. Rome, 1975. 20 x 28. 106 pp., 31 pls. Paper. $23.50
Egyptian and Egyptianizing scarabs and ring bezels from this important Phoenician site in the Western Mediterranean.

567.520 De Serres, J.-P. Hotel Drouot.
Antiquités Égyptiennes; Antiquités Grecques et Romaines; Haute Curiosité. Paris, 1981. 20.5 x 17. 43 pp., 6 illus. Paper. $4.50
Auction catalogue of amulets, gems and some jewelry. Most objects are shown in color on the outside covers of the catalogue.

75.55 Thaplyal, K.K.
Studies in Ancient Indian Seals. Lucknow, 1972. 25 x 18. 437 pp., 36 pls. $48.50
Lengthy study of seals and their history in India from ca. 3rd century B.C. to 7th century A.D. A thorough presentation.

89.68 Tillot, M.
Mille ans d'art à Carthage. Tunis, 1978. 20.5 x 20. 80 pp., 88 color pls. $18.50
Handsomely presents gems, amulets and jewelry from ancient Phoenician and Roman sites.

8.69 Tufnell, O. and Ward, W.A.
Relations between Byblos, Egypt and Mesopotamia at the end of the third Millenium B.C., a study of the Montet Jar. (**Syria**, vol. XLIII, 1966). Paris, 1966. 77 pp., 6 pls., 10 figs. Paper. $18.50
Large closed find of jewelry, scarabs and beads, all illustrated and dated.

496.451 Vercoutter, J.
Les Objets Égyptiens et Égyptisants du Mobilier Funéraire Carthaginois.
Paris, 1945. 23 x 28.5. 397 pp., 29 pls., num. figs., folding pls. and maps. Paper.
$78.00
Important book illustrates, classifies and translates 936 Egyptian and Phoenician scarabs and amulets, both in hardstone and in faience, some mounted as rings or stampseals. Uncut copy. Rare!

85.64 Vollenweider, M.-L. Musée d'Art et d'Histoire.
Catalogue raisonné des sceaux, cylindres et intailles. I. Geneva, 1967. 21.5 x 30. 217 pp., 95 pls. Paper. $95.00
Beautiful collection, expertly presented! Now out of print.

463.423 Vollenweider, M.-L. Musée d'Art et d'Histoire.
Catalogue raisonne des sceaux, cylindres, intailles et camées. III: La Collection du Révérend Dr. V.E.G. Kenna et d'autres acquisitions et dons récents.
Mainz, 1983. 22 x 30. xx, 242 pp., 115 pls. $85.00
Third volume of the Geneva Collections; especially strong in Near Eastern material of all periods.

606.555 Weber, O.
Altorientalische Siegelbilder. Leipzig. 1920. 22.5 x 14. v, 133 pp.; and viii, 117 pp., 596 illus. $148.00
Two volumes bound together. The plate section shows all 596 seals discussed in the text.

480.437 Zazoff, P.
Die Antiken Gemmen. Munich, 1983. 24.5 x 16.5. 446 pp., 132 pls., 82 figs.
$110.00
Attempt at an update of Furtwaengler's **Die antiken Gemmen**. Most helpful survey, many photographs, line drawings and a concise text help to increase the usefulness of this handbook. Recommended as a quick but thorough reference tool.

Egyptian Scarabs

79.58 Acquaro, E.
Amuletti Egiziani ed Egittizanti del Museo Nazionale di Cagliari. Rome, 1977. 20 x 28. 158 pp., 61 pls. Paper. $32.50
Catalogues 1271 amulets and illustrates these mostly Egyptian and Aegypto-Phoenician amulets from Sardina.

90.70 Blankenberg-Van Delden, C.
The large commemorative scarabs of Amenhotep III. Leiden, 1969. xi, 198 pp., 35 pls. $87.50
First attempt at a corpus of these historically important "documents".

565.518 The Brooklyn Museum.
Africa in Antiquity: The Arts of Ancient Nubia and the Sudan. I: The Essays. II: The Catalogue.. Brooklyn, 1978. 32 x 22. 143 pp., 100 figs., 19 in color., 3 maps; and 112 pp., 84 figs., 9 in color. $48.00
Two volumes illustrating the "provincial arts of Egypt", the jewelry is especially noteworthy for its many different influences and barbaric splendor. Recommended!

495.450 Cintas, P.
Amulettes Puniques. Tunis, 1946. 21.5 x 28. 171 pp., 19 pls., num. illus., tables. Paper. $87.50
Scarce publication describes and shows many amulets, scarabs and jewelry from Carthaginian sites.

93.73 Hornung, E. and Staehelin, E.
Skarabaeen und andere Siegelelemente aus Basler Sammlungen. (Aegypt. Denkmaeler in d. Schweiz, vol. I). 400 pp., 129 pls. $185.00
Illustrates more than 3000 scarabs and related objects.

94.74 Matouk, F.S.
Corpus du Scarabée Égyptien. I: Les Scarabées Royaux. Beirut, 1971. 28.5 x 22. vi, 222 pp., 18 pls., 25 figs. $77.50
Presents 904 scarabs arranged by dynasty with transliterations and translations.

95.75 Matouk, F.S.
Corpus du Scarabée Égyptien. II: Analyse thématique. Beirut, 1977. 28.5 x 22. 416 pp., 41 pls., 52 figs. $115.00
Presents 2,480 scarabs in line drawings, photographs and translations. Discusses symbols and their meaning.

96.76 Newberry, P.E.
Scarab-shaped seals. 384 pp., 22 pls. $185.00
Reprint of the 1907 ed. Standard work for the study of scarabs.

97.77 Niccacci, A.
Hyksos Scarabs. Jerusalem, 1980. 17 x 24. 86 pp., 12 pls. Paper. $18.00
Presents 317 scarabs from the Flagellation Museum, Jerusalem, and a private collection in Israel; all are illustrated.

98.78 Petrie, Sir, W.M.F.
Scarabs and Cylinders with Names illustrated by the Egyptian Collection in University College, London. London, 1917. 25 x 31.5. viii, 46 pp., 73 pls. $185.00
Extensive collection of scarabs, all carefully translated, dated and illustrated.

546.500 Petrie, Sir, W.M.F.
Buttons and Design Scarabs. London, 1974. 32 x 23. 34 pp., 30 pls. $60.00
Reprint of the 1925 edition, now itself out-of-print.

88.67 Scandone, G.M.
Scarabei e Scaraboidi Egiziani ed Egittizanti del Museo Nazionale di Cagliari. Rome, 1975. 20 x 28. 106 pp., 31 pls. Paper. $23.50
Egyptian and Egyptianizing scarabs and ring bezels from this important Phoenician site in the western Mediterranean.

706.685 Tufnell, O.
Studies on Scarab Seals. II: Scarab Seals and their Contribution to History in the Second Millenium B.C.. Warminster, 1984. 21.5 x 30. Two vols.: 397 pp.; and num. pls., index. Paper. $85.00
Two fascicules, sold as a set. Volume two is available separately as our no. 705.684, below.

8.69 Tufnell, O. and Ward, W.A.
Relations between Byblos, Egypt and Mesopotamia at the end of the third Millenium BC, a study of the Montet Jar. (Syria, vol. XLIII, 1966). Paris, 1966. 77 pp., 6 pls., 10 figs. Paper. $18.50
Large closed find of jewelry, scarabs and beads, all illustrated and dated.

496.451 Vercoutter, J.
Les Objets Égyptiens et Égyptisants du Mobilier Funéraire Carthaginois. Paris, 1945, 23 28.5. 397 pp., 29 pls., num. figs., folding pls. and maps. Paper. $78.00
Important book illustrates, classifies and translates 936 Egyptian and Phoenician scarabs and amulets, both in hardstone and in faience, some mounted as rings or stampseals. Uncut copy. Rare!

91.71 Vodoz, I. Musée d'Art et d'Histoire.
Catalogue raisonné des scarabées gravés du Musée d'Art et d'Histoire de Genève. Geneva, 1979. 26 x 20. 175 pp., 37 pls., num. figs. Paper. $36.00
A large collection of Egyptian scarabs is carefully catalogued and translated, all are illustrated.

92.72 Von Beste. Hanover. Kestner Museum.
Corpus Antiquitatum Aegyptiacarum.
vol. I: **Skarabaeen.** 1979. 21 x 30. $28.50
vol. II: **Skarabaeen.** 1979. 21 x 30. $28.50
vol. III: **Skarabaeen.** 1979. 21 x 30. $28.50
Three loose leaf folders illustrating and describing the collection in Hanover.

705.684 Ward, W.
Studies on Scarab Seals. I: Pre-Twelfth Dynasty Scarab Amulets. Warminster, 1978. 21.5 x 30.5. 116 pp., 16 pls., 52 figs. $57.50
Sequel to our no. 706.685, above.

Minoan · Mycenaean Gems and Vessels

99.196 Amandry, P.
Collection Hélène Stathatos. I: Les Bijoux Antiques. Strasbourg, 1953. 28.5 x 38. 149 pp., 44 pls., 80 figs. Paper. $650.00
Very scarce and important catalogue of this major collection of ancient jewelry of the Mycenaean through Hellenistic periods.

101.80 Brandt, E. Staatliche Muenzsammlung, Muenchen.
Antike Gemmen in deutschen Sammlungen. I-1: Griechische Gemmen von minoischer Zeit bis zum spaeten Hellenismus. Munich, 1968. 106 pp., 68 pls., illustrates 367 gems. $87.50

104.80 Zwierlein-Diehl, E.
Antike Gemmen in deutschen Sammlungen. II: Staatliche Museen preussischer Kulturbesitz, Antikenabteilung Berlin. Munich, 1969. 198 pp., 106 pls., illustrates 564 gems. $125.00

108.410 Battaglia, G.B.
Gioelli Antichi dall'eta Micenea all'Ellenismo. Rome, 1982. 24.5 x 31. 38 pp., 82 color illus. Paper. $22.50
Handsomely illustrated catalogue of the famous Castellani Collection of ancient jewelry, now in the Villa Giulia, Rome.

119.653 Betts, J.H.
Die schweizer Sammlungen. (**CMS**, vol. X.). Berlin, 1980. 296 pp. $77.50
Describes and illustrates 323 gems.

619. 568 Bielefeld, E.
Schmuck. (**Archaeologia Homerica**, vol. I, 1968.). Munich, 1968. 24.5 x 17. 70 pp., 6 pls, incl. 1 color., 8 figs. Paper. $18.50
Study of earliest Greek jewelry from the Helladic through the Geometric Period, based on numerous quotes from Homer and thorough research into the archaeological record.

115.649 Caskey, J.L., (et. al.).
Kleinere griechische Sammlungen. (**CMS**, vol. V. 1-2.). 2 vols: $205.00
v.I: Berlin, 1975. xliv, 623 pp., 10 pls. Catalogues 316 gems.
v.2: Berlin, 1976. 374 pp., 10 pls. Catalogues 751 gems.

601.551 Catling, H.W.
Kouklia: Evreti Tomb 8. (**BCH**, vol. XCII, 1968.). Paris, 1968. 7 pp., 2 figs. Paper.
$11.50
Also contains: Kenna, V.E.G., **The seal use of Cyprus in the Bronze Age III**, and Kenna, V.E.G., **The Kouklia ring from Evreti**.

118.652 Effenterre, H. and M.
Cabinet des Médailles de la Bibliothèque Nationale, Paris. (**CMS**, vol. IX.). Berlin, 1972, xxiv, 259 pp. $67.50
Describes and illustrates 228 gems.

642.610 Furtwaengler, A.
Die Antiken Gemmen. Geschichte der Steinschneidekunst im klassischen Altertum. 3 vols.: xvi, 67 pls.; and viii, 330 pp.; and xii, 464 pp., 3 pls. $650.00
Three volume reprint of the original 1900 edition, now out-of-print. Contains the full text and all plates of the original edition at a fraction of the cost. A classic!

132.92 Higgins, R.A.
The Aegina Treasure; An Archaeological Mystery. London, 1979. 23.5 x 15.5. 72 pp., 65 illus. Paper. $24.00
Fascinating history of the discovery of the treasure, with careful description of its parts. Now out-of-print.

124.84 Hoffmann, H. and von Claer, V. Museum fuer Kunst und Gewerbe. Hamburg.
Antiker Gold- und Silberschmuck; Katalog mit Untersuchung der Objekte auf technischer Grundlage. Mainz, 1968. 23.5 x 19. x, 246 pp., num. illus. $38.50
Catalogues and illustrates 137 pieces of ancient jewelry. Includes a thorough section on technology with many close-up photographs.

116.650 Kenna, V.E.G.
Die englischen Museen. II: London, British Museum; Cambridge, Fitzwilliam Museum; Liverpool, City Museum; Birmingham, City Museum. (**CMS**, vol. VII.). Berlin, 1967. xx, 336 pp. $47.50
Describes and illustrates 264 gems.

117.651 Kenna, V.E.G.
Die englischen Privatsammlungen. (**CMS**, vol. VIII.). Berlin, 1966. xviii, 224 pp. $35.00
Catalogues 152 gems.

120.654 Kenna, V.E.G.
Nordamerika I: New York. The Metropolitan Museum of Art. (**CMS**, vol. XII.). Berlin, 1972. xx, 416 pp. $97.50
Catalogues 325 gems.

121.655 Kenna, V.E.G. and Eberhard, T.
Nordamerika II: Kleinere Sammlungen. (**CMS**, vol. XIII.). Berlin, 1974. xvi, 176 pp. $45.00
Catalogues 166 gems.

125.85 Kenna, V.E.G.
The Cretan Talismanic Stone in the Late Minoan Age. (**SIMA**, XXIV). Lund, 1969. 30.5 x 22.5. 35 pp., 26 pls., 279 figs. Paper. $28.50
Distinct series of Minoan gems; illustrates many iconographical details.

126.86 Kenna, V.E.G.
Quelques Aspects de la Glyptique Chypriote. (**Syria**, vol. XLIV, 1967.). $4.50

127.87 Kenna, V.E.G.
Studies of Birds on Seals of the Aegean and Eastern Mediterranean. (**Op. Ath.**, vol. XLIV, 1968). Paper. $5.50

128.88 Kenna, V.E.G.
Catalogue of the Cypriote Seals of the Bronze Age in the British Museum.
(**SIMA**, XX:3). 30 x 22. 41 pp., 32 pls. Paper. $26.00
Useful catalogue of finger rings and engraved gems, their use and history, together with a brief history of this pivotal island.

494.449 Kenna, V.E.G.
Cretan Seals with a Catalogue of the Minoan Gems in the Ashmolean Museum. Oxford, 1960. 24 x 32. xiii, 163 pp., 25 pls., 172 figs. $175.00
Standard work describing the important collection of early gems in Oxford. Scarce and long out-of-print.

599.551 Kenna, V.E.G.
The seal use of Cyprus in the Bronze Age, III. (**BCH**, vol. XCII, 1968.). $11.50
Also contains: Kenna, V.E.G., **The Kouklia ring from Evreti** and Catling, H.W., **Kouklia: Evreti Tomb 8.**

129.89 Laffineur, R.
Les vases en métal précieux à l'époque mycénienne. Göteburg, 1977. 21 x 11.5. 171 pp., 47 pls. Paper. $38.50
Discussion of silver and gold vessels with their decorations.

130.90 Marshall, F. British Museum.
Catalogue of the Jewellery, Greek, Etruscan, and Roman in the Department of Antiquities, British Museum. London, 1969. 28 x 23. lxii, 400 pp., 73 pls. $95.00
The standard reference work describing 3,168 items. Now out-of-print.

122.83 Niemeier, W.-D., (Ed.).
Studien zur minoischen und helladischen Glyptik. (**CMS**, Beiheft I.). Berlin, 1981. 19 x 25.5. 282 pp., num. illus. $87.50
Text of nineteen lectures in English, French and German, given at the symposium in Marburg, 1978.

493.656 Onassoglu, A.
Die "Talismanischen" Siegel. (**CMS**, Beiheft II.). Berlin, 1985. 308 pp., 68 pls., 20 figs., fold-out table. $105.00
Attempt to classify the gems of the MM III - LM IB according to their general iconography; includes a chapter on cutting technique.

134.94 Persson, A.W.
The Royal Tombs at Dendra near Midea. Lund, 1931. 23 x 29. viii, 152 pp., 4 color pls., 86 figs. $48.50
Mycenaean jewelry, metal vessels and engraved gems from a controlled excavation are well published in this scarce report.

135.95 Persson, A.W.
New Tombs at Dendra near Midea. Lund, 1942. 23 x 29. 210 pp., 8 pls., 139 pls. $46.50
Additional finds of metal vessels, jewelry, seals and beads from Mycenaean shaft graves.

113.647 Pini, I.
Iraklion. Archaeologisches Museum: Die Siegeldruecke von Phaestos. (**CMS**, vol. II.5.). Berlin, 1970. xxiv, 292 pp. $52.50
Describes and illustrates 829 gem impressions.

634.646 Pini, I.
Iraklion. Archaeologisches Museum: Die Siegel der Nachpalastzeit und undatierte spaetminoische Siegel. (**CMS**, vol. II.4.). Berlin, 1985. 18.5 x 25. 376 pp., 729 illus., map. $105.00
The most recently published volume of the **CMS**.

11.643 Platon, N.
Iraklion. Archaeologisches Museum: Die Siegel der Vorpalastzeit. (**CMS**, vol. II.1). Berlin, 1969. xxvi, 606 pp., 1 color pl. $85.00
Describes and illustrates 503 gems.

492.645 Platon, N. and Pini, I.
Iraklion. Archaeologisches Museum, Die Siegel der Neupalastzeit. (**CMS**, vol. II.3.). Berlin, 1984. 470 pp., 1400 illus. $110.00

133.93 Richter, G.M.A. Metropolitan Museum of Art.
Catalogue of the Engraved Gems of the Classical Style. New York, 1920. 14 x 22. lxxiv, 232 pp., 88 pls. $115.00
Limited edition of 1000. Includes the Minoan and Mycenaean gems omitted from the 1956 edition. Scarce!

114.648 Sakellarakis, J.A. and Kenna, V.E.G.
Iraklion. Sammlung Metaxas. (**CMS**, vol. IV.). Berlin, 1969. 426 pp., 1 color pl. $67.50

110.82 Sakellariou, A.
Die minoischen und mykenischen Siegel des Nationalmuseums in Athen. (**CMS**, vol. I.). Berlin, 1965. xxii, 544 pp.
Describes and illustrates 517 gems. Now out-of-print, requests will be filled when copies are secured.

136.96 Sakellariou, A.
Die Mykenische Siegelglyptik. (**SIMA**, vol. IX, 1961). 28 x 22. 11 pp., 14 figs. Paper. $8.50
Introduction to the iconography of Mycenaean seals and ring bezels.

131.91 Tait, H., (Ed.). British Museum.
Jewellery through 7000 years. London, 1976. 24 x 19. 276 pp., num color and B. & W. illus. Paper. $22.50
Presents 466 pieces of jewelry from around the world. Excellent general survey; well illustrated. Out-of-print.

85.64 Vollenweider, M.-L. Musée d'Art et d'Histoire.
Catalogue raisonné des sceaux, cylindres et intailles. I. Geneva, 1967. 21.5 x 30. 217 pp., 95 pls. Paper. $95.00
Beautiful collection, expertly presented! Now out-of-print.

463.423 Vollenweider, M.-L. Musée d'Art et d'Histoire.
Catalogue raisonne des sceaux, cylindres, intailles et camées. III: La Collection du Révérend Dr. V.E.G. Kenna et d'autres acquisitions et dons récents.
Mainz, 1983. 22 x 30. xx, 242 pp., 115 pls. $85.00
Third volume of the Geneva Collections; especially strong in Near Eastern material of all periods.

139.99 Xenaki-Sakellariou, A.
Les Cachets minoens de la collection Giamalakis. (Études Crétoises, X). Paris, 1958. 28 x 22. xix, 100 pp., 30 pls. Paper. $36.00
Impressive collection of 426 Minoan seals.

657.427 Younger, J.G.
Creating A Sealstone. (**Expedition**, vol. 23, 1981.). 8 pp., 23 illus. Paper. $5.50
Study showing the tools and techniques used to create Minoan and Mycenaean seals; evidence includes unfinished seals and tool marks.

140.100 Yule, P.
Early Cretan Seals: A Study of Chronology. (Marburger Studien zur Vor-und Fruehgeschichte, vol. IV.). Mainz, 1980. xiv, 246 pp., 41 pls., num. figs. $72.50
A systematic definition of technical terms and of the criteria used to date shapes and motifs.

480.437 Zazoff, P.
Die Antiken Gemmen. Munich, 1983. 24.5 x 16.5. 446 pp., 132 pls., 83 figs.
$110.00
Attempt at an update of Furtwaengler's **Die antiken Gemmen**. Most helpful survey, many photographs, line drawings and a concise text help to increase the usefulness of this handbook. Recommended as a quick but thorough reference tool.

137.97 Zwierlein-Diehl, E. Kunsthistorisches Museum.
Die antiken Gemmen des Kunsthistorischen Museums in Wien. I: Die Gemmen von der minoischen Zeit bis zur fruehen roemischen Kaiserzeit. Munich, 1973. 168 pp., 94 pls. $125.00
Thorough presentation of famous collection originally formed by the Habsburgs.

Greek Gems, incl. Graeco-Persian and Cypriot

100.80
Antike Gemmen in deutschen Sammlungen.
The following have been published and are available either individually or as a set: THE EIGHT VOLUME SET $825.00

101.80 Brandt, E. Staatliche Muenzsammlung, Muenchen.
Antike Gemmen in deutschen Sammlungen. I-1: Griechische Gemmen von minoischer Zeit bis zum spaeten Hellenismus. Munich, 1968. 106 pp., 68 pls., illustrates 367 gems. $87.50

102.80 Brandt, E., (et. al.). Staatliche Muenzsammlung, Muenchen.
Antike Gemmen in deutschen Sammlungen. I-2: Italische Gemmen etruskisch bis roemisch-republikanisch; Italische Glaspasten vorkaiserzeitlich. Munich, 1970. 230 pp., 187 pls. illustrates 2,170 gems. $135.00

103.80 Brandt, E., (et. al.). Staatliche Muenzsammlung, Muenchen.
Antike Gemmen in deutschen Sammlungen. I-3: Gemmen und Glaspasten der roemische Kaiserzeit sowie Nachtraege. Munich, 1972. 221 pp., 336 pls., illustrates 3,584 gems. $150.00

104.80 Zwierlein-Diehl, E.
Antike Gemmen in deutschen Sammlungen. II: Staatliche Museen preussischer Kulturbesitz, Antikenabteilung Berlin. Munich, 1969. 198 pp., 106 pls., illustrates 564 gems. $125.00

105.80 Scherf, V., (et. al.).
Antike Gemmen in deutschen Sammlungen. III: Braunschweig; Goettingen; Kassel. Wiesbaden, 1970. 2 vols.: viii, 272 pp.; and 118 pls., illustrates 1,037 gems. $115.00

106.80 Schluter, M., (et. al.).
Antike Gemmen in deutschen Sammlungen. IV: Hannover, Kestner-Museum; Hamburg, Museum fuer Kunst und Gewerbe. Wiesbaden, 1975. 2 vols.: viii, 437 pp.; and 287 pls., illustrates 1,922 gems. $245.00

107.81 Babelon, E.
Collection Pauvert de la Chapelle, Intailles et Camées Paris, 1899. 20.5 x 29. xxiv, 63 pp., 10 pls. $425.00
Famous collection of gems, now part of the Bibliothèque Nationale.

160.120 Babelon, E. Bibliothèque Nationale.
Catalogue des Camées Antiques et Modernes. Paris, 1897. 463 pp., 13 figs. Paper. $85.00
Scarce text volume of the French national collection. Photocopies of the 76 plates can be supplied for an additional $45.00.

161.121 Babelon, E. Bibliothèque Nationale.
Les Pierres Gravées, Guide du Visiteur. Paris, 1930. 14 x 19. 155 pp., 32 pls.
     $57.50
Illustrates 158 important gems from the French national collection.

142.102 Boardman, J.
Island Gems, A study of Greek Seals in the Geometric and Early Archaic Periods. London, 1963. 22 x 14. 176 pp., 20 pls., 19 figs. Paper. $27.50
Out-of-print.

143.103 Boardman, J.
Archaic Greek Gems; schools and artists in the sixth and early fifth centuries B.C. Evanston, 1968. 25.5 x 19.5. 236 pp., 3 color pls., 40 pls. $36.00
Major study of the origins and development of Greek glyptic arts.

144.104 Boardman, J.
Engraved Gems: the Ionides Collection. Evanston, 1968. 114 pp., 30 pls. $43.00
Catalogues and illustrates 99 intaglios and cameos from this important collection, now dispersed. Out-of-print.

145.105 Boardman, J.
Greek Gems and Finger Rings: Early Bronze Age to Late Classical. New York, 1972. 32 x 24. 458 pp., 9 color pls., 1015 illus. $85.00
An important basic survey of ancient glyptics. Out-of-print.

146.106 Boardman, J.
Intaglios and Rings: Greek, Etruscan and Eastern. London, 1975. 25 x 18. 118 pp., 32 pls. $36.00
In-depth catalogue of a hitherto unpublished private collection of 214 rings and engraved gems.

147.107 Boardman, J. and Scarisbrick, D.
The Ralph Harari Collection of Finger Rings. London, 1977. 25 x 19. 149 pp., 52 pls., incl. 2 color pls. $38.50
Outstanding collection of 216 finger rings, and engraved gems, from Ancient to Neo-Classical, expertly presented.

159.119 Boardman, J. and Vollenweider, M.-L. Ashmolean Museum.
Catalogue of the Engraved Gems and Finger Rings. I: Greek and Etruscan. Oxford, 1978. 28 x 22. vi, 122 pp., 64 pls., 13 figs. $65.00
First volume in planned series publishing all gems and rings in the Ashmolean Museum. A beautiful collection!

641.608 Boardman, J. Museo Arqueologico Nacional.
Escarabeos de Piedra Procedentes de Ibiza. Madrid, 1984. 25 x 20. 103 pp., 41 pls. $18.00
Long awaited book on the Phoenician and Graeco-Phoenician scarabs from the Western Mediterranean.

149.109 Burlington Fine Arts Club.
Exhibition of Greek Art. London, 1904. 32 x 41.5. xxxii, 265 pp., 112 pls. $450.00
Oversized catalogue illustrating all branches of Greek art, includes many engraved gems from major English collections, now mostly dispersed. Scarce!

462.422 Contenau, G.
La Question des Origines Comparées les Cylindres Chypriotes. (Revue d'Assyriologie, vol. XV, 1918). 11 pp., 15 figs. Paper. $4.50
Attempt to link Cypriote and Elamite seals.

558.511 Cote, C. Hotel Drouot.
Catalogue des Antiquités Romaines et des Objets d'Art et de Haute Curiosité. Paris, 1936, 23.5 x 20.5 x 20.5. 22 pp. Paper. $12.50
This auction catalogue lists Roman silver spoons, Greek and Roman gems, Dark Age jewelry and other objects. Photocopies of the original plates can be supplied for an additional $5.00. Scarce.

704.683 De Juliis, M., (Ed.).
Gli Ori di Taranto in Eta Ellenistica. Milan, 1985. 27 x 23.5. 529 pp., num. ills. incl. num. color. $45.00
Major new exhibition catalogue of Greek jewelry - all from dated tombs in the Tarentum region. Includes a 60 page section on finger rings and 65 pages on different earring types. All are illustrated - many in detailed photographs. Recommended.

84.63 Densmore Curtis, C.
Sardis. XIII: Jewelry and Goldwork. Rome, 1925. 28 x 34.5. 48 pp., 11 pls. $115.00
Scarce publication showing all the gems and jewelry from this important East Greek site.

642.610 Furtwaengler, A.
Die Antiken Gemmen. Geschichte der Steinschneidekunst im klassischen Altertum. 3 vols.: xvi, 67 pls.; and viii, 330 pp.; and xii, 464 pp., 3 pls. $650.00
Three volume reprint of the original 1900 edition, now out-of-print. Contains the full text and all plates of the original edition at a fraction of the cost. A classic!

608.557 Gebhart, H.
Gemmen und Kameen. Berlin, 1925. 24 x 16. viii, 232 pp., 255 illus. $165.00
Excellent overview with a strong section on Post-Byzantine gems, the later artists and their signatures as they appear on gems. With 254 illustrations of individual stones.

152.112 Horster, G.
Statuen auf Gemmen. (Habelts Dissertationsdruecke, Reihe klassische Archaeologie, 1972.). Bonn, 1970. 21 x 15. 136 pp., 23 pls. Paper. $32.50
Ancient sculpture, often lost in the original, as shown on ancient gems. Out-of-print.

153.113 Karageorghis, G.
Un Cylindre de Chypre. (Syria, vol. XXXVI, 1959). 8 pp., 1 fig. Paper. $3.50

599.551 Kenna, V.E.G.
The seal use of Cyprus in the Bronze Age, III. (BCH, vol. XCII, 1968.). Paris, 1968. 14 pp., 6 figs. Paper. $11.50
Also contains: Kenna, V.E.G.,**The Kouklia ring from Evreti** and Catling, H.W., **Kouklia: Evreti Tomb 8.**

156.116 Lippold, G.
Gemmen und Kameen des Altertums und der Neuzeit. Stuttgart, 1921. 23 x 30. xii, 190 pp., 167 pls. $185.00
Clearly illustrates and briefly identifies 1695 engraved gems. Scarce!

167.129 Maaskant-Kleibrink, M. Royal Coin Cabinet.
Catalogue of the Engraved Gems in the Royal Coin Cabinet. The Hague, 1978. 2 vols.: 380 pp., 37 figs.; and 189 pls. $225.00
Major research into the technology of glyptic arts applied to a collection of 1172 gems, particularly strong in Roman gems. All are illustrated, with many technical details enlarged.

157.117 Masson, O.
Quelques Intailles Chypriotes Inscrites. (Syria, vol. XLIV, 1967). 11 pp., 2 pls., 5 figs. Paper. $6.50
Describes Graeco-Cypriot scarabs.

154.114 Neverov, O. Hermitage Museum.
Antique Cameos in the Hermitage Collection. Leningrad, 1971. 14 x 18. 95 pp., 107 color pls. $36.00
Attractive presentation of major ancient cameos. Out-of-print.

155.115 Neverov, O. Hermitage Museum.
Antique Intaglios in the Hermitage Collection. Leningrad, 1976. 14 x 18. 112 pp., 290 pls., incl. 107 color pls. $36.00
Elegantly illustrates and describes 145 superb gems in color and B. & W. Out-of-print.

531. 485 Nicholls, R.
The Wellcome Gems: A Fitzwilliam Museum Catalogue. Cambridge, 1983. 15 x 21. 57 pp., num. illus. Paper. $12.50
Supplementary catalogue of 250 Ancient and Later gems to the soon to be published **Classical Gems: Ancient and Modern Intaglios and Cameos in the Fitzwilliam Museum, Cambridge.**, most are illustrated.

71.51 Porada, E., (Ed.).
Ancient Art in Seals. Princeton, 1980. 24 x 16. 131 pp., 27 pls., 2 maps. $28.50
Essays by P. Amiet, N. Ozguec and J. Boardman with a lengthy introduction by Dr. Porada on various aspects of ancient glyptics.

164.124 Reinach, S.
Pierres Gravées. Paris, 1895. 20 x 29. 195 pp., 138 pls. Paper. $245.00
Illustrates, on 137 engraved plates, 2,150 engraved gems from famous European collections; incorporates early research by Eckel, Gori, Levesque de Gravelle, Mariette, Millin and Stosch.

133.93 Richter, G.M.A. Metropolitan Museum of Art.
Catalogue of the Engraved Gems of the Classical Style. New York, 1920. 14 x 22. lxxxiv, 232 pp., 88 pls. $115.00
Limited edition of 1000. Includes the Minoan and Mycenaean gems omitted from the 1956 edition. Scarce!

158.118 Richter, G.M.A. Metropolitan Museum of Art.
Catalogue of the Engraved Gems, Greek, Etruscan and Roman. Rome, 1956. xliii, 143 pp., 75 pls., num. illus. Paper. $175.00
America's premier collection, expertly catalogued and annotated. Out-of-print.

165.126 Richter, G.M.A.
The Engraved Gems of the Greeks, Etruscans and Romans. I: A History of Greek Art in Miniature. London, 1968. 24 x 33.5. x, 339 pp., 2 color pls., num. figs. $140.00

510.465 Richter, G.M.A. Metropolitan Museum of Art.
Ancient Gems from the Evans and Beatty Collections. New York, 1942. 19 x 13. 32 pp., 54 illus. Paper. $28.50
Scarce publication shows 63 gems newly acquired by The Museum from the Evans and Beatty Collections, all are shown in enlargements.

163.123 Scarisbrick, D.
The Wellington Gems. London, 1977. 23 x 15.5. 72 pp. Paper. $18.50
Together with: Scarisbrick, D., **Further Wellington Gems and Historic Rings**. London, 1978. 22 pp., 4 pls. Two privately printed handlists of a large and varied collection of ancient and later gems.

74.54 Six, J.
De la Glyptique Syro-Hittite jusqu'a Praxitéle. (Syria, 1925). 28 x 22. 10 pp., 15 figs. Paper. $5.50
East meets West in art on cylinder seals.

454.127 Story-Maskelyne, N.M.H.
Catalogue of the Marlborough Gems, being a collection of Works in Cameo and Intaglio, formed by George, 3rd Duke of Marlborough. London, 1899. 17 x 25.5. xix, 122 pp., 14 pls. Full leather binding. $450.00
Extremely scarce sale catalogue of the Marlborough Collection with a lenghty introduction by Story-Maskelyne; our copy includes prices realized written in the margins. A superbly bound copy in full red morocco with gold stamping and gilt top edge.

162.122 Vermeule, C.C. The University Museum.
Cameo and Intaglio, Engraved Gems from the Sommerville Collection. Philadelphia, 1957. 15 x 21.5. 35 pp., 2 pls. Paper. $12.50
Exhibition catalogue of 650 gems of all periods.

572.525 Vermeule, C.C. Museum of Fine Arts.
A Collection of Greek and Roman Gems. (**Bulletin**, vol. LXI, 1963). Boston, 1963. 27 x 17. 15 pp., 20 figs. Paper. $15.00
Publishes 18 newly acquired intaglii, all are illustrated.

148.108 Vermeule, C.C. Museum of Fine Arts.
Greek and Roman Gems: Recent Additions to the Collections. (**Bulletin**, vol. LXIV, 1966). 17 pp., 23 figs. Paper. $12.50
Publishes and illustrates 23 additional gems.

85.64 Vollenweider, M.-L. Musée d'Art et d'Histoire.
Catalogue raisonné des sceaux, cylindres et intailles. I. Geneva, 1967. 21.5 x 30. 217 pp., 95 pls. Paper. $95.00
Beautiful collection, expertly presented! Now out-of-print.

150.110 Vollenweider, M.-L. Musée d'Art et d'Histoire.
Catalogue raisonné des sceaux, cylindres, intailles et camées. II: Les portraits, les masques de théatre, les symboles politiques; une contribution à l'histoire des civilisations hellénistique et romaine. Mainz, 1076. 30 x 21. 9 pp., 144 pls. $90.00
Second volume of the Geneva Collection Catalogues.

151.111 Vollenweider, M.-L. Musée d'Art et d'Histoire.
Catalogue raisonné des sceaux, cylindres, intailles et camées. II: Les portraits, les masques de théatre, les symboles politiques; une contribution à l'histoire des civilisations hellénistique et romaine. Mainz, 1979. 30 x 22. xxi, 563 pp., 8 color pls., 10 figs. $135.00
Eagerly awaited text volume describing the gems in the previously published volume of plates, our no. 150.110, above.

463.423 Vollenweider, M.-L. Musée d'Art et d'Histoire.
Catalogue raisonné des sceaux, cylindres, intailles et camées. III: La Collection du Révérend Dr. V.E.G. Kenna et d'autres acquisitions et dons récents. Mainz, 1983. 22 x 30. xx, 242 pp., 115 pls. $85.00
Third volume of the Geneva Collections; especially strong in Near Eastern material of all periods.

511.466 Vollenweider, M.-L.
Deliciae Leonis: Antike geschnittene Steine und Ringe aus einer Privatsammlung. Mainz, 1984. 22 x 30.5. ix, 322 pp., 8 color pls., 105 pls., 5 figs. $87.50
It is easy to like these "Deliciae Leonis"! A worthy tribute to a superb collection of, mostly, Greek, Etruscan and Roman engraved gems and rings.

480.437 Zazoff, P.
Die Antiken Gemmen. Munich, 1983. 24.5 x 16.5. 446 pp., 132 pls., 82 figs.
$110.00
Attempt at an update of Furtwaengler's **Die antiken Gemmen**. Most helpful survey, many photographs, line drawings and a concise text help to increase the usefulness of this handbook. Recommended as a quick but thorough reference tool.

137.97 Zwierlein-Diehl, E. Kunsthistorisches Museum.
Die antiken Gemmen des Kunsthistorischen Museums in Wien. I: Die Gemmen von der minoischen Zeit bis zur fruehen roemischen Kaiserzeit. Munich, 1973. 168 pp., 94 pls. $125.00
Thorough presentation of famous collection originally formed by the Habsburgs.

138.98 Zwierlein-Diehl, E. Kunsthistorisches Museum
Die antiken Gemmen des Kunsthistorischen Museums in Wien. II: Die Glasgemmen – Die Glaskameen; Nachtraege zu Band I: Die Gemmen der spaeteren roemischen Kaiserzeit. Part I: Gotter. Munich, 1979. 414 pp., 166 pls. $145.00
Continuation of our no. 137.97 above.

Etruscan Gems

100.80
Antike Gemmen in deutschen Sammlungen
The following have been published and are available either individually or as a set: THE EIGHT VOLUME SET $825.00

101.80 Brandt, E. Staatliche Muenzsammlung, Muenchen.
Antike Gemmen in deutschen Sammlungen. I-1: Griechische Gemmen von minoischer Zeit bis zum spaeten Hellenismus. Munich, 1968. 106 pp., 68 pls., illustrates 367 gems. $87.50

102.80 Brandt, E., (et al.). Staatliche Muenzsammlung, Muenchen.
Antike Gemmen in deutschen Sammlungen. I-2: Italische Gemmen etruskisch bis roemisch-republikanisch; Italische Glaspasten vorkaiserzeitlich. Munich, 1970. 230 pp., 187 pls. illustrates 2,170 gems. $135.00

103.80 Brandt, E., (et al.). Staatliche Muenzsammlung, Muenchen.
Antike Gemmen in deutschen Sammlungen. I-3: Gemmen und Glaspasten der roemischen Kaiserzeit sowie Nachtraege. Munich, 1972. 221 pp., 336 pls., illustrates 3,584 gems. $150.00

104.80 Zwierlein-Diehl, E.
Antike Gemmen in deutschen Sammlungen. II: Staatliche Museen preussischer Kulturbesitz, Antikenabteilung Berlin. Munich, 1969. 198 pp., 106 pls., illustrates 564 gems. $125.00

105.80 Scherf, V., (et al.).
Antike Gemmen in deutschen Sammlungen. III: Braunschweig; Goettingen; Kassel. Wiesbaden, 1970. 2 vols.: viii, 272 pp.; and 118 pls., illustrates 1,037 gems. $115.00

106.80 Schluter, M., (et al.).
Antike Gemmen in deutschen Sammlungen. IV: Hannover, Kestner-Museum; Hamburg, Museum fuer Kunst und Gewerbe. Wiesbaden, 1975. 2 vols.: viii, 437 pp.; and 287 pls., illustrates 1,922 gems. $245.00

107.81 Babelon, E.
Collection Pauvert de la Chapelle, Intailles et Camées. Paris, 1899. 20.5 x 29. xxiv, 63 pp., 10 pls. $245.00
Famous collection of gems, now part of the Bibliothèque Nationale.

161.121 Babelon, E. Bibliothèque Nationale.
Les Pierres Gravées, Guide du Visiteur. Paris, 1930. 14 x 19. 155 pp., 32 pls.
$57.50
Illustrates 158 important gems from the French national collection.

108.410 Battaglia, G.B.
Gioelli Antichi dall'eta Micenea all'Ellenismo. Rome, 1982. 24.5 x 31. 38 pp., 82 color illus. Paper. $22.50
Handsomely illustrated catalogue of the famous Castellani Collection of ancient jewelry, now in the Villa Giulia, Rome.

146.106 Boardman, J.
Intaglios and Rings: Greek, Etruscan and Eastern. London, 1975. 25 x 18. 118 pp., 32 pls. $36.00
In-depth catalogue of a hitherto unpublished private collection of 214 rings and engraved gems.

147.107 Boardman, J. and Scarisbrick, D.
The Ralph Harari Collection of Finger Rings. London, 1977. 25 x 19. 149 pp., 52 pls., incl. 2 color. $38.50
Outstanding collection of 216 finger rings, and engraved gems, from Ancient to Neo-Classical, expertly presented.

159.119 Boardman, J. and Vollenweider, M.-L. Ashmolean Museum.
Catalogue of the Engraved Gems and Finger Rings. I: Greek and Etruscan. Oxford, 1978. 28 x 22. vi, 122 pp., 64 pls., 13 figs. $65.00
First volume in planned series publishing all gems and rings in the Ashmolean Museum. A beautiful collection!

483.440 Cristofani, M. and Martelli, M.
L'Oro degli Etruschi. Novara, 1983. 23 x 31. 343 pp., 310 color illus., 17 figs. Slipcase. $110.00
Superbly illustrated publication shows the full range and splendor of Etruscan gold and bead jewelry, some set with gems, of all periods. Includes a separate section on technique. Likely to become a standard reference!

529.483 Forber, B.A.
Catalogue of Engraved Gems in the Art Museum, Princeton University. Berkeley, 1978. 16 x 21. 236 pp., 75 pls., fig. Paper. $60.00
Xerographic copy of a doctoral thesis, plates are of mediocre quality, text describes nearly 200 gems, mostly of Roman date, some of doubtful age.

642.610 Furtwaengler, A.
Die Antiken Gemmen. Geschichte der Steinschneidekunst im klassischen Altertum. 3 vols.: xvi, 67 pls.; and viii, 330 pp.; and xii, 464 pp., 3 pls. $650.00
Three volume reprint of the original 1900 edition, now out-of-print. Contains the full text and all plates of the original edition at a fraction of the cost. A classic!

608.557 Gebhart, H.
Gemmen und Kameen. Berlin, 1925. 24 x 16. viii, 232 pp., 255 illus. $165.00
Excellent overview with a strong section on Post-Byzantine gems, the later artists and their signatures as they appear on gems. With 254 illustrations of individual stones.

166.128 Guzzo, P.G.
Le Gemme a scarabeo del Museo Nazionale di Napoli. (MEFRA, vol. 83, 1971). 24 x 16. 42 pp., 7 pls. Paper. $12.50
First publication and illustration of 77 scarabs and 9 finger rings from 15 known findspots.

167.129 Maaskant-Kleibrink, M. Royal Coin Cabinet.
Catalogue of the Engraved Gems in the Royal Coin Cabinet. The Hague, 1978. 2 vols.: 380 pp., 37 figs.; and 189 pls. $225.00
Major research into the technology of glyptic arts applied to a collection of 1172 gems, particularly strong in Roman gems. All are illustrated, with many technical details enlarged.

168.130 Martini, W.
Die Etruskische Ringsteinglyptik. (Mitteilungen des deutschen archaeologischen Instituts, 18). Heidelberg, 1971. 28.5 x 20. 169 pp., 40 pls. Paper. $55.00
Illustrates 336 scarabs and shows how they developed into the Italic ringstones of the first century BC.

133.93 Richter, G.M.A. Metropolitan Museum of Art.
Catalogue of the Engraved Gems of the Classical Style. New York, 1920. 14 x 22. lxxiv, 232 pp., 88 pls. $115.00
Limited edition of 1000. Includes the Minoan and Mycenaean gems omitted from the 1956 edition. Scarce!

158.118 Richter, G.M.A. Metropolitan Museum of Art.
Catalogue of the Engraved Gems, Greek, Etruscan and Roman. Rome, 1956. xliii, 143 pp., 75 pls., num. illus. Paper. $175.00
America's premier collection, expertly catalogued and annotated. Out-of-print.

165.126 Richter, G.M.A.
The Engraved Gems of the Greeks, Etruscans and Romans. I: A History of Greek Art in Miniature. London, 1968. 24 x 33.5. x, 339 pp., 2 color pls., num. figs. $140.00

510.465 Richter, G.M.A. Metropolitan Museum of Art.
Ancient Gems from the Evans and Beatty Collections. New York, 1942. 19 x 13. 32 pp., 54 illus. Paper. $28.50
Scarce publication shows 63 gems newly acquired by The Museum from the Evans and Beatty Collections, all are shown in enlargements.

611.560 Scarpignato, M.
Oreficerie etrusche arcaiche del Museo Gregoriano-Etrusco. (Monumenti Musei e Gallerie Pontificie, n.d.). 21.5 x 24. 69 pp., 120 pls., incl. 35 color.
$65.00
Newly published museum catalogue of Archaic Etruscan jewelry.

454.127 Story-Maskelyne, N.M.H.
Catalogue of the Marlborough Gems, being a collection of Works in Cameo and Intaglio, formed by George, 3rd Duke of Marlborough. London, 1899. 17 x 25.5. xix, 122 pp., 14 pls. Full leather binding. $450.00
Extremely scarce sale catalogue of the Marlborough Collection with a lenghty introduction by Story-Maskelyne; our copy includes prices realized written in the margins. A superbly bound copy in full red morocco with gold stamping and gilt top edge.

162.122 Vermeule, C.C. The University Museum.
Cameo and Intaglio, Engraved Gems from the Sommerville Collection. Philadelphia, 1957. 15 x 21.5. 35 pp., 2 pls. Paper. $12.50
Exhibition catalogue of 650 gems of all periods.

463.423 Vollenweider, M.-L. Musée d'Art et d'Histoire.
Catalogue raisonné des sceaux, cylindres, intailles et camées. III: La Collection du Révérend Dr. V.E.G. Kenna et d'autres acquisitions et dons récents. Mainz, 1983. 22 x 30. xx, 242 pp., 115 pls. $85.00
Third volume of the Geneva Collections; especially strong in Near Eastern material of all periods.

511.466 Vollenweider, M.-L.
Deliciae Leonis: Antike geschnittene Steine und Ringe aus einer Privatsammlung. Mainz, 1984. 22 x 30.5. ix, 322 pp., 8 color pls., 105 pls., 5 figs. $87.50
It is easy to like these "Deliciae Leonis"! A worthy tribute to a superb collection of, mostly Greek, Etruscan and Roman engraved gems and rings.

169.131 Zazoff, P.
Etruskische Skarabaeen. Mainz, 1968. 32 x 23. vii, 227 pp., 55 pls. $65.00
Thorough study of all aspects of Etruscan gem engraving; describes 1,580 examples. With extensive bibliography.

480.437 Zazoff, P.
Die Antiken Gemmen. Munich, 1983. 24.5 x 16.5. 446 pp., 132 pls., 82 figs.
$110.00
Attempt at an update of Furtwaengler's **Die antiken Gemmen**. Most helpful survey, many photographs, line drawings and a concise text help to increase the usefulness of this handbook. Recommended as a quick but thorough reference tool.

Roman Gems, incl. "Gnostic" Gems

100.80
Antike Gemmen in deutschen Sammlungen.
The following have been published and are available either individually or as a set: THE EIGHT VOLUME SET $825.00

101.80 Brandt, E. Staatliche Muenzsammlung, Muenchen.
Antike Gemmen in deutschen Sammlungen. I-1: Griechische Gemmen von minoischer Zeit bis zum spaeten Hellenismus. Munich, 1968. 106 pp., 68 pls. illustrates 367 gems. $87.50

102.80 Brandt, E., (et al.). Staatliche Muenzsammlung, Muenchen.
Antike Gemmen in deutschen Sammlungen. I-2: Italische Gemmen etruskisch bis roemisch-republikanisch; Italische Glaspasten vorkaiserzeitlich. Munich, 1970. 230 pp., 187 pls. illustrates 2,170 gems. $135.00

103.80 Brandt, E., (et al.). Staatliche Muenzsammlung, Muenchen.
Antike Gemmen in deutschen Sammlungen. I-3: Gemmen und Glaspasten der roemische Kaiserzeit sowie Nachtraege. Munich, 1972. 221 pp., 336 pls., illustrates 3,584 gems. $150.00

104.80 Zwierlein-Diehl, E.
Antike Gemmen in deutschen Sammlungen. II: Staatliche Museen preussischer Kulturbesitz, Antikenabteilung Berlin. Munich, 1969. 198 pp., 106 pls., illustrates 564 gems. $125.00

105.80 Scherf, V., (et al.).
Antike Gemmen in deutschen Sammlungen. III: Braunschweig; Goettingen; Kassel. Wiesbaden, 1970. 2 vols.: viii, 272 pp.; and 118 pls., illustrates 1,037 gems. $115.00

106.80 Schluter, M., (et al.).
Antike Gemmen in deutschen Sammlungen. IV: Hannover, Kestner-Museum; Hamburg, Museum fuer Kunst und Gewerbe. Wiesbaden, 1975. 2 vols.: viii, 437 pp.; and 287 pls., illustrates 1,922 gems. $245.00

107.81 Babelon, E.
Collection Pauvert de la Chapelle, Intailles et Camées. Paris, 1899. 20.5 x 29. xxiv, 63 pp., 10 pls. $425.00
Famous collection of gems, now part of the Bibliothèque Nationale.

160.120 Babelon, E. Bibliothèque Nationale.
Catalogue des Camées Antiques et Modernes. Paris, 1897. 463 pp., 13 figs. Paper. $85.00
Scarce text volume of the French national collection. Photo-copies of the 76 plates can be supplied for an additional $45.00.

161.121 Babelon, E. Bibliothèque Nationale.
Les Pierres Gravées, Guide du Visiteur. Paris, 1930. 14 x 19. 155 pp., 32 pls. $57.50
Illustrates 158 important gems from the French national collection.

170.132 Le Blant, E.
750 Inscriptions de Pierres Gravées Inédites ou peu connues. Paris, 1896. 23 x 28. 210 pp., 2 pls. Paper. $72.50
Most useful compilation of inscriptions on ancient gems, both cameos and intaglios. Rare!

171.133 Berry, B.Y. Indiana University.
Ancient gems from the collection of Burton Y. Berry. Bloomington, 1968. 25 x 21. 151 pp., num. illus. Paper. $30.00
Catalogues and illustrates 259 ancient, mostly Roman, gems.

147.107 Boardman, J. and Scarisbrick, D.
The Ralph Harari Collection of Finger Rings. London, 1977. 25 x 19. 149 pp., 52 pls., incl. 2 color pls. $38.50
Outstanding collection of 216 finger rings, and engraved gems, from Ancient to Neo-Classical, expertly presented.

172.134 Bruns, G.
Staatskameen des 4. Jahrhunderts nach Christi Geburt. (**BWP**, 104, 1948). 31 x 23. 40 pp., 27 figs. Paper. $36.50
Cameos as historical documents, depicted in official Court Style.

173.135 Buehler, H.-P.
Antike Gefaesse aus Edelsteinen. Mainz, 1973. 30 x 21. 85 pp., 40 pls., incl. 2 color pls., 1 fig. $65.00
First attempt at a corpus of surviving hardstone vessels, with discussion of shapes, dates.

597.549 Mesnil du Buisson.
Les Tessères et les Monnaies de Palmyre. Paris, 1944 - 1962. 22 x 28.5. 2 vols.: 834 pp., 324 figs.; and 16 pp., 125 pls. 1 text vol., 1 portfolio of loose pls. $170.00
Scarce study of Palmyran culture and philosophy, illustrated with many hundreds of detailed photographs and figures of the tesserae and coins with their distinct iconography, so similar to that found on the gems. Recommended!

174.136 Chiesa, G.S.
Gemme di Luni. Rome, 1978. 24 x 17. 141 pp., 25 pls. Paper. $55.00
Elaboration of earlier theories, exemplified by intaglios from a second Roman gem engraving center.

558.511 Cote, C. Hotel Drouot.
Catalogue des Antiquités Romaines et des Objets d'Art et de Haute Curiosité. Paris, 1936. 23.5 x 20.5. 22 pp. Paper. $12.50
This auction catalogue lists Roman silver spoons, Greek and roman gems, Dark Age jewelry and other objects. Photocopies of the original plates can be supplied for an additional $5.00. Scarce.

175.137 Cumont, F.
Un Intaille Provenant d'Emèse. (**Syria**, 1926). 6 pp., 1 fig. Paper. $4.50
Shows an intaglio engraved on both sides with inscriptions and images of the Tyche of Rome and of Antioch.

177.139 Dacos, N., (et al.). Museo Mediceo.
Il Tesoro di Lorenzo il Magnifico: Le Gemme. Catalogue della Mostra, Palazzo Medici Riccardi, Firenze, 1972. Florence, 1973. 24 x 17. vi, 167 pp., 15 color pls., 99 illus. Paper. $32.50
Contains descriptions of ancient and Neo-Classical gems and an important 15th century invention.

178.140 Dacos, N., (et al.). Museo Mediceo.
Il Tesoro di Lorenzo il Magnifico, repertorio delle gemme e dei vasi. Florence, 1980. 17.5 x 25. 302 pp., 23 color pls., 208 illus. $45.00
Contains all of the above plus the 1974 catalogue of the hardstone vases and other carvings, now in a 2nd edition combined in one volume.

87.66 De Ridder, A.
Collection de Clercq. VII: Les Bijoux et les Pierres Gravées. Paris, 1911. 28 x 36.5. Paper. $190.00
Part II: **Les Pierres Gravées.** 438 pp., 15 pls. Catalogues 1135 ancient gems. Scarce!

507.462 Delatte, A. and Derchain, Ph. Bibliothèque Nationale
Les Intailles Magiques Gréco - Egyptiennes. Paris, 1964. 24 x 15.5. 380 pp., 527 figs., 4 color pls. Paper. $125.00
Scarce catalogue of the "Gnostic" gems in the Bibliothèque Nationale, all are illustrated, transliterated and translated. With numerous references to other collections. Recommended.

176.138 Deonna, W.
Gemmes Antiques de la Collection Duval. (Aréthuse, 1925). 20 x 25. 18 pp., 5 pls. Paper. $16.50
A collection of 129 gems, all illustrated and described.

188.150 Dimitrova-Milcheva, A.
Antique Engraved Gems and Cameos in the National Archaeological Museum in Sofia. Sofia, 1981. 21 x 29. 171 pp., 4 color pls., 64 pls. $22.50
Well presented catalogue of 326 gems, all illustrated in enlargements, mostly with known find-spots within Bulgaria.

489.446 Hotel Drouot.
Pierres Gravées, Camées Objets Divers: Antiques, de la Renaissance et Modernes. Paris, 1926. 26 x 18. 12 pp., 1 pl. Paper. $18.50

623.572 Hotel Drouot.
Bijoux Antiques - Camées - Intailles. Paris, 1959. 26.5 x 21. 24 pp., 7 pls. Paper. $12.50
Catalogue of an auction that dispersed, among others, 51 pairs of ancient earrings, (Roman and earlier), 110 engraved gems, (all illustrated). With prices realized marked in the margin.

193.156 Eichler, F. and Kris, E. Kunsthistorisches Museum.
Die Kameen im Kunsthistorischen Museum. Vienna, 1927. 24 x 31. x, 246 pp., 84 pls., 83 figs. $550.00
Indispensable text on cameo carving, long out-of-print.

179.141 Foerschner, G. Historisches Museum.
Glaspasten, Geschnittene Steine, Arabische Muenzgewichte. Melsungen, 1982. 17 x 22. 111 pp., 7 color pls., num. illus. Paper. $18.50
Large and varied collection of interesting material in new publication.

529.483 Forber, B.A.
Catalogue of Engraved Gems in the Art Museum, Princeton University. Berkeley, 1978. 16 x 21. 236 pp., 75 pls., fig. Paper. $60.00
Xerographic copy of a doctoral thesis, plates are of mediocre quality, text describes nearly 200 gems, mostly of Roman date, some of doubtful age.

9.155 Fremersdorf, F. Museo Sacro.
Antikes, Islamisches und Mittelalterliches Glas sowie kleinere Arbeiten aus Stein, Gagat und verwandten Stoffen in den Vatikanischen Sammlungen Roms. Vatican City, 1975. 23.5 x 41. 133 pp., 2 color pls., 92 pls. $250.00
Large format catalogue; contains lengthy sections on beads, gems and hardstone carvings-in-the-round in the Vatican Museums.

642.610 Furtwaengler, A.
Die Antiken Gemmen. Geschichte der Steinschneidekunst im klassischen Altertum. 3 vols.: xvi, 67 pls.; and viii, 330 pp.; and xii, 464 pp., 3 pls. $650.00
Three volume reprint of the original 1900 edition, now out-of-print. Contains the full text and all plates of the original edition at a fraction of the cost. A classic!

508.463 Goldstein, S., (et al.).
Cameo Glass: Masterpieces from 2000 Years of Glassmaking. Corning, N.Y., 1982. 27.5 x 20. 140 pp., 158 illus. incl. many color. Paper. $18.50
Glass vessels and gems, Roman, Islamic, Oriental and Neo-Classical, all created by wheel cutting and other glyptic skills. Well catalogued and illustrated, with a glossary and bibliography.

180.142 Gramatopol, M.
Les pierres gravées du Cabinet Numismatique de l'Académie Roumaine. (Collection Latomus, 138). Brussels, 1974. 130 pp., 47 pls. Paper. $32.00
Catalogues and illustrates 965 gems, mostly Roman and Later.

516.470 Grand Palais.
Le Trésor de Saint-Marc de Vénise. Paris, 1974. 23 x 26. 337 pp., num. pls., incl. color. Paper. $37.50
Superbly produced catalogue of a superb exhibition of major Antique hardstone vessels and related objects. Many additional treasures from the French national collections are added. Recommended! English version also available.

181.143 Hafner, G.
Der Adlerkameo und die "Auffindung des Telephos". (Aachener Kunstblaetter, 38). Aachen, 1969. 29 pp., 42 illus. Paper. $12.50
Iconographical study illustrated with detailed photographs.

182.144 Hamburger, A.
Gems from Caesarea Maritima. ('Atiqot, VIII). Jerusalem, 1968. 37 pp., 8 pls. Paper. $24.00
Catalogues and illustrates 165 gems from this important Roman city in Israel. Out-of-print.

183.145 Henig, M.
Corpus of Roman Engraved Gemstones from British Sites. (BAR, 8). Oxford, 1978. 391 pp., 76 pls., 3 figs. Paper. $48.50
Most interesting general discussion of Roman glyptic arts combined with a catalogue of all known gems from Britain. Recommended!

184.146 Henig, M.
The Lewis collection of engraved gemstones in Corpus Christi College, Cambridge. (BAR, S-1). Oxford, 1975. 94 pp., 29 pls. Paper. $12.50
Finally illustrates and newly discusses the gems first published by J.H. Middleton in 1892, **The Lewis collection of gems and rings in the possission of Corpus Christi College, Cambridge.**

152.112 Horster, G.
Statuen auf Gemmen. (**Habelts Dissertationsdruecke, Reihe klassische Archaeologie**, 1972.). Bonn, 1970. 21 x 15. 136 pp., 23 pls. Paper. $32.50
Ancient sculpture, often lost in the original, as shown on ancient gems. Out-of-print.

185.147 Kaehler, H., (Ed.).
Alberti Rubeni Dissertatio de Gemme Augustea. (**Monumente Artis Romanae**, IX). Berlin, 1968. 40 pp., 1 color pl., 24 pls. $48.50
Includes a facsimile of the text and illustration by Rubens from ca. 1625. With 24 superbly detailed photographs of this famous cameo. Out-of-print.

186.148 Kibaltchich, T.W.
Gemmes de la Russie Méridionale. Berlin, 1910. 88 pp., 20 pls. Edition limited to 250 copies. $325.00
Collection of 511 items; mostly Roman gems, with many interesting "Gnostic" types.

187.149 Krug. A.
Antike Gemmen im Roemisch-Germanischen Museum Koeln. Frankfurt, a/M., 1981. 18 x 28. 113 pp., 73 pls. Paper. $22.50
Collection of 481 mostly Roman gems, all illustrated and described.

156.116 Lippold, G.
Gemmen und Kameen des Altertums und der Neuzeit. Stuttgart, 1921. 23 x 30. xii, 190 pp., 167 pls. $185.00
Clearly illustrates and briefly identifies 1695 engraved gems. Scarce!

167.129 Maaskant-Kleibrink, M. Royal Coin Cabinet.
Catalogue of the Engraved Gems in the Royal Coin Cabinet. The Hague, 1978. 2 vols.: 380 pp., 37 figs.; and 189 pls. $225.00
Major research into the technology of glyptic arts applied to a collection of 1172 gems, particularly strong in Roman gems. All are illustrated, with many technical details enlarged.

154.114 Neverov, O. Hermitage Museum.
Antique Cameos in the Hermitage Collection. Leningrad, 1971. 14 x 18. 95 pp., 107 color pls. $36.00
Attractive presentation of major ancient cameos. Out-of-print.

155.115 Neverov, O. Hermitage Museum.
Antique Intaglios in the Hermitage Collection. Leningrad, 1976. 14 x 18. 112 pp., 290 pls., incl. 107 color pls. $36.00
Elegantly illustrates and describes 145 superb gems in color and B. & W. Out-of-print.

531.485 Nicholls, R.
The Wellcome Gems: A Fitzwilliam Museum Catalogue. Cambridge, 1983. 15 x 21. 57 pp., num. illus. Paper. $12.50
Supplementary catalogue of 250 Ancient and Later gems to the soon to be published **Classical Gems: Ancient and Modern Intaglios and Cameos in the Fitzwilliam Museum, Cambridge.**, most are illustrated.

648. 616 Philipp, H.
Mira et Magica: Gemmen im Aegyptischen Museum Berlin-Charlottenburg. Mainz, 1984. 136 pp., 55 pls., 207 illus. $72.50
Approximately 200 "magical gems", many originally from the collection of Philipp Stosch in 1764, later scorned by Furtwaengler, who refused to include them in his publication of the gems in the Antiquarium, (1896), finally published and interpreted.

509.464 Platz-Horster, G.
Die antiken Gemmen im Rheinischen Landesmuseum Bonn. Bonn, 1984. 24.5 x 17. 141 pp., 36 pls. $18.50
Large collection of mostly Roman gems, mounted and unmounted, with known dates and findspots from the Bonn area.

164.124 Reinach, S.
Pierres Gravées. Paris, 1895. 20 x 29. 195 pp., 138 pls. Paper. $245.00
Illustrates, on 137 engraved plates, 2,150 engraved gems from famous European collections; incorporates early research by Eckel, Gori, Levesque de Gravelle, Mariette, Millin and Stosch.

133.93 Richter, G.M.A. Metropolitan Museum of Art.
Catalogue of the Engraved Gems of the Classical Style. New York, 1920. 14 x 22. lxxiv, 232 pp., 88 pls. $115.00
Limited edition of 1000. Includes the Minoan and Mycenaean gems omitted from the 1956 edition. Scarce!

158.118 Richter, G.M.A. Metropolitan Museum of Art.
Catalogue of the Engraved Gems, Greek, Etruscan and Roman. Rome, 1956. xliii, 143 pp., 75 pls., num. illus. Paper. $175.00
America's premier collection, expertly catalogued and annotated. Out-of-print.

510.465 Richter, G.M.A. Metropolitan Museum of Art.
Ancient Gems from the Evans and Beatty Collections. New York, 1942. 19 x 13. 32 pp., 54 illus. Paper. $28.50
Scarce publication shows 63 gems newly acquired by The Museum from the Evans and Beatty Collections, all are shown in enlargements.

679.658 Richter, G.M.A.
The Engraved Gems of the Greeks, Etruscans and Romans. II: Engraved Gems of the Romans, a Supplement to the History of Roman Art. London, 1971. 24 x 33.5. x, 307 pp., 120 pls. $140.00

190.152 Righetti, R.
Gemme e cammei delle collezioni comunali. (Cataloghi dei musei comunali di Roma, 4). Rome, 1955. 115 pp., 20 pls. Paper. $13.50
Catalogues 276 gems, Roman and Neo-Classical, from three museums.

191.153 Righetti, R.
Opere di Glittica dei Museo Sacro e Profano. Vatican City, 1955. 52 pp., 17 pls. Paper. $16.50
Collection strong in Byzantine gems, some Roman and Neo-Classical.

163.123 Scarisbrick, D.
The Wellington Gems. London, 1977. 23 x 15.5. 72 pp. Paper. $18.50
Together with: Scarisbrick, D., **Further Wellington Gems and Historic Rings.** London, 1978. 22 pp., 4 pls. Two privately printed handlists of a large and varied collection of ancient and later gems.

192.154 Stenico, A.
Un intaglio magico Greco-Orientale al Museo di Pavia. (**Boll. Soc. Pavese di Storia Patria**, vol. XXII-XXIII, 1973.). 17 x 24. 10 pp., 4 illus. Paper. $7.50
Large magical gem with lengthy inscriptions on both sides, with parallels from other collections.

454.127 Story-Maskelyne, N.M.H.
Catalogue of the Marlborough Gems, being a collection of Works in Cameo and Intaglio, formed by George, 3rd Duke of Marlborough. London, 1899. 17 x 25.5. xix, 122 pp., 14 pls. Full leather binding. $450.00
Extremely scarce sale catalogue of the Marlborough Collection with a lengthy introduction by Story-Maskelyne; our copy includes prices realized written in the margins. A superbly bound copy in full red morocco with gold stamping and gilt top edge.

89.68 Tillot, M.
Mille ans d'art à Carthage. Tunis, 1978. 20.5 x 20. 80 pp., 88 color pls. $18.50
Handsomely presents gems, amulets and jewelry from ancient Phoenician and Roman sites.

189.151 Veillard, J.-Y. Musée de Rennes.
Catalogue des Intailles et Camées de la Collection du Président de Robien. Rennes, 1972. 44 pp., 18 pls. Paper. $20.00
Presents an obscure collection of, mostly, Roman gems.

162.122 Vermeule, C.C. The University Museum.
Cameo and Intaglio, Engraved Gems from the Sommerville Collection. Philadelphia, 1957. 15 x 21.5. 35 pp., 2 pls. Paper. $12.50
Exhibition catalogue of 650 gems of all periods.

572.525 Vermeule, C.C. Museum of Fine Arts.
A Collection of Greek and Roman Gems. (**Bulletin**, vol. LXI, 1963). Boston, 1963, 27 x 17. 15 pp., 20 figs. Paper. $15.00
Publishes 18 newly acquired intaglii, all are illustrated.

148.108 Vermeule, C.C. Museum of Fine Arts.
Greek and Roman Gems: Recent Additions to the Collections. (**Bulletin**, vol. LXIV, 1966). 17 pp., 23 figs. Paper. $12.50
Publishes and illustrates 23 additional gems.

150.110 Vollenweider, M.-L. Musée d'Art et d'Histoire.
Les portraits, les masques de théatre, les symboles politiques; une contribution à l'histoire des civilisations hellénistique et romaine. Mainz, 1976. 30 x 21. 9 pp., 144 pls. $90.00
Second volume of the Geneva Collection Catalogues.

150.111 Vollenweider, M.-L. Musée d'Art et d'Histoire.
Les portraits, les masques de théatre, les symboles politiques; une contribution à l'histoire des civilisations hellénistique et romaine. Mainz, 1979. 30 x 22. xxi, 563 pp., 8 color pls., 10 figs. $135.00
Eagerly awaited text volume describing the gems in the previously published volume of plates, our no. 150.110, above.

194.157 Vollenweider, M.-L.
Die Steinschneidekunst und ihre Kuenstler in Spaetrepublikanischer und Augusteischer Zeit. Baden, 1966. 20 x 29. 148 pp., 100 pls. $125.00
Basic text on artists, their known repertoire and characteristics of style. Out-of-print.

195.158 Vollenweider, M.-L.
Die Portraetgemmen der roemischen Republik. Mainz, 1974. 2 vols.: xiii, 316 pp.; and v, 110 pp., 168 pls. $250.00
Wide ranging study on the origins and development of Roman portraiture. Recommended!

463.423 Vollenweider, M.-L. Musée d'Art et d'Histoire.
Catalogue raisonné des sceaux, cylindres, intailles et camées. III: La Collection du Révérend Dr. V.E.G. Kenna et d'autres acquisitions et dons récents. Mainz, 1983. 22 x 30. xx, 242 pp., 115 pls. $85.00
Third volume of the Geneva Collections; especially strong in Near Eastern material of all periods.

511.466 Vollenweider, M.-L.
Deliciae Leonis: antike geschnittene Steine und Ringe aus einer Privatsammlung. Mainz, 1984. 22 x 30.5. ix, 322 pp., 8 color pls., 105 pls., 5 figs. $87.50
It is easy to like these "Deliciae Leonis"! A worthy tribute to a superb collection of, mostly, Greek, Etruscan and Roman engraved gems and rings.

515.469 Zahlhaas, G.
Fingerringe und Gemmen: Sammlung Dr. E. Pressmar. Munich, 1985. 69 pp., 161 illus. Paper. $14.50
First publication of a private collection of 100 finger rings, all are illustrated and classified as to origin and date. The collection is strongest in the more commonly encountered types, Roman, Byzantine and Islamic, some others.

196.159 Zahn, R.
Sammlung Baurat Schiller/Berlin. Berlin, 1929. 136 pp., 65 pls. Full leather binding. $275.00
A scholarly catalogue of a famous collection of ancient jewelry and glass, now dispersed. Scarce!

480.437 Zazoff, P.
Die Antiken Gemmen. Munich, 1983. 24.5 x 16.5. 446 pp., 132 pls., 82 figs. $110.00
Attempt at an update of Furtwaengler's **Die antiken Gemmen.** Most helpful survey, many photographs, line drawings and a concise text help to increase the usefulness of this handbook. Recommended as a quick but thorough reference tool.

137.97 Zwierlein-Diehl, E. Kunsthistorisches Museum.
Die antiken Gemmen des Kunsthistorischen Museums in Wien. I: die Gemmen von der minoischen Zeit bis zur fruehen roemischen Kaiserzeit. Munich, 1973. 168 pp., 94 pls. $125.00
Thorough presentation of famous collection originally formed by the Habsburgs.

138.98 Zwierlein-Diehl, E. Kunsthistorisches Museum.
Die antiken Gemmen des Kunsthistorischen Museums in Wien. II: Die Glasgemmen - Die Glaskameen; Nachtraege zu Band I: Die Gemmen der spaeteren roemischen Kaiserzeit. part I: Gotter.. Munich, 1979. 414 pp., 166 pls. $145.00
Continuation of our no. 137-97, above.

Sasanian Gems

197.160 Bivar, A.D.H.
Kushan and Kushano-Sasanian Seals and Kushano-Sasanian Coins: Sasanian Seals in the British Museum. (Corpus Inscriptionum Iranicarum). London, 1968. 25 pp., 30 pls. $36.50
Professionally produced portfolio of loose plates illustrating mostly gems and sealings from several allied cultures.

212.175 Bivar, A.D.H. British Museum.
Catalogue of the Western Asiatic Seals in the British Museum. Stamp Seals. II: The Sasanian Dynasty. London, 1969. 28.5. x 22. vii, 145 pp., 32 pls. $32.50
Comprehensive study of ca. 800 gems.

605.554 Borisov, A.Y. and Lukonin, V.G.
Sasanidskie gemmby. Katalog sobraniya gosudarstvennogo ermitzaha. Leningrad, 1962. 26.5 x 21. 220 pp., 20 pls., 14 illus. $165.00
Publishes the largest collection of Sasanian gems in the world. 158 gems are illustrated; more than 800 are classified and described. Includes English synopsis.

214.177 Brunner, C.J. Metropolitan Museum of Art.
Sasanian Stamp Seals in the Metropolitan Museum of Art. New York, 1978. 24 x 17. 149 pp., num. illus. $40.00
Descriptive catalogue of 224 gems in the MMA, all are illustrated and transliterated.

529.483 Forber, B.A.
Catalogue of Engraved Gems in the Art Museum, Princeton University. Berkeley, 1978. 16 x 21. 236 pp., 75 pls., fig. Paper. $60.00
Xerographic copy of a doctoral thesis, plates are of mediocre quality, text describes nearly 200 gems, mostly of Roman date, some of doubtful age.

198.161 Frye, R.N., (Ed.).
Sasanian remains from Quasr-i Abu Nasr: seals, sealings, coins. Cambridge, MA., 1973. 133 pp., 25 pls. $24.50
Presents gems from datable contexts.

199.162 Frye, R.N., (Ed.).
Sasanian Seals in the Collection of Mohsen Foroughi. (Corpus Inscriptionum Iranicarum). London, 1971. 24 pls. $34.50
Private collection of 209 inscribed Sasanian gems, generously published in a large format loose-leaf portfolio.

200.163 Gignoux, P.
Intailles Sassanides de la Collection Pirouzan. $65.00
Contained in: **Hommages et Opera Minora**, vol. III: **Monumentum H.S.** Nyberg, 1975.

201.164 Gignoux, P. and Curiel, R.
Sur un intaille sasanide du Cabinet des Médailles de Paris. (Studia Iranica, vol. 4, 1975). $27.50
This same issue also contains: Gignoux, P. **Sur les sceaux sassanides de la Societé numismatique américaine.**

202.165 Gignoux, P. and Gyselen, R.
Cachets sasanides de la collection Azizbeglu. (Studia Iranica, vol. 6, 1977).
$37.50
This same issue also contains: Gignoux, P. and Muller, K.J. **Quelques sceaux sasanides de Bonn.**

203.166 Gignoux, P. and Gyselen, R.
Nouveaux cachets sasanides de la collection Pirouzan. (Studia Iranica, vol. 7, 1978). $37.50

204.167 Gignoux, P. Bibliothèque Nationale
Catalogue des Sceaux, Camées, et Bulles Sasanides. II: Les Sceaux et Bulles Inscrits. Paris, 1978. 30.5 x 21.5. 159 pp., 81 pls. $90.00
Beautifully illustrated catalogue of one of Europe's leading collections.

205.168 Gignoux, P.
Un bulle sasanide du Musée d'État de Tbilissie (Georgie). (Studia Iranica, vol. 8, 1979). $37.50
This same issue also contains: Gyselen, R. **Ateliers monétaires et cachets officiels sasanides.**

206.169 Gignoux, P.
Sceaux Chrétiens d'époque sasanide. (Iranica Antiqua. vol. XV, 1979). $77.50
This volume contains, among other articles: Amiet, P. **Antiquités de Serpentine**; Pottier, M.-H. **Un cachet en argent de Bactriane**; Porada, E. **A Lapis Lazuli Figurine from Hierakonpolis in Egypt.**

207.170 Gignoux, P. and Gyselen, R.
Nouveaux sceaux sasanides de la collection M.I. Mochiri. (Studia Iranica, vol. 10, 1981). $42.50
This issue also includes: Denisov, E.P. and Grenet, F. **Boucles d'oreilles en or à images de coqs découvertes en Bactrianes.**

209.172 Gignoux, P. and Gyselen, R.
Sceaux Sasanides de diverses collections privées. Louvain, 1982. 26 x 17. 208 pp., 30 pls., 6 figs. Paper. $42.50
Describes, classifies and illustrates 576 Sasanian gems from several collections, some now dispersed. Includes tables of iconographical details, shapes and inscriptions. Very well illustrated with enlarged photographs of the gems.

208.171 Gignoux, P. and Kalus, L.
Les formules des sceaux sasanides et islamiques: continuité ou mutation. (Studia Iranica, vol. 11, 1982). $47.50
Interesting comparison between Sasanian and early Islamic seal inscriptions.

210.173 Goebl, R.
Der sasanidische Siegelkanon. (**Handbuecher der mittelasiatischen Numismatik**, IV). Brunswick, 1973. x, 72 pp., 42 pls. $65.00
Useful classification of the gem motifs of this period.

516.470 Grand Palais.
Le Trésor de Saint-Marc de Vénise. Paris, 1984. 23 x 26. 337 pp., num. pls., incl. color. Paper. $37.50
Superbly produced catalogue of a superb exhibition of major Antique hardstone vessels and related objects. Many additional treasures from the French national collections are added. Recommended! English version also available.

213.176 Harper, P.O. Asia House Gallery.
The Royal Hunter: Art of the Sasanian Empire. New York, 1978. 175 pp., num. illus., incl. color. $32.50
Exhibition catalogue illustrating many aspects of Sasanian life. With important sections on precious metals and engraved gems.

211.174 Lerner, J.
Christian Seals of the Sasanian Period. (**Uitgaven van het Nederlands Historisch-Archaeologisch Instituut**, 41). Leiden, 1977. 26 x 19. 74 pp., 8 pls. Paper.
$21.50
Catalogues and discusses 65 examples of these important early Christian depictions.

531.485 Nicholls, R.
The Wellcome Gems: A Fitzwiliam Museum Catalogue. Cambridge, 1983. 15 x 21. 57 pp., num. illus. Paper. $12.50
Supplementary catalogue of 250 Ancient and Later gems to the soon to be published **Classical Gems: Ancient and Modern Intaglios and Cameos in the Fitzwilliam Museum, Cambridge.**, most are illustrated.

215.178 Speleers, L.
Les Intailles du Docteur Jousset de Bellesme. (Syria, 1923). 9 pp., 1 pl. Paper.
$4.50
Obscure collection of 42, mostly Sasanian, gems. All illustrated.

480.437 Zazoff, P.
Die Antiken Gemmen. Munich, 1983. 24.5 x 16.5. 446 pp., 132 pls., 82 figs
$110.00
Attempt at an update of Furtwaengler's **Die antiken Gemmen**. Most helpful survey, many photographs, line drawings and a concise text help to increase the usefulness of this handbook. Recommended as a quick but thorough reference tool.

Byzantine Gems and Mediaeval Seals

170.132 Le Blant, E.
750 Inscriptions de Pierres Gravées Inédites ou peu connues. Paris, 1896. 23 x 28. 210 pp., 2 pls. Paper. $72.50
Most useful compilation of inscriptions on ancient gems, both cameos and intaglios. Rare!

592.544 Chandon de Briailles.
Sur Deux Bulles de L'Orient Latin. (Mélanges Syriens, n.d.). 28 x 22. 11 pp., 4 illus. Paper. $6.50

593.545 Chandon de Briailles.
Bulle de Clérembaut de Broyes, Archévèque de Tyr. (Syria, 1940.). 28.5 x 23. 7 pp., 2 illus. Paper. $5.50
Descriptions of the bulla, and the history of the archbishop of Tyre in 1215, during the crusades.

594.546 Chandon de Briailles.
Lignages d'Outre-Mer: Les Seigneurs de Margat. (Syria, vol. XXV, 1946-48.). 28.5 x 23. 27 pp., 1 illus. Paper. $6.50
Lineage and seal of a crusader's family in the 12th - 15th c.

595.547 Chandon de Briailles.
Bulles de L'Orient Latin. (Syria, vol. XXVII, 1950). 28.5 x 23. 16 pp., 2 pls., 7 figs. Paper. $6.50
Bullae from the Frankish Kingdom in southern Lebanon during the 11th - 13th c.

597.549 Mesnil du Buisson.
Les Tessères et les Monnaies de Palmyre. Paris, 1944 - 1962. 22 x 28.5. 2 vols.: 834 pp., 324 figs.; and 16 pp., 125 pls. 1 text vol., 1 portfolio of loose pls. $170.00
Scarce study of Palmyran culture and philosophy, illustrated with many hundreds of detailed photographs and figures of the tesserae and coins with their distinct iconography, so similar to that found on the gems. Recommended!

507.462 Delatte, A. and Derchain, Ph.
Les Intailles Magiques Gréco - Egyptiennes. Paris, 1964. 24 x 15.5. 380 pp., 527 figs., 4 color pls. Paper. $125.00
Scarce catalogue of the "Gnostic" gems in the Bibliothèque Nationale, all are illustrated, transliterated and translated. With numerous references to other collections. Recommended.

608.557 Gebhart, H.
Gemmen und Kameen. Berlin, 1925. 24 x 16. viii, 232 pp., 255 illus. $165.00
Excellent overview with a strong section on Post-Byzantine gems, the later artists and their signatures as they appear on gems. With 254 illustrations of individual stones.

516.470 Grand Palais.
Le Trésor de Saint-Marc de Vénise. Paris, 1984. 23 x 26. 337 pp., num. pls., incl. color. Paper. $37.50
Superbly produced catalogue of a superb exhibition of major Antique hardstone vessels and related objects. Many additional treasures from the French national collections are added. Recommended! English version also available.

211.174 Lerner, J.
Christian Seals of the Sasanian Period. (Uitgaven van het Nederlands Historisch-Archaeologisch Instituut, 41). Leiden, 1977. 26 x 19. 74 pp., 8 pls. Paper.
$21.50
Catalogues and discusses 65 examples of these important early Christian depictions.

648.616 Philipp, H.
Mira et Magica: Gemmen im Aegyptischen Museum Berlin-Charlottenburg.
Mainz, 1984. 136 pp., 55 pls., 207 illus. $72.50
Approximately 200 "magical gems", many originally from the collection of Philipp Stosch in 1764, later scorned by Furtwaengler, who refused to include them in his publication of the gems in the Antiquarium, (1896), finally published and interpreted.

576.528 Popovich, L.
A Byzantine Cameo. (Expedition, vol. 4, 1962). 20.5 x 26.5. 6 pp., 9 illus. Paper.
$6.50
A discussion of the large Byzantine cameo from the Maxwell Sommerville Collection. The article places the gem in its context and compares it to others of similar workmanship.

555.509 Ross, M.C.
Catalogue of the Byzantine and Early Mediaeval Antiquities in the Dumbarton Oaks Collection. I: Metalwork, Ceramics, Glass, Glyptics, Painting. Washington, D.C., 1962. 29 x 22. xv, 115 pp., 65 pls. $38.50
Illustrates, and carefully publishes, Byzantine and early Mediaeval silver objects, the engraved gems and engraved glass vessels and other small objects from the Dumbarton Oaks Collection.

613.562 Schlumberger, G., (et al.).
Sigillographie de l'Orient Latin. Paris, 1943. 29 x 23. xix, 281 pp., 22 pls. Paper.
$68.50
Catalogues and shows ca. 450 seals, mostly in lead or wax, from the Kingdom of Jerusalem, the Kingdom of Cyprus and from Constantinople. Both ecclesiastic and temporal seals are shown and translated. Scarce!

455.415 Vikan, G. and Nesbitt, J.
Security in Byzantium: Locking, Sealing, Weighing. Washington, 1980. 21.5 x 28. 39 pp., 88 figs. Paper. $6.50
First attempt to describe security related Byzantine objects; with careful descriptions and numerous illustrations of "ring-keys", gems, stamp-seals and finger rings. Recommended!

661.627 Wentzel, H.
Beitraege zur Kunst des Mittelalters. Festschrift fuer Hans Wentzel zum 60. Geburtsdag. Berlin, 1975. 16.5 x 23.5. viii, 268 pp., 150 pls. Paper. $55.00
"Festchrift" containing numerous specialized articles on Byzantine and Mediaeval glyptics, jewelry, ivories and allied fields. Recommended.

Renaissance and Later Gems

160.120 Babelon, E. Bibliothèque Nationale.
Catalogue des Camées Antiques et Modernes. Paris, 1897. 463 pp., 13 figs. Paper. $85.00
Scarce text volume of the French national collection. Photocopies of the 76 plates can be supplied for an additional $45.00.

161.121 Babelon, E. Bibliothèque Nationale.
Les Pierres Gravées, Guide du Visiteur. Paris, 1930. 14 x 19. 155 pp., 32 pls. $57.50
Illustrates 158 important gems from the French national collection.

434.388 Chadour, A.B.
Antonio Gentili und der Altarsats von St. Peter. Muenster, 1980. 330 pp., 132 pls. Paper. $45.00
Privately printed Ph.D. dissertation about the gems, materials used and iconography of the famous altar pieces in Rome and the artist who created them.

177.139 Dacos, N., (et al.). Museo Mediceo.
Il Tesoro di Lorenzo il Magnifico: Le Gemme. Catalogue della Mostra, Palazzo Medici Riccardi, Firenze, 1972. Florence, 1973. 24 x 17. vi, 167 pp., 15 color pls., 99 illus. Paper. $32.50
Contains descriptions of Ancient and Neo-Classical gems and an important 15th century inventory.

178.140 Dacos, N., (et al.). Museo Mediceo.
Il Tesoro di Lorenzo il Magnifico, repertorio delle gemme e dei vasi. Florence, 1980. 17.5 x 25. 302 pp., 23 color pls., 208 illus. $45.00
Contains all of the above plus the 1974 catalogue of the hardstone vases and other carvings, now in a 2nd edition combined in one volume.

499.454 Egger, G.
Buergerlicher Schmuck: 15. - 20. Jahrhundert. Munich, 1984. 25 x 28. 224 pp., 52 color pls., 410 illus. $65.00
Interesting book shows the ordinary jewelry that common people used to wear. Emphasis is on the Italian Renaissance, Dutch 17th c. and the German speaking countries of the 19th c.

193.156 Eichler, F. and Kris, E. Kunsthistorisches Museum.
Die Kameen im Kunsthistorischen Museum. Vienna, 1927. 24 x 31. x, 246 pp., 84 pls., 83 figs. $550.00
Indispensable text on cameo carving, long out-of-print.

500.455 Evans, J.
Magical Jewels of the Middle Ages and Renaissance. New York, 1976. 13.5 x 21.5. 264 pp., 3 pls., indexes. Reprint of the 1922 ed. Paper. $9.50
Basic book on early Western lapidaries; includes extensive quotes from the original manuscripts.

179.141 Foerschner, G. Historisches Museum.
Glaspasten, Geschnittene Steine, Arabische Muenzgewichte. Melsungen, 1982. 17 x 22. 111 pp., 7 color pls., num. illus. Paper. $18.50
Large and varied collection of interesting material in new publication.

389.343 Gallo, R.
Il Tesoro di S. Marco e la sua Storia. Venice, 1967. 18 x 25. xvi, 424 pp., 80 pls. $45.00
Presentation of Venetian church treasure which contains Antique hardstone and glass vessels and gem-set objects.

608.557 Gebhart, H.
Gemmen und Kameen. Berlin, 1925. 24 x 16. viii, 232 pp., 255 illus. $165.00
Excellent overview with a strong section on Post-Byzantine gems, the later artists and their signatures as they appear on gems. With 254 illustrations of individual stones.

180.142 Gramatopol, M.
Les pierres gravées du Cabinet Numismatique de l'Académie Roumaine. (**Collection Latomus**, 138). Brussels, 1974. 130 pp., 47 pls. Paper. $32.50
Catalogues and illustrates 965 gems, mostly Roman and Later.

516.470 Grand Palais.
Le Trésor de Saint-Marc de Vénise. Paris, 1984. 23 x 26. 337 pp., num. pls., incl. color. Paper. $37.50
Superbly produced catalogue of a superb exhibition of major Antique hardstone vessels and related objects. Many additional treasures from the French national collections are added. Recommended! English version also available.

438.392 Hackenbroch, Y.
Renaissance Jewellery. Munich, 1979. 424 pp., 35 color pls., 927 B. & W. illus. $135.00
An impressive compendium of Renaissance jewelry. History, artists, and the development of iconography are discussed for each of the various schools that produced the jewelry.

563.516 Hackenbroch, Y. Metropolitan Museum of Art.
Commessi. (**Bulletin**, vol. XXIV, 1966). New York, 1966. 25 x 20.5. 12 pp., 29 illus. Paper. $12.50
Important article on commessi, the combination of carved gems with enamel and goldsmiths' work. The article describes all known examples. Scarce!

489.446 Hotel Drouot.
Pierres Gravées, Camées, Objets Divers Antiques de la Renaissance et Modernes. Paris, 1926. 26 x 18. 12 pp., 1 pl. Paper. $18.50
Illustrates 40 engraved gems of all periods.

442.396 Kagan, Hermitage Museum.
Western European Cameos in the Hermitage Collection. Leningrad, 1973. 14 x 18. 96 pp., 103 color pls. $32.50
Attractive presentation of 13th C. and later cameos. Out-of-print.

441.395 Kris, E.
Renaissance-Kleinkunst in Italien, Gefaesse, Gemmen, Schmuckstuecke und Skulpturen in Bergkristall und Edelstein. Leipzig, n.d. 23 x 28.5. 12 pp., 200 pls.
$245.00
Very scarce copy of this basic book on Italian Renaissance glyptics and hardstone objects in the round.

560.513 Lemaitre, J.-L., (Ed.). Musée du Pays d'Ussel.
Sceaux des Archives communales d'Ussel. Paris, 1982. 19 x 19. 63 pp., 21 illus., 1 color pl. Paper. $14.50
Shows detailed photographs of the wax seals in the Archives, all date from the 13th - 18th c.

430.384 Lesley, P. Baltimore Museum of Art.
Renaissance jewels and jeweled objects from the Melvin Gutman collection. Baltimore, 1968. 23 x 28.5. 194 pp., 5 color pls., num. illus. $28.50
Catalogues and illustrates 70 major pieces. Out-of-print.

156.116 Lippold, G.
Gemmen und Kameen des Altertums und der Neuzeit. Stuttgart, 1921. 23 x 30. xii, 190 pp., 167 pls. $185.00
Clearly illustrates and briefly identifies 1695 engraved gems. Scarce!

531.485 Nicholls, R.
The Wellcome Gems: A Fitzwilliam Museum Catalogue. Cambridge, 1983. 15 x 21. 57 pp., num. illus. Paper. $12.50
Supplementary catalogue of 250 Ancient and Later gems to the soon to be published **Classical Gems: Ancient and Modern Intaglios and Cameos in the Fitzwilliam Museum, Cambridge.**, most are illustrated.

677.640 Philippe, J.
Réliquaires Médiévaux de l'Orient Chrétien en Verre et en Cristal de Roche conservés en Belgique. Liège, 1975. 24 x 16. 45 pp., 21 figs. Paper. $16.50
Obscure publication shows important Mediaeval and Islamic rock crystal and cut glass vessels preserved in church treasures. Parallels from other treasures are listed and illustrated.

164.124 Reinach, S.
Pierres Gravées. Paris, 1895. 20 x 29. 195 pp., 138 pls. Paper. $245.00
Illustrates, on 137 engraved plates, 2,150 engraved gems from famous European collections; incorporates early research by Eckel, Gori, Levesque de Gravelle, Mariette, Millin and Stosch.

190.152 Righetti, R.
Gemme e cammei delle collezioni comunali. (Cataloghi dei musei comunali di Roma, 4). Rome, 1955. 115 pp., 20 pls. Paper. $13.50
Catalogues 276 gems, Roman and Neo-Classical, from three museums.

191.153 Righetti, R.
Opere di Glittica dei Museo Sacro e Profano. Vatican City, 1955. 52 pp., 17 pls. Paper. $16.50
Collection strong in Byzantine gems, some Roman and Neo-Classical.

485.442 Rowe, D.F. The Martin D'Arcy Gallery of Art.
The Art of Jewelry 1450-1650. Chicago, 1975. 19 x 26. 72 pp., 88 illus. Paper.
$9.50
Publishes 52 pieces of Renaissance jewelry, some set with engraved gems, all from private collections.

163.123 Scarisbrick, D.
The Wellington Gems. London, 1977. 23 x 15.5. 72 pp. Paper. $18.50
Together with: Scarisbrick, D., **Further Wellington Gems and Historic Rings.** London, 1978. 22 pp., 4 pls. Two privately printed handlists of a large and varied collection of ancient and later gems.

505.460 Somers Cocks, A. and Truman, C.
Renaissance jewels, gold boxes and objets de vertu. (Catalogue of the Thyssen-Bornemisza Collection). London, 1984. 384 pp., 150 color pls., 200 illus.
$115.00
Important general discussion of Renaissance and later history of jewelry, as well as a careful catalogue of a major collection.

547.501 Sotheby's.
The Thomas F. Flannery Jr. Collection; Medieval and Later Works of Art.. London, 1983. 27 x 19. 291 pp., ca 400 illus., many in color. $36.00
Hardbound, single owner, auction sale catalogue, showing large collection of finger rings, medieval and Renaissance jewels, gems and enamels, now dispersed. Very well illustrated with numerous color photographs.

454.127 Story-Maskelyne, N.M.H.
Catalogue of the Marlborough Gems, being a collection of Works in Cameo and Intaglio, formed by George, 3rd Duke of Marlborough. London, 1899. 17 x 25.5. xix, 122 pp., 14 pls. Full leather binding. $450.00
Extremely scarce sale catalogue of the Marlborough Collection with a lenghty introduction by Story-Maskelyne; our copy includes prices realized written in the margins. A superbly bound copy in full red morocco with gold stamping and gilt top edge.

445.399 Tait, H., (Ed.). British Museum.
The Art of the Jeweller: A Catalogue of the Hull Grundy Gift to the British Museum of Jewellery, Engraved Gems and Goldsmiths' work. London, 1983. 27.5 x 22. 2 vols.: 208 pp.; and 372 pp., 116 color pls., 1400 B. & W. illus. 2 Vols., Cased.
$245.00
Limited edition describing and illustrating nearly 1200 pieces of jewelry and engraved gems from the late 17th to the mid 20th Century. Recommended!

162.122 Vermeule, C.C. The University Museum.
Cameo and Intaglio, Engraved Gems from the Sommerville Collection. Philadelphia, 1957. 15 x 21.5. 35 pp., 2 pls. Paper. $12.50
Exhibition catalogue of 650 gems of all periods.

Egyptian Jewelry

216.179 Aldred, C.
Jewels of the Pharaohs, Egyptian Jewelry of the Dynastic Period. New York, 1978. 28.5 x 21. 128 pp., 173 illus., incl. 109 color. $18.00
Good general survey, well illustrated.

218.181 Andrews, C.A.R. British Museum.
Catalogue of Egyptian Antiquities in the Britsh Museum. vol. VI: Jewellery I: From the earliest times to the Seventeenth Dynasty. London, 1981. 36 x 28. 152 pp., 48 pls. $125.00
First volume in a planned series of scientific catalogues of Egyptian jewelry; 675 objects are listed, 200 illustrated, with comparative material and dates.

565.518 The Brooklyn Museum.
Africa in Antiquity: The Arts of Ancient Nubia and the Sudan. I: The Essays II: The Catalogue. Brooklyn, 1978. 32 x 22. 143 pp., 100 figs., 19 in color., 3 maps; and 112 pp., 84 figs., 9 in color. $48.00
Two volumes illustrating the "provincial arts of Egypt", the jewelry is especially noteworthy for its many different influences and barbaric splendor. Recommended!

521.475 Delange-Bazin, E. Musée du Louvre.
Les Bijoux de l'Antiquité Égyptienne. Paris, 1983. 11.5 x 23.5. 18 pp., num. illus. Paper. $5.50
Introduction to the vast holdings of Egyptian jewelry in the Musée du Louvre, Paris.

217.180 Garside, A., (Ed.). Walters Art Gallery.
Jewelry, Ancient to Modern. Baltimore, 1979 32 x 23. 256 pp., num. illus. incl. 116 color. $40.00
Scholarly catalogue, beautifully produced, of jewelry from all periods.

537.491 Gerlach, M., (Ed.).
Primitive and Folk Jewelry. New York, 1971. 28 x 21. 218 pp., 109 pls. with 1900 illus. Paper. $11.50
Quality reprint of the 1906 edition of **Voelkerschmuck**; still an excellent quick reference for ancient, ethnic and unusual jewelry with more than 1900 items illustrated.

591.543 De Morgan, J.
Fouilles à Dahchour: Mars-Juin, 1894. Vienna, 1895. 32.5 x 26.5. 166 pp., 40 pls., incl. 7 color., 274 figs. Paper. $185.
Scarce excavation report of the XI-XII Dynasty jewelry and beads found by De Morgan in 1894. Major finds of datable royal jewelry and other objects; well illustrated.

221.184 Ogden, J.M.
A Private Collection of Egyptian Gold Jewellery. London, 1979. 30 pp., 3 color pls., 8 pls. Paper. $9.50
Auction catalogue, (Christie, Manson & Woods, Ltd.), of Egyptian jewelry of many periods.

88.67 Scandone, G.M.
Scarabei e Scaraboidi Egiziani ed Egittizanti del Museo Nazionale di Cagliari.
Rome, 1975. 20 x 28. 106 pp., 31 pls. Paper. $23.50
Egyptian and Egyptianizing scarabs and ring bezels from this important Phoenician site in the Western Mediterranean.

8.69 Tufnell, O. and Ward, W.A.
Relations between Byblos, Egypt and Mesopotamia at the end of the third Millenium BC, a study of the Montet Jar. (Syria, vol. XLIII, 1966). Paris, 1966. 77 pp., 6 pls., 10 figs. Paper. $18.50
Large closed find of jewelry, scarabs and beads, all illustrated and dated.

496.451 Vercoutter, J.
Les Objets Égyptiens et Égyptisants du Mobilier Funéraire Carthaginois.
Paris, 1945. 23 x 28.5. 397 pp., 29 pls., num. figs., folding pls. and maps. Paper. $78.00
Important book illustrates, classifies and translates 936 Egyptian and Phoenician scarabs and amulets, both in hardstone and in faience, some mounted as rings or stampseals. Uncut copy. Rare!

221.185 Vilimkova, M.
Egyptian Jewellery. Prague, 1969. 20.5 x 28.5. 142 pp., 94 color illus. $47.50
Interesting survey with excellent illustrations.

219.182 Williams, C.R. The New York Historical Society.
Catalogue of Egyptian Antiquities ... Gold and Silver and Related Objects.
New York, 1924. 23.5 x 31.5. 281 pp., 38 pls. Paper. $225.00
One of the earliest catalogues to utilize both technological and stylistic criteria to determine authenticity and dates.

220.183 Winlock, H.E. Metropolitan Museum of Art.
The Treasure of El Lahun. New York, 1973. xvi, 80 pp., 16 pls., 5 figs. $30.00
Large find of 12th Dynasty jewelry, elegantly described. (Reprint of the 1920 ed.).

Near Eastern - Phoenician Jewelry

685.664 Abrahamian, V.A., (Ed.).
Armenian Jewelry Art: From the Ancient Period to the Present Day. Leningrad, 1985. 222 pp., 154 color pls. $24.50
Early Near Eastern and Armenian jewelry from the third millenium B.C. to the present is shown on 154 color plates. Text in English, Armenian and Russian.

79.58 Acquaro, E.
Amuletti Egiziani ed Egittizanti del Museo Nazionale di Cagliari. Rome, 1977. 20 x 28. 158 pp., 61 pls. Paper. $32.50
Catalogues 1271 amulets and illustrates these mostly Egyptian and Aegypto-Phoenician amulets from Sardina.

533.487 Akishev, K.
The Ancient gold of Kazakhstan. Alma Ata, 1983. 17.5 x 22. 261 pp., 178 color pls., figs. Text in three languages. Slipcase. $26.50
Rich finds of gold jewelry, from 12th c. BC. - 14th c. AD., with the majority of the objects shown of the Scytho-Siberian cultures of the 6th c. BC to the 3rd c. AD., some superb gem-encrusted pieces show many different influences.

25.6 Amiet, P.
Éléments Émaillés du Décor Architectural Néo-Élamite. (**Syria**, vol. XLIV, 1967). 28 x 22.5. 24 pp., 2 pls., 15 figs. Paper. $7.50
Bound together with: Lambert, M. **Shutruk-Nahunte et Shutur-Nahunte**.

80.59 Amiet, P.
Bactriane Proto-Historique. (**Syria**, vol. LIV, 1977). 28 x 22. 32 pp., 4 pls., 2 figs. Paper. $9.50
Important article on recent finds of beads, jewelry, seals and other 3rd Millenium objects in the Iranian-Afghani plateau.

81.60 Amiet, P.
Antiquités de Serpentine. (**Iranica Antiqua**, vol. XV, 1980). 27.5 x 19. xv, 314 pp., 36 pls., 41 figs. $77.50
this volume also contains, among others: Gignoux, P. **Sceaux chrétiens d'époque sasanide**.; Pottier, M.-H. **Un cachet en argent de Bactriane**; Porada, E. **A Lapis Lazuli Figurine from Hierakonpolis in Egypt**.

223.411 Amiet, P.
Les Ivoires Achéménides de Suse. (**Syria**, vol. LIV, 1977). 42 pp., 4 pls., 71 illus. Paper. $12.50

1.412 Arnaud, D., (et al.).
Ilsu-Ibnisu Orfèvre de l'E. Babbar de Larsa. (**Syria**, vol. LVI, 1979). 64 pp., 4 pls., 82 figs. Paper. $22.50
Important find of beads, weights, tools and jewelry from the mid 18th Century BC.; many illustrations of beads and jewelry.

237.199 Blinkenberg, C.
Fibules Grecques et Orientales. (Lindiaka, V). Copenhagen, 1926. 24 x 15. 312 pp., 320 illus. Paper. $62.50
Investigation of development of fibulae in Greece and Near East, from Mycene to miniature Italic types, profusely illustrated. Scarce.

331.604 Caner, E.
Fibeln in Anatolien I. (PBF, vol. XIV. 8, 1983.). 350 pp., 90 pls. $95.00

224.413 Chandra, R.G.
Studies in the development of Ornaments and Jewellery in Proto-Historic India. Varanasi, 1964. xviii, 342 pp., 48 pls. $45.00
Carefully publishes the origin and development of the jewelry from the Mohenjodaro-Harappa and Indus Valley cultures.

495.450 Cintas, P.
Amulettes Puniques. Tunis, 1946. 21.5 x 28. 171 pp., 19 pls., num. illus., tables. Paper. $87.50
Scarce publication describes and shows many amulets, scarabs and jewelry from Carthaginian sites.

617.566 Cintas, P.
Carthage, sa Naissance, sa Grandeur: Les Collections Puniques des Musées du Bardo, de Carthage et d'Utique. (Archéologie Vivante, vol. I-2.). Paris, 1968-1969. 28.5 x 21.5. 155 pp., 181 illus. incl. 45 color., 36 figs., 3 maps. Paper. $28.50
This issue of the short-lived quarterly **Archaeologia Viva** contains 15 separate articles by different scholars each describing a different aspect of Carthaginian culture. Phoenician gems and jewelry are discussed and well illustrated.

225.360 Contenau, G.
L'Incrustation sur Métal et l'Orfèvrerie Cloisonnée en Mésopotamie. (Syria, vol. XXXIII, 1956). 5 pp., Paper. $4.50

226.186 Culican, W.
Jewelry from Sarafand and Sidon. (Op. Ath, vol. XII). 7 pp., 25 figs. Paper. $7.50
Well illustrated survey of jewelry from the Phoenician homeland.

227.187 De Clercq-Fobe, D.
Épingles Votives du Luristan (Iran). Leiden, 1978. viii, 300 pp., 63 pls., 126 figs. $72.50
First study of often encountered but hitherto poorly documented class of Iranian jewelry. See, also, our no. 229.189.

84.63 Densmore Curtis, C.
Sardis. XIII: Jewelry and Goldwork. Rome, 1925. 28 x 34.5. 48 pp., 11 pls. $115.00
Scarce publication showing all the gems and jewelry from this important East Greek site.

217.180 Garside, A., (Ed.). Walters Art Gallery.
Jewelry, Ancient to Modern. Baltimore, 1979 32 x 23. 256 pp., num illus. incl. 116 color. $40.00
Scholarly catalogue, beautifully produced, of jewelry from all periods.

588.540 Genouillac, H., (et al.).
Fouilles de Telloh. I: Époques Présargoniques. II: époques d'Ur IIIe Dynastie et de Larsa. Paris, 1934-1936. 29.5 x 23. xii, 106 pp., 96 pls., incl. 2 color, figs.; and 70 pp., 103 pls., incl. 2 color. 2 portfolios. $550.00
Two very scarce portfolios publishing the finds from Telloh; shows many cylinder seals, beads and other small finds as well as the pottery and idols.

228.188 Ghirshman, R.
Anneaux destinés à tendres la corde de l'Arc. (Syria, vol. XXXV, 1958). $5.50
An often encountered ornament described and explained.

473.431 Graham, K.
Scientific Notes on the Finds from Ur. (The Museum Journal, 1929). 17 x 27.5. 12 pp., 8 illus. Paper. $5.50
Technical information about the cleaning of the silver objects and jewelry found in Ur. This issue of **The Museum Journal** contains two additional articles of related interest.

686.665 Harper, P.O. The Metropolitan Museum of Art.
Ancient Near Eastern Art. (Bulletin, vol. XLI, 1984.). New York, 1984. 29 x 21.5. 56 pp., 80 illus. incl. 40 color. Paper. $9.50
Special issue of the **Bulletin** to commemorate the opening of the new Near Eastern Galleries; shows silver vessels and precious jewelry produced over a six thousand year period.

229.189 Huot, J.-L.
La Diffusion des Épingles a tête a double enroulement. (Syria, vol. XLVI, 1969). 36 pp., 5 pls., map. Paper. $9.50
Attempt to classify a common Near Eastern ornament; see, also, our No. 227.187.

557.510 Legrain, L.
Nippur's Gold Treasure. (The Museum Journal, 1920). 17 x 25.5. 7 pp., 1 fig. Paper. $5.50
Translation and background of an inscribed cuneiform tablet which contains a catalogue of 125 jewels and seals dating from the 14th c. BC.

666.431 Legrain L.
The Boudoir of Queen Shubad. (The Museum Journal, 1929). 17 x 27.5. 34 pp., 12 pls., 4 illus. Paper. $5.50
Precious metal and stone regalia from early Ur, 3500 BC, are shown and discussed. Cylinder seals show the fashions that complemented the metal and bead jewelry.

609.558 Markoe, G.
Phoenician Bronze and Silver Bowls from Cyprus and the Mediterranean. Berkeley, 1985. 508 pp., num. pls., and illus. Paper. $45.00
A fully illustrated corpus of all extant decorated bronze and silver repoussé bowls from the Mediterranean region.

646.614 Markoe, G., (Ed.).
Ancient Bronzes, Ceramics and Seals: The Nasli M. Heeramaneck Collection of Ancient Near Eastern, Central Asiatic, and European Art. Los Angeles, 1981. 25 x 23.5. 271 pp., 360 illus., incl. 13 color. Paper. $18.50
A catalogue showing 1349 objects ranging from cylinder seals to small Luristan bronzes. Much unusual material from various Steppe Cultures and an extensive series of early stampseals is also included.

130.90 Marshall, F. British Museum.
Catalogue of the Jewellery, Greek, Etruscan, and Roman in the Department of Antiquities, British Museum. London, 1969. 28 x 23. lxii, 400 pp., 73 pls. $95.00
The standard reference work describing 3,168 items. Now out-of-print.

230.190 Maxwell-Hyslop, K.R.
Western Asiatic Jewellery c. 3000-612 BC. London, 1971. 16 x 24. 286 pp., 259 illus., 167 figs. $45.00
Authoritative survey of hitherto poorly documented jewelry from Near Eastern sites.

231.191 Negbi, O.
The Hoards of Goldwork from Tell El-Ajjul. (SIMA, vol. XXV, 1970). Göteburg, 1970. 54 pp., 5 pls. Paper. $18.50
Important hoard of gold jewelry from ca. 1500 BC.; well catalogued and illustrated.

234.195 Palazzo Chiablese.
Ori e Argenti dell'Italia Antica. Turin, 1961. 17 x 23.5. 276 pp., 12 color illus., 106 pls. $65.00
Scarce exhibition catalogue of ancient jewelry of many periods found in Italy.

478.435 Parrot, A.
Le "Trésor" d'Ur. (Mission Archéologique de Mari, vol. IV). Paris, 1968. 21.5 x 27.5. 67 pp., 3 color pls., 22 pls., 42 figs. $45.00
Illustrates jewelry, many seals and small precious objects from Ur.

548.502 Perry, R.
Schmuck der Antike, Gefaesse und Geraete aus Bronze. (Sonderliste T). Basel, 1981. 24 x 17. 48 pp., 1 color pl., 124 illus. Paper. $12.50
Carefully catalogued group of ancient jewelry from the 2nd millenium to early Islamic. Illustrates ca. 75 pieces.

232.192 Pisano, G.Q.
I Gioielli Fenici di Tharros nel Museo Nazionale di Cagliari. Rome, 1974. 199 pp., 30 pls., 17 figs. Paper. $28.50
In-depth study of Phoenician jewelry, well illustrated.

6.193 Quillard, B.
Bijoux Carthaginois. I: Les Colliers. Louvain, 1979. 133 pp., 20 color pls., 2 tables. $48.50
Welcome addition to small but growing number of books on ancient necklace components.

628,577 Sarianidi, V.
L'Or de la Bactriane: Fouilles de la Nécropole de Tillia-Tepe en Afghanistan Septentrional. Leningrad, 1985. 36 x 26. 259 pp., 426 illus. incl. 166 color pls.
$75.00
Sumptuously illustrated book publishes the recent finds of gem set-gold jewelry from Bactria, dating from the 1st c. BC. - 1st c. AD., many different stylistic influences may be recognized.

131.91 Tait, H., (Ed.). British Museum.
Jewellery through 7000 years. London, 1976. 24 x 19. 276 pp., num. color and B. & W. illus. Paper. $22.50
Presents 466 pieces of jewelry from around the world. Excellent general survey; well illustrated. Out-of-print.

89.68 Tillot, M.
Mille ans d'art à Carthage. Tunis, 1978. 20.5 x 20. 80 pp., 88 color pls. $18.50
Handsomely presents gems, amulets and jewelry from ancient Phoenician and Roman sites.

233.194 Tual, A.
Pour un typologie des bijoux de femmes en Iran. (Studia Iranica, vol. 9, 1980).
$38.50

8.69 Tufnell, O. and Ward, W.A.
Relations between Byblos, Egypt and Mesopotamia at the end of the third Millenium BC, a study of the Montet Jar. (Syria, vol. XLIII, 1966). Paris, 1966. 77 pp., 6 pls., 10 figs. Paper. $18.50
Large closed find of jewelry, scarabs and beads, all illustrated and dated.

496.451 Vercoutter, J.
Les Objets Égyptiens et Égyptisants du Mobilier Funéraire Carthaginois. Paris, 1945. 23 x 28.5. 397 pp., 29 pls., num. figs., folding pls. and maps. Paper.
$78.00
Important book illustrates, classifies and translates 936 Egyptian and Phoenician scarabs and amulets, both in hardstone and in faience, some mounted as rings or stampseals. Uncut copy. Rare!

Greek Jewelry

533.487 Akishev, K.
The Ancient Gold of Kazakhstan. Alma Ata, 1983. 17.5 x 22. 261 pp., 178 color pls., figs. Text in three languages. Slipcase. $26.50
Rich finds of gold jewelry, from 12th c. BC. - 14th c. AD., with the majority of the objects shown of the Scytho-Siberian cultures of the 6th c. BC. to the 3rd c. AD., some superb gem-encrusted pieces show many different influences.

99.196 Amandry, P.
Collection Hélène Stathatos. I: Les Bijoux Antiques. Strasbourg, 1953. 28.5 x 38. 149 pp., 44 pls., 80 figs. Paper. $650.00
Very scarce and important catalogue of this major collection of ancient jewelry of the Mycenaean through Hellenistic periods.

621.570 Amandry, P.
Rapport Préliminaire sur les Statues Chryséléphantines de Delphes. (BCH, vol. LXIII, 1939.). Paris, 1939. 25 x 18.5. 33 pp., 23 pls., 13 figs. Paper. $26.50
Important article describing the small finds in precious materials, ivory, gold and silver made during the excavations of 1938. Most date from the 6th and 5th c. BC.

108.410 Battaglia, G.B.
Gioelli Antichi dall'eta Micenea all'Ellenismo. Rome, 1982. 24.5 x 31. 38 pp., 82 color illus. Paper. $22.50
Hansomely illustrated catalogue of the famous Castellani Collection of ancient jewelry, now in the Villa Giulia, Rome.

235.197 Benaki Museum.
Jewelry. Athens, 1970. 14 x 15.5. 3 pp., 48 illus. Paper. $8.50
Well illustrated booklet shows, in 48 detailed photographs, highlights of the collection which covers 5000 years of jewelry.

242.588 Berge, L. and Alexander, K.
Ancient Gold work and Jewelry from Chicago Collections. (The Ancient World, vol. XI, 1985.). Chicago, 1985. 28 x 21.5. 29 pp., 16 pls. Paper. $11.50
Exhibition catalogue of 172 pieces of ancient gold jewelry from private collections in the Chicago area. Emphasis is on jewelry and objects from the 4th c. BC - 4th c. AD.

619.568 Bielefeld, E.
Schmuck. (Archaeologia Homerica, vol. I, 1968.). Munich, 1968. 24.5 x 17. 70 pp., 6 pls. incl. 1 color., 8 figs. Paper. $18.50
Study of earliest Greek jewelry from the Helladic through the Geometric Period, based on numerous quotes from Homer and thorough reserach into the archaeological record.

237.199 Blinkenberg, C.
Fibules Grecques et Orientales. (Lindiaka, V). Copenhagen, 1926. 24 x 15. 312 pp., 310 illus. Paper. $62.50
Investigation of development of fibulae in Greece and Near East, from Mycene to miniature Italic types, profusely illustrated. Scarce.

253.212 Breglia, L. Museo Nazionale de Napoli.
Catalogo delle Oreficerie. Rome, 1941. 193 pp., 45 pls. Paper. $42.50
Leading Italian collection, comprehensively published and illustrated. Out-of-print and now quite scarce.

601.551 Catling, H.W.
Kouklia: Evreti Tomb 8. (**BCH**, vol. XCII, 1968.). Paris, 1968. 7 pp., 2 figs. Paper.
$11.50
Also contains: Kenna, V.E.G., **The seal use of Cyprus in the Bronze Age, III** and Kenna, V.E.G., **The Kouklia ring from Evreti.**

668.633 Chadour, A.B. and Joppien, R. Kunstgewerbemuseum.
Schmuck, Bestandskatalog des Kunstgewerbemuseums. Cologne, 1985. 2 vols. with num. illus., incl. color. $45.00
Major new museum catalogue with a lengthy introduction and 910 entries, especially strong in Ancient, Migration Period, Renaissance and 19th c. jewelry. A fine group of 355 rings is shown in two views each. Recommended!

239.201 Chandra, R.G.
Indo-Greek Jewellery. New Delhi, 1979. 136 pp., 25 pls. $32.50
Most interesting study on unfamiliar aspects of ancient Greek jewelry, includes chapter on technology.

540.494 Coarelli, F.
Greek and Roman Jewellery. Feltham, 1970. 19.5 x 13.5. 157 pp., 68 color pls.
$18.50
Well illustrated introduction to ancient jewelry.

240.202 Coche de la Ferté, É.
Les Bijoux Antiques. Paris, 1956. 13.5 x 21.5. 122 pp., 28 pls., 8 figs. Paper.
$40.00
Careful study examining ancient jewelry and its techniques. Includes a section on forgeries.

241.203 Cologne. Roemisch-germanisches Museum.
Gold der Thraker, Archaeologische Schaetze aus Bulgarien. Cologne, 1979. 240 pp., 35 color pls., num. illus. $22.50
Richly illustrated exhibition catalogue of provincial Greek toreutics. Now out-of-print.

698.677 Davidson, P.F. and Oliver, A. The Brooklyn Museum.
Ancient Greek and Roman Gold Jewelry in the Brooklyn Museum. Brooklyn, 1984. 29 x 23. 214 pp., 224 figs. $45.00
Recent museum catalogue of a large collection of Hellenistic and Roman jewelry. Each object is illustrated and carefully described with bibliography.

704.683 De Juliis, M., (Ed.).
Gli Ori di Taranto in Eta Ellenistica. Milan, 1985. 27 x 23.5. 529 pp., num. ills. incl. num. color. $45.00
Major new exhibition catalogue of Greek jewelry - all from dated tombs in the Tarentum region. Includes a 60 page section on finger rings and 65 pages on different earring types. All are illustrated - many in detailed photographs. Recommended.

84.63 Densmore Curtis, C.
Sardis. XIII: Jewelry and Goldwork. Rome, 1925. 28 x 34.5. 48 pp., 11 pls.
$115.00
Scarce publication showing all the gems and jewelry from this important East Greek site.

564.517 Deppert-Lippitz, B.
Spaethellenistische Goldschmiede-Arbeiten. (Antike Kunst, 1972.). 28 x 22.5. 12 pp., 8 pls. Paper. $18.00
Important article on Late Hellenistic jewelry, illustrated with many datable examples.

123.609 Deppert-Lippitz, B.
Griechischer Goldschmuck. Mainz, 1985. 320 pp., 32 color pls., 225 illus.
$32.50
A thorough examination of Greek jewelry from the Mycenaean to the late Hellenistic Period based on dated finds, vase painting, sculpture and coins.

255.214 Dusenberry, E.B. The Newark Museum.
Greek Vases, Jewelry, Terracottas and Other Objects in the Eugene Schaeffer Collection. (The Museum, vol. III, 1951). 16 pp., 24 illus. Paper. $4.50
Includes some 4th - 3rd Century Scythian and Greek jewelry.

530.484 Ergil, T.
Kuepeler / Earrings: The Catalogue of the Istanbul Archaeological Museum. Istanbul, 1983. 19 x 27.5. 71 pp., num. illus., incl. color. Paper. $26.50
Catalogues earrings of all periods of Turkish history, illustrates Hellenistic and Roman types mostly, some others.

627.576 Gagochidze, J.
L'Ornament de la Femme Georgienne. Khelovneba, 1981. 16.5 x 13. 221 pp., 91 color illus., 5 figs. Paper. $14.50
Jewelry from Georgia, (USSR), from the IVth Millenium to the 19th c. AD. The plates are poorly printed but show interesting jewelry: many beads and necklace elements, some ancient rings and cameos. Text in French, Russian and Georgian.

217.180 Garside, A., (Ed.). Walters Art Gallery.
Jewelry, Ancient to Modern. Baltimore, 1979 32 x 23. 256 pp., num. illus. incl. 116 color. $40.00
Scholarly catalogue, beautifully produced, of jewelry from all periods.

236.198 Greifenhagen, A. Staatliche Museen Preussischer Kulturbesitz. Antikenabteilung. **Schmuckarbeiten in Edelmetall.** $550.00
The two portfolios include:
    I: **Fundgruppen.** Berlin, 1970. 102 pp., 73 illus., 90 pls., 8 color.
    II: **Einzelstuecke.** Berlin, 1975. 141 pp., 50 illus., 92 pls., 4 color.
Two boxed volumes. Superbly produced! Now out-of-print.

246.205 Greifenhagen, A.
Schmuck der Alten Welt. Berlin, 1979. 72 pp., 27 color pls. Paper. $12.50
Attractively illustrated introduction to ancient jewelry.

247.206 Hackens, T., (Ed.).
Studies in Ancient Jewelry. (**Aurifex**, I.). Louvain, 1980. 154 pp., num. color pls., num. illus. $48.50
Contains six lengthy articles on ancient jewelry and technology, incl. four articles on various aspects of Greek toreutics.

248.207 Hackens, T. and Winkes, R., (Eds.).
Gold Jewelry; Craft, Style and Meaning from Mycenae to Constantinopolis. (**Aurifex**, V.). Louvain, 1983. 17.5 x 26. 227 pp., num. illus., incl. 21 color. $36.00
Descriptive catalogue of 46 items, with 40 page section on Greek jewelry and photographs showing technical details.

260.219 Hackens, T. Rhode Island School of Design, Museum of Art.
Catalogue of the Classical Collections: classical jewelry. Providence 1976. 159 pp., num. illus. Paper. $45.00
Carefully catalogues and illustrates 79 pieces of jewelry and 11 ancient gems. Out-of-print.

249.208 Higgins, R.A.
Greek and Roman Jewellery. London, 1981. 16 x 23.5. 304 pp., 64 pls., 28 figs. $45.00
Second edition of this basic work, newly illustrated, extensively revised and updated.

553.507 Higgins, R.A.
Jewellery from Classical Lands. Oxford, 1969. 21.5 x 14. 32 pp., 4 color pls., 16 pls. Paper. $14.50
Introduction to ancient jewelry of the Classical world.

124.84 Hoffmann, H. and von Claer, V. Museum fuer Kunst und Gewerbe Hamburg.
Antiker Gold- und Silberschmuck; Katalog mit Untersuchung der Objekte auf technischer Grundlage. Mainz, 1968. 23.5 x 19. x, 246 pp., num. illus. $38.50
Catalogues and illustrates 137 pieces of ancient jewelry. Includes a thorough section on technology with many close-up photographs.

238.200 Hoffmann, H. and Davidson, P.F. The Brooklyn Museum.
Greek Gold, Jewelry from the Age of Alexander. Brooklyn, 1965. xi, 311 pp., 8 color pls., 138 illus. Paper. $40.00
Significant catalogue surveying both the technology and the iconography of Early Hellenistic jewelry.

244.586 Kilian, K.
Fibeln in Thessalien. (**PBF**, vol. XIV.2, 1975.). viii, 233 pp., 99 pls. $57.50

250.209 Laffineur, R.
L'Orfèvrerie Rhodienne Orientalisante. Paris, 1978. 226 pp., 27 pls. Paper. $95.00
Comprehensive study of Greek island jewelry with discussion of iconography and careful illustrations.

488.445 Laffineur, R.
Collection Paul Canellopoulos (XV): Bijoux en Or Grecs et Romains. (**BCH**,, vol. CIV, 1980). Paris, 1980. 19 x 25. 112 pp., 192 illus. Paper. $45.00
Descriptive catalogue of a large private collection, (169 pieces, all are illustrated) of jewelry from the Greek Bronze Age to the Roman Imperial Period.

602.552 Lévy, E.
Nouveaux bijoux à Délos. (**BCH**, vol. XCII, 1968.). Paris, 1968. 19 x 25. 16 pp., 13 figs. Paper. $18.00
Publishes and illustrates a dated 2nd century BC. treasure. Additionally contains, among many other articles,: Buchanan, B., **A Cypriote Cylinder at Yale (Newell Collection 358).**

130.90 Marshall, F. British Museum.
Catalogue of the Jewellery, Greek, Etruscan, and Roman in the Department of Antiquities, British Museum. London, 1969. 28 x 23. lxii, 400 pp., 73 pls. $95.00
The standard reference work describing 3,168 items. Now out-of-print.

486.443 Metzger, C. Musée du Louvre.
Bijoux Grecs, Étrusques et Romains. Paris, 1983. 11.5 x 23.5. 18 pp., 30 illus. Paper. $5.50
Illustrates highlights from the French national collections.

251.210 Miller, S.G.
Two Groups of Thessalian Gold. Berkeley, 1979. xii, 78 pp., 32 pls. Paper.
$16.00
Careful study of Northern Greek Hellenistic jewelry; an attempt is made to distinguish between workshops.

252.211 Muscarella, O.W.
Phrygian Fibulae from Gordion. London, 1967. viii, 91 pp., 20 pls. Paper.
$18.50
Studies the dates and origins of one class of fibulae to help increase our understanding of cultural relations in the Near East.

264.223 Ninou, K., (Ed.). Archaeological Museum.
Treasures of Ancient Macedonia. Thessalonika, n.d. 110 pp., 25 color pls., 37 pls. Paper. $34.50
First exhibition catalogue of recent finds from the tomb of Philip II of Macedon, with many equally impressive objects added.

256.215 Ondrejova, I.
Les Bijoux Antiques du Pont Euxin Septentrional. Prague, 1975. 83 pp., 14 pls.
$21.50
Substantial find of Hellenistic and Roman jewelry; well illustrated and catalogued.

234.195 Palazzo Chiablese.
Ori e Argenti dell'Italia Antica. Turin, 1961. 17 x 23.5. 276 pp., 12 color illus., 106 pls. $65.00
Scarce exhibition catalogue of ancient jewelry of many periods found in Italy.

548.502 Perry, R.
Schmuck der Antike, Gefaesse und Geraete aus Bronze. (Sonderliste T). Basel, 1981. 24 x 17. 48 pp., 1 color pl., 124 illus. Paper. $12.50
Carefully catalogued group of ancient jewelry from the 2nd millenium to early Islamic. Illustrates ca. 75 pieces.

258.217 Philipp, H.
Bronzeschmuck aus Olympia. (Olympische Forschungen, vol. XIII). Berlin, 1981. 21 x 28. xvi, 403 pp., 82 pls. Paper. $95.00
Valuable contribution to study of early jewelry types from this major site.

259.218 Pierides, A.
Jewellery in the Cyprus Museum. Nicosia, 1971. 59 pp., 2 color pls., 38 pls. Paper. $28.50
Large format, well illustrated catalogue of ancient jewelry from Cyprus.

261.220 Raddatz, K.
Die Schatzfunde der Iberischen Halbinsel vom Ende des dritten bis zur Mitte des ersten Jahrhunderts vor Chr. Geb. (Madrider Forschungen, vol. V). Berlin, 1969. 22 x 32. 2 vols.: x, 289 pp., 1 pl., 35 figs.; and 98 pls., 11 maps. $115.00
Large finds of jewelry and some metal vessels from Iberia are carefully described and illustrated.

487.444 Ruxer, M.S. and Kubczak, J.
Naszyjnik Grecki w Okresach Hellenistycznym i Rzymskim / Greek Necklace of the Hellenistic and Roman Ages. Warsaw, 1972. 17 x 24. 271 pp., 6 color pls., 74 pls., 32 figs. Paper. $110.00
Describes the differences in conception and construction between the necklaces of the Greek and Roman periods; illustrated with many examples from obscure or lost collections. Rare!

245.587 Sapouna-Sakellaris, E.
Die Fibeln der griechischen Inseln. (PBF, vol. XIV.4, 1978.). x, 150 pp., 56 pls. $62.50

628.577 Sarianidi, V.
L'Or de la Bactriane: Fouilles de la Nécropole de Tillia-Tepe en Afghanistan Septentrional. Leningrad, 1985. 36 x 26. 259 pp., 426 illus. incl. 166 color pls.
$75.00
Sumptuously illustrated book publishes the recent finds of gem-set gold jewelry from Bactria, dating from the 1st c. BC. - 1st c. AD., many different stylistic influences may be recognized.

262. 221 Segall, B.
Tradition und Neuschoepfung in der fruehalexandrinischen Kleinkunst. (BWP, 119/120). Berlin, 1966. 63 pp., 22 figs. Paper. $52.50
Study of development of Hellenistic preciosa in various media.

263.222 Segall, B.
Zur Griechischen Goldschmiedekunst des vierten Jahrhunderts v. Chr. Wiesbaden, 1966. 24 x 31. viii, 51 pp., 47 pls., 3 figs. $48.50
Thorough examination of Classical Greek jewelry, superbly illustrated.

401.356 Svoboda, B. and Concev, D.
Neue Denkmaeler antiker Toreutik. Prague, 1956. 21 x 31. 173 pp., 32 pls., 46 figs. $48.00
Contains: **Zur Geschichte des Rhytons**, and **Der Goldschatz von Panagjuriste**. Rare book describing gold and silver vessels from Eastern European site.

131.91 Tait, H., (Ed.). British Museum.
Jewellery through 7000 years. London, 1976. 24 x 19. 276 pp., num. color and B. & W. illus. Paper. $22.50
Presents 466 pieces of jewelry from around the world. Excellent general survey; well illustrated. Out-of-print.

257.216 Vickers, M. Ashmolean Museum.
Scythian Treasures in Oxford. Oxford, 1979. 15 x 21. 56 pp., 18 pls., 13 figs. Paper. $8.00
Presents mostly jewelry and engraved gems, some pottery, armor.

265.224 Yalouris, N., (Ed.).
The Search for Alexander. New York, 1980. 22 x 28.5. 192 pp., 295 illus., incl. 90 color. $23.50
Well illustrated survey of early Hellenistic jewelry.

Etruscan Jewelry

108.410 Battaglia, G.B.
Gioelli Antichi dall'eta Micenea all'Ellenismo. Rome, 1982. 24.5 x 31. 38 pp., 82 color illus. Paper. $22.50
Handsomely illustrated catalogue of the famous Castellani Collection of ancient jewelry, now in the Villa Guilia, Rome.

242.588 Berge, L. and Alexander, K.
Ancient Gold Work and Jewelry from Chicago Collections. (The Ancient World, vol. XI, 1985.). Chicago, 1985. 28 x 21.5. 29 pp., 16 pls. Paper. $11.50
Exhibition catalogue of 172 pieces of ancient gold jewelry from private collections in the Chicago area. Emphasis is on jewelry and objects from the 4th c. BC - 4th c. AD.

146.106 Boardman, J.
Intaglios and Rings: Greek, Etruscan and Eastern. London, 1975. 25 x 18. 118 pp., 32 pls. $36.00
In-depth catalogue of a hitherto unpublished private collection of 214 rings and engraved gems.

253.212 Breglia, L. Museo Nazionale de Napoli.
Catalogo dello Oreficerie. Rome, 1941. 193 pp., 45 pls. Paper. $42.50
Leading Italian collection, comprehensively published and illustrated. Out-of-print and now quite scarce.

668.633 Chadour, A.B. and Joppien, R. Kunstgewerbemuseum.
Schmuck, Bestandskatalog des Kunstgewerbemuseums. Cologne, 1985. 2 vols. with num. illus., incl. color. $45.00
Major new museum catalogue with a lengthy introduction and 910 entries, especially strong in Ancient, Migration Period, Renaissance and 19th c. jewelry. A fine group of 355 rings is shown in two views each. Recommended!

266.225 Chieco Bianchi, A.M., (Ed.).
Proposta per una tipologia delle fibule di Este. Florence, 1976. 18 x 27. 48 pp., 22 pls. Paper. $17.50
Illustrates the development of Etruscan fibulae.

240.202 Coche de la Ferté, É.
Les Bijoux Antiques. Paris, 1956. 13.5 x 21.5. 122 pp., 28 pls , 8 figs. Paper.
$40.00
Careful study examining ancient jewelry and its techniques. Includes a section on forgeries.

483.440 Cristofani, M. and Martelli, M.
L'Oro degli Etruschi. Novara, 1983. 23 x 31. 343 pp., 310 color illus., 17 figs. Slipcase. $110.00
Superbly illustrated publication shows the full range and splendor of Etruscan gold and bead jewelry, some set with gems, of all periods. Includes a separate section on technique. Likely to become a standard reference.!

562.515 Hotel Drouot.
Collection d'Orfèvrerie Antique. Paris, 1934. 24 x 18. 21 pp., 4 pls., 2 figs. Paper.
$15.00
Catalogue of a sale that dispersed, in 197 lots, a collection of ancient gold jewelry especially strong in Etruscan and Roman jewelry. Scarce.

217.180 Garside, A., (Ed.). Walters Art Gallery.
Jewelry, Ancient to Modern. Baltimore, 1979 32 x 23. 256 pp., num. illus. incl. 116 color. $40.00
Scholarly catalogue, beautifully produced, of jewelry from all periods.

267.226 Guarducci, M.
La Cosidetta Fibula Prenestina Antiquari, Eruditi e Falsari nella Roma dell'Ottocento. (Atti della Accademia Nazionale dei Lincei, vol. XXIV, 1980.). 162 pp., 5 color pls., 6 pls., 9 figs. Paper. $38.50
Most fascinating study proving the famous Etruscan fibula to be a forgery!

247.206 Hackens, T., (Ed.).
Studies in Ancient Jewelry. (**Aurifex**, I.). Louvain, 1980. 154 pp., num. color pls., num. illus. $48.00
Contains six lengthy articles on ancient jewelry and technology, incl. four articles on various aspects of Greek toreutics.

248.207 Hackens, T. and Winkes, R., (Eds.).
Gold Jewelry; Craft, Style and Meaning from Mycenae to Constantinopolis. (**Aurifex**, V.). Louvain, 1983. 17.5 x 26. 227 pp., num. ilus., incl. 21 color. $36.00
Descriptive catalogue of 46 items, with 40 page section on Greek jewelry and photographs showing technical details.

260.219 Hackens, T. Rhode Island School of Design, Museum of Art.
Catalogue of the Classical Collections: classical jewelry. Providence, 1976. 159 pp., num. illus. Paper. $45.00
Carefully catalogues and illustrates 79 pieces of jewelry and 11 ancient gems. Out-of-print.

268.227 Heurgon, J.
Recherches sur la Fibule d'or inscrite de Chiusi: la plus ancienne mention épigraphique du nom des Étrusques. (**MEFRA**, vol. 83, 1971). 19 pp., 9 illus. Paper.
$5.50

249.208 Higgins, R.A.
Greek and Roman Jewellery. London, 1981. 16 x 23.5. 304 pp., 64 pls., 28 figs.
$45.00
Second edition of this basic work, newly illustrated, extensively revised and updated.

553.507 Higgins, R.A.
Jewellery from Classical Lands. Oxford, 1969. 21.5 x 14. 32 pp., 4 color pls., 16 pls. Paper. $14.50
Introduction to ancient jewelry of the Classical world.

124.84 Hoffmann, H. and von Claer, V. Museum fuer Kunst und Gewerbe Hamburg.
Antiker Gold- und Silberschmuck; Katalog mit Untersuchung der Objekte auf technischer Grundlage. Mainz, 1968. 23.5 x 19. x, 246 pp., num. illus. $38.50
Catalogues and illustrates 137 pieces of ancient jewelry. Includes a thorough section on technology with many close-up photographs.

130.90 Marshall, F. British Museum.
Catalogue of the Jewellery, Greek, Etruscan, and Roman in the Department of Antiquities, British Museum. London, 1969. 28 x 23. lxii, 400 pp., 73 pls. $95.00
The standard reference work describing 3,168 items. Now out-of-print.

486.443 Metzger, C. Musée du Louvre.
Bijoux Grecs, Étrusques et Romains. Paris, 1983. 11.5 x 23.5. 18 pp., 30 illus. Paper. $5.50
Illustrates highlights from the French national collections.

234.195 Palazzo Chiablese.
Ori e Argenti dell'Italia Antica. Turin, 1961. 17 x 23.5. 276 pp., 12 color illus., 106 pls. $65.00
Scarce exhibition catalogue of ancient jewelry of many periods found in Italy.

548.502 Perry, R.
Schmuck der Antike, Gefaesse und Geraete aus Bronze. (Sonderliste T). Basel, 1981. 24 x 17. 48 pp., 1 color pl., 124 illus. Paper. $12.50
Carefully catalogued group of ancient jewelry from the 2nd millenium to early Islamic. Illustrates ca. 75 pieces.

611.560 Scarpignato, M.
Oreficerie etrusche arcaiche del Museo Gregoriano-Etrusco. (Monumenti Musei e Gallerie Pontificie, n.d.). 21.5 x 24. 69 pp., 120 pls., incl 35 in color.
$65.00
Newly published museum catalogue of Archaic Etruscan jewelry.

581.533 Siviero, R.
Jewelry and Amber of Italy: A Collection in the National Museum of Naples. New York, 1959. 34.5 x 25. 153 pp., 8 color pls., 274 pls., 115 figs. $185.00
Important, well illustrated book showing the Etruscan and Roman jewelry in the Naples' Museum from the excavations in Pompei and Herculaneum.

131.91 Tait, H., (Ed.). British Museum.
Jewellery through 7000 years. London, 1976. 24 x 19. 176 pp., num. color and B. & W. illus. Paper. $22.50
Presents 466 pieces of jewelry from around the world. Excellent general survey; well illustrated. Out-of-print.

Roman Jewelry

550.504 Baratte, F. and Guyon, J.
Recherches Archéologiques à Sirmium (II). (**MEFRA**, vol. 87, 1975). Paris, 1975. 24.5 x 17. 27 pp., 16 figs. Paper. $4.50
Contains three articles describing the general excavations, the finds of jewelry and of a silver reliquary at Sirmium in a 4th c. context.

512.467 Bateson, J.D.
Enamel-working in Iron Age, Roman and Sub-Roman Britain; The Products and Techniques. (**BAR**, 93, 1981). Oxford, 1981. 167 pp., 15 pls. Paper. $22.50
Comprehensive survey of the enameled objects from Britain from 200 BC - 700 AD. Millefiori enamels and their techniques are studied in detail.

652.620 Battaglia, G.B. Museo Nazionale Romano.
Corredi Funerari di Eta Imperiale e Barbarica nel Museo Nazionale Romano. Rome, 1983. 19.5 x 25.5. 176 pp., 158 illus. $32.50
Roman Imperial and Later jewelry from dated tombs is carefully studied and used to anchor various styles more securely. Well illustrated.

513.468 Beckmann, C.
Metallfingerringe der roemischen Kaiserzeit im freien Germanien. (**Saalburg Jahrbuch**, vol. XXVI, 1969). 32 x 24. 102 pp., 32 illus., 2 pls., 15 maps. Paper.
$45.00
Survey of finger rings coeval with the later Roman Empire but made and worn in the non-Roman parts of Northern Europe, shows styles, types, dates. Includes 15 maps showing distribution patterns. Catalogues 844 finger rings. Recommended.

514.468 Beckmann, B.
Die baltischen Metallnadeln der roemischen Kaiserzeit. (**Saalburg Jahrbuch**, vol. XXVI, 1969). 32 x 24. 13 pp., 1 fig., 4 maps. Paper. $45.00
Catalogue listing of 249 stick pins from Northern Europe. This publication also contains the above listed article which describes finger rings from the same geographical area.

235.197 Benaki Museum.
Jewelry. Athens, 1970. 14 x 15.5. 3 pp., 48 illus. Paper. $8.50
Well illustrated booklet shows, in 48 detailed photographs, highlights of the collection which covers 5000 years of jewelry.

242.588 Berge, L. and Alexander, K.
Ancient Gold Work and Jewelry from Chicago Collections. (**The Ancient World**, vol. XI, 1985.). Chicago, 1985. 28 x 21.5. 29 pp., 16 pls. Paper. $11.50
Exhibition catalogue of 172 pieces of ancient gold jewelry from private collections in the Chicago area. Emphasis is on jewelry and objects from the 4th c. BC - 4th c. AD.

253.212 Breglia, L. Museo Nazionale de Napoli.
Catalogo delle Oreficerie. Rome, 1941. 193 pp., 45 pls. Paper. $42.50
Leading Italian collection, comprehensively published and illustrated. Out-of-print and now quite scarce.

565.518 The Brooklyn Museum.
Africa in Antiquity: The Arts of Ancient Nubia and the Sudan. I: The Essays. II: The Catalogue.. Brooklyn, 1978. 32 x 22. 143 pp., 100 figs., 19 in color., 3 maps; and 112 pp., 84 figs., 9 in color. $48.00
Two volumes illustrating the "provincial arts of Egypt", the jewelry is especially noteworthy for its many different influences and barbaric splendor. Recommended!

570.523 Brown, K.R. Metropolitan Museum of Art.
Guide to Provincial Roman and Barbarian Metalwork and Jewelry in The Metropolitan Museum of Art. New York, 1981. 23 x 15. 28 pp., 38 figs., map. Paper. $7.50
Attractive catalogue of Late Roman and Migration Period jewelry, includes a short history, identifies and dates the various styles.

637.585 Brown, K.R. Roemisch-Germanisches Zentralmuseum.
The Gold Breast Chain From the Early Byzantine Period in the Roemisch-Germanisches Zentralmuseum. Mainz, 1984. 30 x 21. 30 pp., 4 color pls., 18 pls., 25 figs. $32.50
Interesting and readable study of a rare ornament, probably made in Constantinople around 600. Parallels and examples of usage are shown, other pieces of jewelry in the same technique are touched upon.

668.633 Chadour, A.B. and Joppien, R. Kunstgewerbemuseum.
Schmuck, Bestandskatalog des Kunstgewerbemuseums. Cologne, 1985. 2 vols. with num. illus., incl. color. $45.00
Major new museum catalogue with a lengthy introduction and 910 entries, especially strong in Ancient, Migration Period, Renaissance and 19th c. jewelry. A fine group of 355 rings is shown in two views each. Recommended!

540.494 Coarelli, F.
Greek and Roman Jewellery. Feltham, 1970. 19.5 x 13.5. 157 pp., 68 color pls. $18.50
Well illustrated introduction to ancient jewelry.

240.202 Coche de la Ferté, É.
Les Bijoux Antiques. Paris, 1956. 13.5 x 21.5. 122 pp., 28 pls., 8 figs. Paper. $40.00
Careful study examining ancient jewelry and its techniques. Includes a section on forgeries.

274.232 Coche de la Ferté, É.
Antique Jewellery from the second to the eighth century AD. Bern, 1967. 12 x 19. 8 pp., 19 color pls. $11.50
Publishes and illustrates, in color, highlights from the Collection de Clercq.

275.233 Coche de la Ferté, É.
Un Bracelet d'Époque Romaine à usage obstétrique. (**Syria**, vol. LI, 1974). 22 x 28. 24 pp., 4 pls., 4 figs. Paper. $9.50
Interesting example of an unusual class of Roman jewelry.

277.235 Cosack, E.
Die Fibeln der Alteren roemischen Kaiserzeit in der Germania Libera. I. (Goettinger Schriften zur Vor- und Fruehgeschichte.). Goettingen, 1979. 103 pp., 85 pls., 25 maps. $65.00

698.677 Davidson, P.F. and Oliver, A. The Brooklyn Museum.
Ancient Greek and Roman Gold Jewelry in the Brooklyn Museum. Brooklyn, 1984. 29 x 23. 214 pp., 224 figs. $45.00
Recent museum catalogue of a large collection of Hellenistic and Roman jewelry. Each object is illustrated and carefully described with bibliography.

279.237 Dennison, W.A.
A Gold Treasure of the Late Roman Period from Egypt. (UMS, vol. XII). New York, 1918. 21 x 28. 99 pp., 54 pls., 57 figs. $195.00
Bound together with: Morey, C.R. **East Christian Paintings in the Freer Collection.** xiii, 86 pp., 13 pls., 34 figs.

564.517 Deppert-Lippitz, B.
Spaethellenistische Goldschmiede-Arbeiten. (Antike Kunst, 15, 1972.). 28 x 22.5. 12 pp., 8 pls. Paper. $18.00
Important article on Late Hellenistic jewelry, illustrated with many datable examples.

562.515 Hotel Drouot.
Collection d'Orfèvrerie Antique. Paris, 1934. 24 x 18. 21 pp., 4 pls., 2 figs. Paper.
$15.00
Catalogue of a sale that dispersed, in 197 lots, a collection of ancient gold jewelry especially strong in Etruscan and Roman jewelry. Scarce.

623.572 Hotel Drouot.
Bijoux Antiques - Camées - Intailles. Paris, 1959. 26.5 x 21. 24 pp., 7 pls. Paper.
$12.50
Catalogue of an auction that dispersed, among others, 51 pairs of ancient earrings, (Roman and earlier), 110 engraved gems, (all illustrated). With prices realized marked in the margin.

625.574 Hotel Drouot.
Antiques - Art Chrétien: Bijoux d'Or, IVe Siècle - Xe Siècle. Paris, 1959. 27 x 21. 33 pp., 9 pls. Paper. $12.50
Auction catalogue showing Byzantine and earlier gold jewelry, 26 finger rings, as well as pottery and other objects.

530.484 Ergil, T.
Kuepeler / Earrings: The Catalogue of the Istanbul Archaeological Museum. Istanbul, 1983. 19 x 27.5. 71 pp., num. illus., incl. color. Paper. $26.50
Catalogues earrings of all periods of Turkish history, illustrates Hellenistic and Roman types mostly, some others.

280.238 Fontenay, E.
Les Bijoux Anciens et Modernes. Paris, 1887. 19.5 x 27.5. 520 pp., 700 illus.
$160.00
Early, but still relevant, work on the history and technology of jewelry. Rare!

217.180 Garside, A., (Ed.). Walters Art Gallery.
Jewelry, Ancient to Modern. Baltimore, 1979 32 x 23. 256 pp., num. illus. incl. 116 color. $40.00
Scholarly catalogue, beautifully produced, of jewelry from all periods.

537.491 Gerlach, M., (Ed.).
Primitive and Folk Jewelry. New York, 1971. 28 x 21. 218 pp., 109 pls. with 1900 illus. Paper. $11.50
Quality reprint of the 1906 edition of **Voelkerschmuck**; still an excellent quick reference for ancient, ethnic and unusual jewelry with more than 1900 items illustrated.

236.198 Greifenhagen, A. Staatliche Museen Preussischer Kulturbesitz. Antikenabteilung.
Schmuckarbeiten in Edelmetall. $550.00
The two portfolios include:
   I: **Fundgruppen.** Berlin, 1970. 102 pp., 73 illus., 90 pls., 8 color.
   II: **Einzelstuecke.** Berlin, 1975. 141 pp., 50 illus., 92 pls., 4 color.
Two boxed volumes. Superbly produced! Now out-of-print.

246.205 Greifenhagen, A.
Schmuck der Alten Welt. Berlin, 1979. 72 pp., 27 color pls. Paper. $12.50
Attractively illustrated introduction to ancient jewelry.

3.239 Guido, M.
The Glass Beads of the Prehistoric and Roman Periods in Britain and Ireland. London, 1978. xxxvi, 250 pp., 4 color pls., 38 figs. $65.00
Beads from Britain, ca. 700 BC - 410 AD are presented in carefully annotated detail; includes classification tables, typology, etc.

248.207 Hackens, T. and Winkes, R., (Eds.).
Gold Jewelry; Craft, Style and Meaning from Mycenae to Constantinopolis. (**Aurifex**, V.). Louvain, 1983. 17.5 x 26. 227 pp., num. illus., incl. 21 color. $36.00
Descriptive catalogue of 46 items, with 40 page section on Greek jewelry and photographs showing technical details.

260.219 Hackens, T. Rhode Island School of Design, Museum of Art.
Catalogue of the classical Collections: classical jewelry. Providence. 1976. 159 pp., num. illus. Paper. $45.00
Carefully catalogues and illustrates 79 pieces of jewelry and 11 ancient gems. Out-of-print.

281.240 Harhoiu, R.
The fifth-century AD, treasure from Pietroasa, in the light of recent research. (**BAR**, S-24). Oxford, 1977. 57 pp., 13 pls. Paper. $11.50
Famous Rumanian find, representing Late Roman industrial relations with "Barbaricum", newly studied and illustrated.

273.231 Hellenkemper, H., (Ed.). Musées d'Histoire.
Trésors romains-Trésors barbares: Industrie d'art à la fin de l'Antiquité et au début du Moyen Age. Brussels, 1979. 13 x 20. 163 pp., 48 pls. incl. 16 color. Paper. $12.50
Jewelry and related precious objects are carefully described, dated and illustrated. Includes section on technology.

249.208 Higgins, R.A.
Greek and Roman Jewellery. London, 1981. 16 x 23.5. 304 pp., 64 pls., 28 figs. $45.00
Second edition of this basic work, newly illustrated, extensively revised and updated.

553.507 Higgins, R.A.
Jewellery from Classical Lands. Oxford, 1969. 21.5 x 14. 32 pp., 4 color pls., 16 pls. Paper. $14.50
Introduction to ancient jewelry of the Classical world.

124.84 Hoffmann, H. and von Claer, V. Museum fuer Kunst und Gewerbe Hamburg.
Antiker Gold- und Silberschmuck; Katalog mit Untersuchung der Objekte auf technischer Grundlage. Mainz, 1968. 23.5 x 19. x, 246 pp., num. illus. $38.50
Catalogues and illustrates 137 pieces of ancient jewelry. Includes a thorough section on technology with many close-up photographs.

282.241 Johns, C. and Potter, T. British Museum.
The Thetford Treasure: Roman Jewellery and Silver. London, 1983. 22.5 x 28.5. 136 pp., 4 color pls., 16 B. & W. pls., 45 figs. $45.00
Major recent find of Late 4th c. jewelry, incl. 22 gold rings and 33 silver spoons, expertly described and illustrated. With a technical examination of the Treasure and an arthistorical interpretation of its significance.

488.445 Laffineur, R.
Collection Paul Canellopoulos (XV): Bijoux en Or Grecs et Romains. (BCH,, vol. CIV, 1980). Paris, 1980. 19 x 25. 112 pp., 192 illus. Paper. $45.00
Descriptive catalogue of a large private collection, (169 pieces, all are illustrated) of jewelry from the Greek Bronze Age to the roman Imperial Period.

284.243 Lerat, L.
Les Fibules d'Alésia dans les Musées d'Alise-Sainte-Reine. Dijon, 1979. 21 x 29.5. 124 pp., 1 color pl. 35 pls., 1 fig. Paper. $32.50
Catalogue of 380 Gallo-Roman fibulae of many different types.

130.90 Marshall, F. British Museum.
Catalogue of the Jewellery, Greek, Etruscan, and Roman in the Department of Antiquities, British Museum. London, 1969. 28 x 23. lxii, 400 pp., 73 pls. $95.00
The standard reference work describing 3,168 items. Now out-of-print.

269.414 Martin, M. and S. Roemermuseum.
Schmuck und Tracht zur Roemerzeit. Augst, 1979. 32 pp., 29 figs. Paper. $7.50
Lucid introduction to the wearing of jewelry; illustrated with many finds from the area.

569.522 Martin, M.
Roemische Schatzfunde aus Augst und Kaiseraugst. Augst, 1977. 21 x 15. 47 pp., 23 figs. Paper. $7.50

486.443 Metzger, C. Musée du Louvre.
Bijoux Grecs, Étrusques et Romains. Paris, 1983. 11.5 x 23.5. 18 pp., 30 illus. Paper. $5.50
Illustrates highlights from the French national collections.

285.244 Michon, E.
À Propos d'un bandeau d'or Palestinien. (**Syria**, 1922). 5 pp. Paper. $3.50
3rd Century Roman gold head band with a Greek inscription.

283.242 Naumann, F. Staatliche Kunstsammlungen.
Antiker Schmuck. Kassel, 1980. 79 pp., 3 color pls., 36 pls., 2 figs. $18.50
Presents a collection of almost 200 objects, strong in East Roman and early Byzantine types.

286.245 Oberlin, OH. Allen Memorial Art Museum.
Melvin Gutman Collection of Ancient and Medieval Gold. (**Bulletin**, vol XVIII, 1961). 298 pp., 2 color pls. Paper. $14.00
Catalogues and describes 180 pieces of jewelry and illustrates all, many in close-up detail.

256.215 Ondrejova, I.
Les Bijoux Antiques du Pont Euxin Septentrional. Prague, 1975. 83 pp., 14 pls. $21.50
Substantial find of Hellenistic and Roman jewelry; well illustrated and catalogued.

234.195 Palazzo Chiablese.
Ori e Argenti dell'Italia Antica. Turin, 1961. 17 x 23.5. 267 pp., 12 color illus., 196 pls. $65.00
Scarce exhibition catalogue of ancient jewelry of many periods found in Italy.

548.502 Perry, R.
Schmuck der Antike, Gefaesse und Geraete aus Bronze. (Sonderliste T). Basel, 1981. 24 x 17. 48 pp., 1 color pl., 124 illus. Paper. $12.50
Carefully catalogued group of ancient jewelry from the 2nd millenium to early Islamic. Illustrates ca. 75 pieces.

287.246 Pfeiler, B.
Roemischer Goldschmuck des ersten und zweiten Jahrhunderts n. Chr. nach datierten Funden. Mainz, 1970. xii, 136 pp., 32 pls. $26.50
Serious attempt to establish chronology of early Roman jewelry.

259.218 Pierides, A.
Jewellery in the Cyprus Museum. Nicosia, 1971. 59 pp., 2 color pls., 38 pls. Paper. $28.50
Large format, well illustrated catalogue of ancient jewelry from Cyprus.

509.464 Platz-Horster, G.
Die antiken Gemmen im Rheinischen Landesmuseum Bonn. Bonn, 1984. 24.5 x 17. 141 pp., 36 pls. $18.50
Large collection of mostly Roman gems, mounted and unmounted, with known dates and findspots from the Bonn area.

270.228 Riha, E. Roemermuseum.
Die roemische Fibeln von Augst und Kaiseraugst. Augst, 1979. 220 pp., 1 color pl., 70 pls., 30 figs., map. $78.50
Serious attempt to establish a typology of Roman fibulae from datable context.

272.230 Rudolph, W. and E. Indiana University Art Museum.
Ancient Jewelry from the collection of Burton Y. Berry. Bloomington, 1973. xxiv, 247 pp., num. illus. Paper. $30.00
Describes and illustrates most of 197 pieces of jewelry from various periods, the majority Roman from Turkey and Syria.

487.444 Ruxer, M.S. and Kubczak, J.
Naszyjnik Grecki w Okresach Hellenistycznym i Rzymskim / Greek Necklace of the Hellenistic and Roman Ages. Warsaw, 1972. 17 x 24. 271 pp., 6 color pls., 74 pls., 32 figs. Paper. $110.00
Describes the differences in conception and construction between the necklaces of the Greek and Roman periods; illustrated with many examples from obscure or lost collections. Rare!

628.577 Sarianidi, V.
L'Or de la Bactriane: Fouilles de la Nécropole de Tillia-Tepe en Afghanistan Septentrional. Leningrad, 1985. 36 x 26. 259 pp., 426 illus. incl. 166 color pls.
$75.00
Sumptuously illustrated book publishes the recent finds of gem-set gold jewelry from Bactria, dating from the 1st c. BC. - 1st c. AD., many different stylistic influences may be recognized.

567.520 De Serres, J.-P. Hotel Drouot.
Antiquités Égyptiennes; Antiquités Grecques et Romaines; Haute Curiosité. Paris, 1981. 20.5 x 17. 43 pp., 6 illus. Paper. $4.50
Auction catalogue of amulets, gems and some jewelry. Most objects are shown in color on the outside covers of the catalogue.

581.533 Siviero, R.
Jewelry and Amber of Italy: A Collection in the National Museum of Naples. New York, 1959. 34.5 x 25. 153 pp., 8 color pls., 274 pls., 115 figs. $185.00
Important, well illustrated book showing the Etruscan and Roman jewelry in the Naples' Museum from the excavations in Pompei and Herculaneum.

131.91 Tait, H., (Ed.). British Museum.
Jewellery through 7000 years. London, 1976. 24 x 19. 276 pp., num. color and B. & W. illus. Paper. $22.50
Presents 466 pieces of jewelry from around the world. Excellent general survey; well illustrated. Out-of-print.

632.581 Tempelmann-Maczynska, M.
Die Perlen der roemischen Kaiserzeit und der fruehen Phase der Voelkerwanderungszeit im mitteleuropaeischen Barbaricum. (Roemisch-Germanische Forschungen, 47). Mainz, 1985. xii, 339 pp., 14 color pls. with 707 illus., 66 pls. with 207 illus., charts. $67.50
Shows Roman and early Migration Period beads, all types are illustrated and described.

276.234 Werner, J. Roemisch-Germanisches Museum.
Katalog der Sammlung Diergardt. vol. I: Die Fibeln. Cologne, 1961. xii, 68 pp., 50 pls., 12 maps. $45.00
Large collection of fibulae.

Finger Rings, all periods

288.247 Abeler, J.
Vom Siegelring zum Liebesring. Wuppertal, n.d. 15 x 24. num. illus, incl. color. Paper. $12.50
Large and varied private collection of rings from all periods. Most are illustrated.

289.248 Battke, H.
Geschichte des Ringes in Beschreibung und Bildern. Baden Baden, 1953. 21 x 27. 111 pp., 1 color pl., 29 pls. $265.00
Lengthy catalogue of a collection of 160 rings, now mostly in the Schmuckmuseum, Pforzheim. Scarce.

290.249 Battke, H.
Ringe aus vier Jahrtausenden. Frankfurt, 1963. 49 pp., 15 color pls. Paper.
$12.50
Presents 55 finger rings from the Schmuckmuseum's collection.

513.468 Beckmann, C.
Metallfingerringe der römischen Kaiserzeit im freien Germanien. (Saalburg Jahrbuch, vol. XXVI, 1969). 32 x 24. 102 pp., 23 illus., 2 pls., 15 maps. Paper.
$45.00
Survey of finger rings coeval with the later Roman Empire but made and worn in the non-Roman parts of Northern Europe, shows styles, types, dates. Includes 15 maps showing distribution patterns. Catalogues 844 finger rings. Recommended.

145.105 Boardman, J.
Greek Gems and Finger Rings: Early Bronze Age to Late Classical. New York, 1972. 32 x 24. 458 pp., 9 color pls., 1015 illus. $85.00
An important basic survey of ancient glyptics. Out-of-print.

146.106 Boardman, J.
Intaglios and Rings: Greek, Etruscan and Eastern. London, 1975. 25 x 18. 118 pp., 32 pls. $36.00
In-depth catalogue of a hitherto unpublished private collection of 214 rings and engraved gems.

147.107 Boardman, J. and Scarisbrick, D.
The Ralph Harari Collection of Finger Rings. London, 1977. 25 x 19. 149 pp., 52 pls., incl. 2 color pls. $38.50
Outstanding collection of 216 finger rings, and engraved gems, from Ancient to Neo-Classical, expertly presented.

159.119 Boardman, J. and Vollenweider, M.-L. Ashmolean Museum.
Catalogue of the Engraved Gems and Finger Rings. I: Greek and Etruscan. Oxford, 1978. 28 x 22. vi, 122 pp., 64 pls., 13 figs. $65.00
First volume in planned series publishing all gems and rings in the Ashmolean Museum. A beautiful collection!

BOOK LIST NO. 7

ORDER FORM
(If desired, institutions may substitute their purchase slips).

No.	Short Title	Price
.		
.		
.		
.		
.		
.		
.		
.		
.		
.		
.		
.		
.		
.		
.		
.		
.		
	TOTAL FOR BOOKS	
FOR CHARGES SEE INSIDE FRONT COVER	Shipping	
	Insurance	
	Bank Charges (where required; see inside front cover)	
	AMOUNT ENCLOSED	

NAME: ....
ADDRESS: ....
CITY: ....
COUNTRY: ....

FOR FUTURE REFERENCE.

Please send updated lists on the following subjects, (check as desired):

— ALL GLYPTIC ARTS.

— Cylinder Seals - Stamp Seals.
— Eastern - Phoenician Gems.
— Egyptian Scarabs.
— Minoan - Mycenaean Gems and Vessels.
— Greek Gems, incl. Graeco-Persian and Cypriot.
— Etruscan Gems.
— Roman Gems, incl. "Gnostic" Gems.
— Sasanian Gems.
— Byzantine Gems and Mediaeval Seals
— Renaissance and Later Gems

— ALL JEWELRY.

— Egyptian Jewelry.
— Near Eastern - Phoenician Jewelry.
— Greek Jewelry.
— Etruscan Jewelry.
— Roman Jewelry.
— Finger Rings, all periods.
— Pre-Historic European Jewelry.
— Medieval, Anglo Saxon and Dark Ages Jewelry.
— Byzantine Gems and Jewelry.
— Sasanian Jewelry - Silver Vessels.
— Islamic Gems and Jewelry.
— Ethnic Jewelry.
— Amber.
— Beads.
— Ancient "Kleinkunst", Metal Vessels, Objects.
— Renaissance and Later Gems and Jewelry.
— Technology - Ancient Texts - Varia

— CONTINUE TO SEND ALL COMPLETE LISTS.

— OTHER SUBJECTS, please specify ....

I AM LOOKING FOR THE FOLLOWING BOOKS; PLEASE QUOTE WHEN YOU FIND A COPY:

1) ....
2) ....
3) ....
4) ....
5) ....

PLEASE DETACH AND MAIL THIS ORDER FORM TO:

DEREK J. CONTENT RARE BOOKS, INC.
CROW HILL
HOULTON, MAINE 04730
U.S.A.

TELEPHONE:

(207) 532-7794

668.633 Chadour, A.B. and Joppien, R. Kunstgewerbemuseum.
Schmuck, Bestandskatalog des Kunstgewerbemuseums. Cologne, 1985. 2 vols. with num. illus., incl. color. $45.00
Major new museum catalogue with a lengthy introduction and 910 entries, especially strong in Ancient, Migration Period, Renaissance and 19th c. jewelry. A fine group of 355 rings is shown in two views each. Recommended!

558.511 Cote, C. Hotel Drouot.
Catalogue des Antiquités Romaines et des Objets d'Art et de Haute Curiosité. Paris, 1936. 23.5 x 20.5. 22 pp. Paper. $12.50
This auction catalogue lists Roman silver spoons, Greek and Roman gems, Dark Age jewelry and other objects. Photocopies of the original plates can be supplied for an additional $5.00. Scarce.

291.250 Deloche, M.
Le Port des Anneaux dans l'Antiquité Romaine et dans les Premiers Siècles du Moyen Age. Paris, 1896. 22.5 x 28. 112 pp. Paper. $45.00
Discussion of sumptuary laws, economics and fashions, and their effect on the wearing of finger rings in the ancient world.

625.574 Hotel Drouot.
Antiques - Art Chrétien: Bijoux d'Or, IVe Siècle - Xe Siècle. Paris, 1959. 27 x 21. 33 pp., 9 pls. Paper. $12.50
Auction catalogue showing Byzantine and earlier gold jewelry, 26 finger rings, as well as pottery and other objects.

280.238 Fontenay, E.
Les Bijoux Anciens et Modernes. Paris, 1887. 19.5 x 27.5. 520 pp., 700 illus.
$160.00
Early, but still relevant, work on the history and technology of jewelry. Rare!

292.252 Hinton, D.
Medieval Jewellery from the eleventh to the fifteenth century. Aylesbury, 1982. 15 x 21. 48 pp., 46 illus. Paper. $9.50
Well illustrated book showing mostly British medieval rings and some other jewelry.

293.253 Jones, W.
Finger-Ring Lore, Historical, Legendary, Anecdotal. London, 1877. 13 x 19.5. xiv, 545 pp., 300 illus. $95.00
First edition of scarce book dealing with all aspects of rings from all periods. Most interesting text, definitely worth reading!

128.88 Kenna, V.E.G.
Catalogue of the Cypriote Seals of the Bronze Age in the British Museum. (**SIMA**, XX:3). 30 x 22. 41 pp., 32 pls. Paper. $26.50
Useful catalogue of finger rings and engraved gems, their use and history, together with a brief history of this pivotal island.

600.551 Kenna, V.E.G.
The Kouklia ring from Evreti. (**BCH**, vol. XCII, 1968.). Paris, 1968. 4 pp., 2 figs. Paper. $11.50
Also contains: Kenna V.E.G., **The Seal Use of Cyprus in the Bronze Age** and Catling, H.W., **Kouklia: Evreti Tomb 8**.

186.148 Kibaltchich, T.W.
Gemmes de la Russie Méridionale. Berlin, 1910. 88 pp., 20 pls. Edition limited to 250 copies. $325.00
Collection of 511 items; mostly Roman gems, with many interesting "Gnostic" types.

536.490 Kunz, G.F.
Rings for the Finger. New York, 1973. 21.5 x 14. xvii., 381 pp., 104 illus. Reprint of the 1917 ed. Paper. $12.50
Excellent reprint of an entertaining survey of rings and ring lore of all periods. With many illustrations of unusual rings.

554.508 Oman, C.C. Victoria and Albert Museum.
Catalogue of Rings. London, 1930. 24.5 x 18.5. xvi, 154 pp., 39 pls., index. Paper.
$325.00
Classic catalogue of 992 rings with ca. 500 rings from ancient Egypt to the 19th c. illustrated. Original paper wrappers. Recommended!

607.556 Oman, C.C.
British Rings 800 - 1914. London, 1974. 25.5 x 19. x, 146 pp., 4 color pls., 96 pls.
$225.00
One of the basic texts on English rings, showing 518 examples, by the former keeper of the Department of Metalwork at the Victoria and Albert Museum, London. Scarce!

548.502 Perry, R.
Schmuck der Antike, Gefässe und Geräte aus Bronze. (Sonderliste T). Basel, 1981. 24 x 17. 48 pp., 1 color pl., 124 illus. Paper. $12.50
Carefully catalogued group of ancient jewelry from the 2nd millenium to early Islamic. Illustrates ca. 75 pieces.

258.217 Philipp, H.
Bronzeschmuck aus Olympia. (Olympische Forschungen, vol. XIII). Berlin, 1981. 21 x 28. xvi, 403 pp., 82 pls. Paper. $95.00
Valuable contribution to study of early jewelry types from this major site.

538.492 Pressmar, E.
Indische Ringe. Frankfurt, 1981. 24.5 x 17. 105 pp., 55 figs. $21.50
Shows, classifies and discusses Indian rings, mostly 18th c. and later.

294.254 De Ricci, S.
Catalogue of a Collection of Ancient Rings formed by the late E. Guilhou. Paris, 1912. vii, 194 pp., 24 pls. $145.00
Large format reprint, (350 copies only), of the privately printed 1912 edition. Illustrates all 1,636 rings. See also No. 295-255.

136.96 Sakellariou, A.
Die Mykenische Siegelglyptik. (**SIMA**, vol. IX, 1961). 28 x 22. 11 pp., 14 figs. Paper. $8.50
Introduction to the iconography of Mycenaean seals and ring bezels.

581.533 Siviero, R.
Jewelry and Amber of Italy: A Collection in the National Museum of Naples. New York, 1959. 34.5 x 25. 153 pp., 8 color pls., 274 pls., 115 figs. $185.00
Important, well illustrated book showing the Etruscan and Roman jewelry in the Naples' Museum from the excavations in Pompei and Herculaneum.

295.255 Sotheby & Co.
Catalogue of the Superb Collection of Rings formed by the Late Monsieur E. Guilhou, of Paris. London, 1937. 18 x 24.5. 178 pp., 1 color pl., 27 B. & W. pls. Paper. $150.00
Rare copy of the sale catalogue which dispersed, in 768 lots, this large collection of finger rings. Very well illustrated, complements No. 294-254.

547.501 Sotheby's.
The Thomas F. Flannery Jr. Collection: Medieval and Later Works of Art. London, 1983. 27 x 19. 291 pp., ca 400 illus., many in color. $36.00
Hardbound, single owner, auction sale catalogue, showing large collection of finger rings, Medieval and Renaissance jewels, gems and enamels, now dispersed. Very well illustrated with numerous color photographs.

296.256 Taylor, G. and Scarisbrick, D.
Finger Rings from Ancient Egypt to the Present Day. London, 1978. 20 x 21. 100 pp., 8 color pls. Paper. $24.50
Catalogues and describes 1000 finger rings, formerly in the Evans and Fortnum Collections. A true compendium! Out-of-print.

455.415 Vikan, G. and Nesbitt, J.
Security in Byzantium: Locking, Sealing, Weighing. Washington, 1980. 21.5 x 28. 39 pp., 88 figs. Paper. $6.50
First attempt to describe security related Byzantine objects; with careful descriptions and numerous illustrations of "ring-keys", gems, stamp-seals and finger rings. Recommended!

511.466 Vollenweider, M.-L.
Deliciae Leonis: antike geschnittene Steine und Ringe aus einer Privatsammlung. Mainz, 1984. 22 x 30.5. ix, 322 pp., 8 color pls., 105 pls., 5 figs. $87.50
It is easy to like these "Deliciae Leonis"! A worthy tribute to a superb collection of, mostly, Greek, Etruscan and Roman engraved gems and rings.

297.257 Ward, A., (et al.).
Rings through the Ages New York, 1981. 25.5 x 28.5. 214 pp., 404 illus., incl. num. color. $75.00
Comprehensive survey; each section written by a different specialist of the period. Well illustrated.

298.258 Woeiriot, P.
Livre d'Anneaux d'Orfèvrerie. Oxford, 1978. Intr. by D. Scarisbrick. vii, 40 pls.
$15.00
Facsimile reprint of the Lyons ed. of 1561. Sumptuous engravings illustrating 16th c. rings.

515.469 Zahlhaas, G.
Fingerringe und Gemmen: Sammlung Dr. E. Pressmar. Munich, 1985. 69 pp., 161 illus. Paper. $14.50
First publication of a private collection of 100 finger rings, all are illustrated and classified as to origin and date. The collection is strongest in the more commonly encountered types, Roman, Byzantine and Islamic, some others.

196.159 Zahn, R.
Sammlung Baurat Schiller/Berlin. Berlin, 1929. 136 pp., 65 pls. Full leather binding. $275.00
A scholarly catalogue of a famous collection of ancient jewelry and glass, now dispersed. Scarce!

Byzantine Jewelry and Silver Objects

580.532 Alborino, V.
Das Silberkästchen von San Nazaro in Mailand. Bonn, 1981. 20.5 x 15. 282 pp., 113 figs. Paper. $22.50
Careful iconographical study of the Late Roman silver reliquary from Milano. A date is established, 375 AD, and the reliquary is fitted into its overall context.

235.197 Benaki Museum.
Jewelry. Athens, 1970. 14 x 15.5. 3 pp., 48 illus. Paper. $8.50
Well illustrated booklet shows, in 48 detailed photographs, highlights of the collection which covers 5000 years of jewelry.

170.132 Le Blant, E.
750 Inscriptions de Pierres Gravées Inédites ou peu connues. Paris, 1896. 23 x 28. 210 pp., 2 pls. Paper. $72.50
Most useful compilation of inscriptions on ancient gems, both cameos and intaglios. Rare!

299.259 Bouras, L. Benaki Museum.
The cross of Adrianople: a silver processional cross of the Middle Byzantine Period. Athens, 1979. 20.5 x 28. 54 pp., 21 pls. Paper. $22.50
Detailed investigation into a 10th c. cross with references to similar crosses in other collections.

300.260 Bréhier, L.
Un Trésor d'Argenterie Ancienne au Musée de Cleveland. (Syria, vol. XXVIII, 1951). Paris, 1951. 9 pp., 4 pls., 3 figs. Paper. $5.50
Three Byzantine silver chalices and a 5th-6th c. paten.

637.585 Brown, K.R. Roemisch-Germanisches Zentralmuseum.
The Gold Breast Chain From the Early Byzantine Period in the Römisch-Germanisches Zentralmuseum. Mainz, 1984. 30 x 21. 30 pp., 4 color pls., 18 pls., 25 figs. $32.50
Interesting and readable study of a rare ornament, probably made in Constantinople around 600. Parallels and examples of usage are shown, other pieces of jewelry in the same technique are touched upon.

624.573 Galerie Charpentier.
Trésor d'Argenterie Romaine. Paris, 1958. 27 x 21. 18 pp., 7 pls. Paper. $14.50
Scarce catalogue that dispersed a 3rd c. Roman silver treasure at auction. Nine silver vessels are illustrated, several with details of the decorations. Noteworthy is a shell-shaped bowl.

274.232 Coche de la Ferté, É.
Antique Jewellery from the second to the eighth century AD. Bern, 1967. 12 x 19. 8 pp., 19 color pls. $11.50
Publishes and illustrates, in color, highlights from the Collection de Clercq.

301.261 Cruikshank Dodd, E.
Byzantine Silver Stamps. Washington, DC., 1962. 29 x 22. 283 pp., 103 pls., 5 fold-out tables, 1 map. $85.00
Comprehensive listing and description of all known Byzantine objects with control stamps, fully illustrated and with a lengthy introduction. Out-of-print.

302.262 Cruikshank Dodd, E.
Byzantine Silver Treasures. Bern, 1973. 24 x 19. 76 pp., 15 pls., 46 figs. Paper. $20.00
Thorough discussion of the Bern Treasure with additional material drawn from other collections. Well illustrated.

279.237 Dennison, W.A.
A Gold Treasure of the Late Roman Period from Egypt. (UMS, vol. XII). New York, 1918. 21 x 28. 99 pp., 54 pls., 57 figs. $195.00
Bound together with: Morey, C.R. **East Christian Paintings in the Freer Collection.** xiii, 86 pp., 13 pls., 34 figs.

303.263 Diehl, C.
Argenteries Syriennes. (Syria, vol. XI, 1930). 7 pp., 3 figs. Paper. $7.50
Describes a hoard of early Christian "apostle spoons".

304.264 Diehl, C.
L'École Artistique d'Antioche et les trésors d'Argenterie Syrienne. 15 pp., 6 pls. some foxing. Paper. $6.50
Discusses Late Antique and Byzantine silver vessels.

615.564 Diehl, C.
Un Nouveau Trésor d'Argenterie Syrienne. (Syria, 1926.). Paris, 1926. 28.5 x 22.5. 17 pp., 13 pls., 1 fig. Paper. $9.50
Twenty three Byzantine silver vessels, discovered together with, but separated from, "The Chalice of Antioch", are published and illustrated.

625.574 Hotel Drouot.
Antiques - Art Chrétien: Bijoux d'Or, IVe Siècle - Xe Siècle. Paris, 1959. 27 x 21. 33 pp., 9 pls. Paper. $12.50
Auction catalogue showing Byzantine and earlier gold jewelry, 26 finger rings, as well as pottery and other objects.

312.272 Dusenbury, E. and Budd, D. The Newark Museum.
Crosses in the Collections of The Museum. (The Museum, 1960). 28 pp., 40 illus. Paper. $4.50
Large collection of crosses of many periods.

305.265 Ebersolt, J.
Sceaux Byzantins du Musée de Constantinople. (Revue Numismatique, 1914). Paris, 1914. 74 pp., 3 pls. Paper. $14.50
Illustrates 18 seals. Rare!

530.484 Ergil, T.
Kuepeler / Earrings: The Catalogue of the Istanbul Archaeological Museum. Istanbul, 1983. 19 x 27.5. 71 pp., num. illus., incl. color. Paper. $26.50
Catalogues earrings of all periods of Turkish history, illustrates Hellenistic and Roman types mostly, some others.

306.266 Falke, O.von
Sammlung Marc Rosenberg. Berlin, 1929. 21 x 28. 68 pp., 27 pls. Paper. $77.50
Illustrated auction catalogue of the sale which dispersed, in 350 lots, the personal collection of this scholar of jewelry. Scarce.

307.267 Galasso, E.
Oreficeria medioevale in Campania. (**Miniature e arte minori in Campania**, 4). Benevento, 1969. 30 x 21. 153 pp., 12 color pls., 25 pls. Paper. $18.50
Byzantine jewelry from South Italy.

217.180 Garside, A., (Ed.). Walters Art Gallery.
Jewelry, Ancient to Modern. Baltimore, 1979. 32 x 23. 256 pp., num. illus. incl. 116 color. $40.00
Scholarly catalogue, beautifully produced, of jewelry from all periods.

516.470 Grand Palais.
Le Trésor de Saint-Marc de Vénise. Paris, 1984. 23 x 26. 337 pp., num. pls., incl. color. Paper. $37.50
Superbly produced catalogue of a superb exhibition of major Antique hardstone vessels and related objects. Many additional treasures from the French national collections are added. Recommended! English version also available.

248.207 Hackens, T. and Winkes, R., (Eds.).
Gold Jewelry: Craft, Style and Meaning from Mycenae to Constantinopolis. (**Aurifex**, V.). Louvain, 1983. 17.5 x 26. 227 pp., num. illus., incl. 21 color. $36.00
Descriptive catalogue of 46 items, with 40 page section on Greek jewelry and photographs showing technical details.

678.641 Hendy, M.F.
Studies in the Byzantine Monetary Economy c. 300 -1450. Cambridge, 1985. 773 pp., 36 pls., 39 maps, tables. $150.00
Extremely thorough study of the economy of the Byzantine Empire, with a wealth of information about trade, both internal and with its neighbors, rations of gold and silver, values of other commodities, professional associations. Recommended.

684.663 Kovacs, E. and Lovag, Z.
The Hungarian Crown and Other Regalia. Budapest, 1984. 97 pp., 42 color pls. $22.50
Detailed color plates show all sides of the Byzantine crown with close-ups of the cloisonne and of the gems, also includes color plates of the mantle, sceptre, orb and sword.

308.268 Lazovic, M., (et al.). Musée d'Art et d'Histoire.
Objects byzantins de la collection du Musée d'Art et d'Histoire. Geneva, 1977.
20 x 25.5. 62 pp., 38 illus. Paper. $12.50
Careful examination of inscribed silver spoons and vessels, with technical analyses.

310.270 Manns, F.
Les Sceaux Byzantins du Musée de la Flagellation. Jerusalem, 1976. 17 x 24. 61 pp., 20 pls. Paper. $24.50

311.271 Millet, G.
Sur les Sceaux des Commerciaires Byzantins. Paris, 1924. 24 pp., 44 figs. Paper. $8.50

283.242 Naumann, F. Staatliche Kunstsammlungen.
Antiker Schmuck. Kassel, 1980. 79 pp., 3 color pls., 36 pls., 2 figs. $18.50
Presents a collection of almost 200 objects, strong in East Roman and early Byzantine types.

286.245 Oberlin, OH. Allen Memorial Art Museum.
Melvin Gutman Collection of Ancient and Medieval Gold. (Bulletin, vol. XVIII, 1961). 298 pp., 2 color pls. Paper. $14.00
Catalogues and describes 180 pieces of jewelry and illustrates all, many in close-up detail.

309.269 Painter, K.S. British Museum.
The Water Newton Early Christian Silver. London, 1977. 48 pp., 35 illus., 11 figs. Paper. $9.50
First publication of a major recent find of Late Antique silver objects.

548.502 Perry, R.
Schmuck der Antike, Gefässe und Geräte aus Bronze. (Sonderliste T). Basel, 1981. 24 x 17. 48 pp., 1 color pl., 124 illus. Paper. $12.50
Carefully catalogued group of ancient jewelry from the 2nd millenium to early Islamic. Illustrates ca. 75 pieces.

259.218 Pierides, A.
Jewellery in the Cyprus Museum. Nicosia, 1971. 59 pp., 2 color pls., 38 pls. Paper. $28.50
Large format, well illustrated catalogue of ancient jewelry from Cyprus.

191.153 Righetti, R.
Opere di Glittica dei Museo Sacro e Profano. Vatican City, 1955. 52 pp., 17 pls. Paper. $16.50
Collection strong in Byzantine gems, some Roman and Neo-Classical.

555.509 Ross, M.C.
Catalogue of the Byzantine and Early Mediaeval Antiquities in the Dumbarton Oaks Collection. I: Metalwork, Ceramics, Glass, Glyptics, Painting. Washington, D.C., 1962. 29 x 22. xv, 115 pp., 65 pls. $38.50
Illustrates, and carefully publishes, Byzantine and early Mediaeval silver objects, the engraved gems and engraved glass vessels and other small objects from the Dumbarton Oaks Collection.

272.230 Rudolph, W. and E. Indiana University Art Museum.
Ancient Jewelry from the collection of Burton Y. Berry. Bloomington, 1973. xxiv, 247 pp., num. illus. Paper. $30.00
Describes and illustrates most of 197 pieces of jewelry from various periods, the majority Roman from Turkey and Syria.

313.273 Schlumberger, G.
Quelques Sceaux de l'Orient Latin au Moyen Age. Paris, 1905. 21 pp., 18 figs. Paper. $6.50

613.562 Schlumberger, G., (et al.).
Sigillographie de l'Orient Latin. Paris, 1943. 29 x 23. xix, 281 pp., 22 pls. Paper. $68.50
Catalogues and shows ca. 450 seals, mostly lead or wax, from the Kingdom of Jerusalem, the Kingdom of Cyprus and from Constantinople. Both ecclesiastic and temporal seals are shown and translated. Scarce!

314.274 Sotheby, London.
Catalogue of the Avar Treasure. London, 1981. 25 x 37. 30 pp., num. illus., color and B. & W., maps. $26.50
Oversize, beautifully illustrated sales catalogue of 122 gold and silver belt fittings of the Avar Period, ca 700 AD., together with two Byzantine silver plates.

162.122 Vermeule, C.C. The University Museum.
Cameo and Intaglio, Engraved Gems from the Sommerville Collection. Philadelphia, 1957. 15 x 21.5. 35 pp., 2 pls. Paper. $12.50
Exhibition catalogue of 650 gems of all periods.

455.415 Vikan, G. and Nesbitt, J.
Security in Byzantium: Locking, Sealing, Weighing. Washington, 1980. 21.5 x 28. 39 pp., 88 figs. Paper. $6.50
First attempt to describe security related Byzantine objects; with careful descriptions and numerous illustrations of "ring-keys", gems, stamp-seals and finger rings. Recommended!

661.627 Wentzel, H.
Beiträge zur Kunst des Mittelalters. Festschrift für Hans Wentzel zum &. Geburtsdag. Berlin, 1975. 16.5 x 23.5. viii, 268 pp., 150 pls. Paper. $55.00
"Festschrift" containing numerous specialized articles on Byzantine and Mediaeval glyptics, jewelry, ivories and allied fields. Recommended.

515.469 Zahlhaas, G.
Fingerringe und Gemmen: Sammlung Dr. E. Pressmar. Munich, 1985. 69 pp., 161 illus. Paper. $14.50
First publication of a private collection of 100 finger rings, all are illustrated and classified as to origin and date. The collection is strongest in the more commonly encountered types, Roman, Byzantine and Islamic, some others.

Pre-Historic European Jewelry

320.593 Audouze, F. and Courtois, J.C.
Les épingles du Sud-Est de la France. (**PBF**, vol. XIII.1, 1970.). v, 75 pp., 30 pls.
$22.50

330.603 Bader, T.
Die Fibeln in Rumänien. (**PBF**, vol. XIV.6, 1982.). 120 pp., 36 pls. $37.50

583.535 Barge, H.
Les Parures du Néolithique Ancien au debut de l'Age des Métaux en Languedoc. Paris, 1982. 29 x 21. 396 pp., 131 figs., 6 pls. Paper. $45.00
Establishes methodology for the earliest beads and related small objects from France. Shows many hundreds of beads and pendants in, mostly, stone, amber, bone and shell. Some metal beads were also found.

512.467 Bateson, J.D.
Enamel-working in Iron Age, Roman and Sub-Roman Britain: The Products and Techniques. (**BAR**, 93, 1981). Oxford, 1981. 167 pp., 15 pls. Paper. $22.50
Comprehensive survey of the enameled objects from Britain from 200 BC - 700 AD. Millefiori enamels and their techniques are studied in detail.

513.468 Beckmann, C.
Metallfingerringe der römischen Kaiserzeit im freien Germanien. (**Saalburg Jahrbuch**, vol. XXVI, 1969). 32 x 24. 102 pp., 23 illus., 2 pls., 15 maps. Paper.
$45.00
Survey of finger rings coeval with the later Roman Empire but made and worn in the non-Roman part of Northern Europe, shows styles, types, dates. Includes 15 maps showing distribution patterns. Catalogues 844 finger rings. Recommended.

514.468 Beckmann, B.
Die baltischen Metallnadeln der römischen Kaiserzeit. (**Saalburg Jahrbuch**, vol. XXVI, 1969). 32 x 24. 13 pp., 1 fig., 4 maps. Paper. $45.00
Catalogue listing of 249 stick pins from Northern Europe. This publication also contains the above listed article which describes finger rings from the same geographical area.

329.602 Betzler, P.
Die Fibeln in Süddeutschland, Österreich und der Schweiz I. (**PBF**, vol. XIV.3, 1974.). viii, 179 pp., 90 pls. $42.50

321.594 Carancini, G.L.
Gli spilloni nell'Italia continentale. (**PBF**, vol. XIII.2, 1975.). xiv, 399 pp., 113 pls.
$77.50

561.514 Duvail, A., (Ed.).
L'art Celtique en Gaule. Paris, 1983-1984. 23.5 x 20.5. 219 pp., 10 color pls., 5 pls., 281 illus., 5 figs., 4 maps. Paper. $19.50
Shows the art of the Celts, 5th - 1st c. BC., as reflected in their objects of daily use with emphasis on the jewelry in gold, silver and bronze.

315.275 Eleure, C.
Les Ors Préhistoriques. Paris, 1982. 19 x 27. 288 pp., 193 illus. $45.00
The earliest gold objects found in France: ingots, jewelry, vessels from the 3rd Millenium to the 7th Century BC.

319.592 Furmanek, V.
Die Anhänger in der Slowakei. (**PBF**, vol. XI.3, 1980.). viii, 61 pp., 45 pls.
$42.50

326.599 Gedl, M.
Die Nadeln in Polen II. (**PBF**, vol. XIII.7, 1982.). 130 pp., 35 pls. $42.50

537.491 Gerlach, M., (Ed.).
Primitive and Folk Jewelry. New York, 1971. 28 x 21. 218 pp., 109 pls. with 1900 illus. Paper. $11.50
Quality reprint of the 1906 edition of **Völkerschmuck**; still an excellent quick reference for ancient, ethnic and unusual jewelry with more than 1900 items illustrated.

3.239 Guido, M.
The Glass Beads of the Prehistoric and Roman Periods in Britain and Ireland. London, 1978. xxxvi, 250 pp., 4 color pls., 38 figs. $65.00
Beads from Britain, ca. 700 BC - 410 AD are presented in carefully annotated detail; includes classification tables, typology, etc.

582.534 Haevernick, T.E., (et al.).
Glasperlen der Vorrömischen Eisenzeit I. (**Marburger Studien zur vor- und Frühgeschichte**, vol. 5). Mainz, 1983. 28.5 x 19.5. viii, 178 pp., 1 color pl., 2 pls., 19 figs. 7 maps. $52.50
Very thorough discussion of the distribution patterns of various types of beads; beads as part of jewelry suites; manner of wearing beads. Vol. II soon to be published, orders now accepted.

332.276 Hardmeyer, B.
Prähistorisches Gold Europas im 3. und 2. Jahrtausend vor Christus. Wadenswill, 1976. 156 pp., 19 illus., 3 maps. Paper. $25.00
Extensive listing of excavated material; with bibliography.

333.277 Hartmann, A.
Prähistorische Goldfunde aus Europa II: Spektralanalytische Untersuchungen und deren Auswertung. (Studien zu den Anfängen der Metallurgie, vol. V.). Berlin, 1983. 21 x 30. 112 pp., 115 pls., 5 maps. $125.00
Shows pre-historic jewelry and trade routes, mostly in Iberia, France, and Denmark.

665.631 Hartmann, A.
Prähistorische Goldfunde aus Europa: Spektralanalytische Untersuchungen und deren Auswertung. (Studien zu den Anfängen der Metallurgie, vol. III.). Berlin, 1970. 129 pp., 3 pls., 59 illus. 87.50

664.630 Junghans, S., (et al.).
Metallanalysen kupferzeitlicher und frühbronzezeitlicher Bodenfund aus Europa. (Studien zu den Anfängen der Metallurgie, vol. I.). Berlin, 1960. 220 pp., 37 pls. $67.50

672.635 Junghans, S., (et al.).
Kupfer und Bronze in der frühen Metallzeit Europas. (Studien zu den Anfängen der Metallurgie, vol. II.). Berlin, 1968. 490 pp., 65 pls., 17 tables., 81 maps.
$225.00
The text is based on 12,000 analyses of early metal objects, all carefully catalogued. Includes 81 maps showing distribution patterns all over Europe.

673.636 Junghans, S., (et al.).
Kupfer und Bronze in der frühen Metallzeit Europas. (Studien zu den Anfängen der Metallurgie, vol. II.). Berlin, 1974. 408 pp. $140.00
Sequel to the above, with a catalogue of 10,000 additional analyses.

244.586 Kilian, K.
Fibeln in Thessalien. (**PBF**, vol. XIV.2, 1975.). viii, 233 pp., 99 pls. $57.50

243.204 Kilian-Dirlmeier, I.
Anhänger und Halsringe in Südwestdeutschland und Nordbayern. (**PBF**, vol. XI.2, 1979.). xii, 283 pp., 11 pls. $77.50

322.595 Kubach, W.
Die Nadeln in Hessen und Rheinhessen. (**PBF**, vol. XIII.3, 1977.). ix, 636 pp., 132 pls., map. $135.00

323.596 Laux, F.
Die Nadeln in Niedersachsen. (**PBF**, vol. XIII.4, 1976.). xii, 159 pp., 63 pls.
$42.50

328.601 Laux, F.
Die Fibeln in Niedersachsen. (**PBF**, vol. XIV.1, 1973.). viii, 67 pp., 58 pls., 4 figs.
$24.00

663.629 MacGregor, M.
Early Celtic Art in North Britain: A study of decorative metalwork from the third century B.C. to the third century A.D. Leicester, 1976. 25.5 x 15.5. 2 Vols.: 240 pp., 16 pls., 7 figs., 22 maps; and 420 pp., 327 figs. $57.50
Vol. I contains an analysis, identifies several "schools", comparative material and maps. Vol. II contains 353 standardized entries, technical notes and details of discovery. Most are illustrated.

254.213 Navarro, R.
Las Fibulas en Cataluna. Barcelona, 1970. 17 x 24. 126 pp., 24 figs., 4 maps. Paper. $11.50
Careful study of early fibulae from Spain, mostly 1st millenium BC.

325.598 Novatna, M.
Die Nadeln in der Slowakei. (**PBF**, vol. XIII.6, 1979.). 220 pp., 53 pls. $42.50

578.530 Pearce, S.
Bronze Age Metalwork in Sourthern Britain. Aylesbury, 1984. 21 x 15. 64 pp., 23 figs. Paper. $5.50
Gold jewelry and bronze objects from early Britain, 2600 - 600 BC.

317.590 Richter, I.
Der Arm- und Beinschmuck der Bronze- und Urnenfelderzeit in Hessen und Rheinhessen. (PBF, vol. X.1, 1970). ix, 197 pp., 98 pls. $42.50

324.597 Rihovsky, J.
Die Nadeln in Mähren und im Ostalpenland. (PBF, vol. XIII.5, 1979.). xi, 261 pp., 87 pls. $95.00

327.600 Rihovsky, J.
Die Nadeln in Westungarn I. (PBF, vol. XIII.10, 1983.). 80 pp., 35 pls. $39.50

245.587 Sapouna-Sakellaris, E.
Die Fibeln der griechischen Inseln. (PBF, vol. XIV.4, 1978.). x, 150 pp., 56 pls. $62.50

631.580 Schumacher-Matthaeus, G.
Studien zu bronzezeitlichen Schmucktrachten im Karpatenbecken: Ein Beitrag zur Deutung der Hortfunde im Karpatenbecken. (Marburger Studien zur Vor- und Frühgeschichte, vol. 6). Mainz, 1984. viii, 266 pp., 77 pls., 51 maps. $68.00
Early East-European jewelry and its distribution throughout the region, a help in establishing trade routes and cultural patterns.

482.439 Soler Garcia, J.M.
El Oro de los Tesoros de Villena. Valencia, 1969. 18 x 25. 22 pp., 46 pls. Paper. $18.50

334.278 Tassinari, S.
La Vaisselle de bronze, romaine et provincale au Musée des Antiquités Nationales. (**Gallia,** Suppl. XXIX). Paris, 1975. 22 x 28. 84 pp., 40 pls. Paper. $11.50
Typology of metal vessels, ladles and strainers from Gaul.

335.279 Taylor, J.J.
Bronze Age Goldwork of the British Isles. London, 1980. 22.5 x 28.5. 199 pp., 64 pls. $105.00
Handsome publication shows the earliest jewelry found in Britain.

318.591 Wels-Weyrauch, U.
Die Anhänger und Halsringe in Südwestdeutschland und Nordbayern. (PBF, vol. XI.1, 1978.). ix, 214 pp., 122 pls. $77.50

Mediaeval, Anglo Saxon and Dark Age Jewelry

336.409 Avent, R.
Anglo-Saxon Disc and Composite Brooches. (**BAR**, vol. 11). Oxford, 1975. 2 vols.: 126 pp., 4 color pls., 30 figs., 6 maps, tables; and 52 pp., 78 pls. Paper. $48.00
Lists and illustrates all 192 known examples. Out-of-print.

512.467 Bateson, J.D.
Enamel-working in Iron Age, Roman and Sub-Roman Britain: The Products and Techniques. (**BAR**, 93). Oxford, 1981. 167 pp., 15 pls. Paper. $22.50
Comprehensive survey of the enameled objects from Britain from 200 BC - 700 AD. Millefiori enamels and their techniques are studied in detail.

652.620 Battaglia, G.B.
Corredi Funerari di Eta Imperiale e Barbarica nel Museo Nazionale Romano. Rome, 1983. 19.5 x 25.5. 176 pp., 158 illus. $32.50
Roman Imperial and Later jewelry from dated tombs is carefully studied and used to anchor various styles more securely. Well illustrated.

582.544 Chandon de Briailles.
Sur Deux Bulles de l'Orient Latin. (**Mélanges Syriens**, n.d.). 28 x 22. 11 pp., 4 illus. Paper. $6.50

593.545 Chandon de Briaillles.
Bulle de Clérembaut de Broyes, Archévèque de Tyr. (**Syria**, 1940.). 28.5 x 23. 7 pp., 2 illus. paper. $5.50
Description of the bulla, and the history of the archbishop of Tyre in 1215, during the crusades.

594.546 Chandon de Briailles.
Lignages d'Outre-Mer: Les Seigneurs de Margat. (**Syria**, vol. XXV, 1946-48.). 28.5 x 23. 27 pp., 1 illus. Paper. $6.50
Lineage and seal of a crusader's family in the 12th - 15th c.

595.547 Chandon de Briailles.
Bulles de L'Orient Latin. (**Syria**, vol. XXVII, 1950). 28.5 x 23. 16 pp., 2 pls., 7 figs. Paper. $6.50
Bullae from the Frankish Kingdom in southern Lebanon during the 11th - 13th c.

570.523 Brown, K.R. Metropolitan Museum of Art.
Guide to Provincial Roman and Barbarian Metalwork and Jewelry in The Metropolitan Museum of Art. New York, 1981. 23 x 15. 28 pp., 38 figs., map. Paper. $7.50
Attractive catalogue of Late Roman and Migration Period jewelry, includes a short history, identifies and dates the various styles.

348.292 Bruce-Mitford, R., (et al.). British Museum.
The Sutton Hoo Ship-Burial. II: Arms, Armour and Regalia. London, 1978. 651 pp., 24 color pls., 443 figs. $160.00
Scientific examination of all aspects of the famous treasure, including chapters on style, provenance and techniques.

316.589 Bruce-Mitford, R., (et al.). British Museum.
The Sutton Hoo Ship-Burial. III fasc. 1-2: Late Roman and Byzantine Silver, Hanging Bowls, Drinking Vessels, Cauldrons and Other Containers, Textiles, The Lyre, Pottery Bottle and Other Items. London, 1983. 32 x 26. xliv, 479 pp., 16 color pls., 340 figs.; and xix, 518 pp., 339 figs. $175.00

2.283 Callmer, J.
Trade beads and bead trade in Scandinavia ca. 800-1000 AD. (Acta Arch. Lund., vol. IV). Lund, 1977. 229 pp., 4 color pls., 22 pls., 16 figs. Paper. $48.50
Clear illustrations show many types of beads previously known from Near Eastern sites, and other evidence of extensive bead trade.

668.633 Chadour, A.B. and Joppien, R. Kunstgewerbemuseum.
Schmuck, Bestandskatalog des Kunstgewerbemuseums. Cologne, 1985. 2 vols. with num. illus., incl. color. $45.00
Major new museum catalogue with a lengthy introduction and 910 entries, especially strong in Ancient, Migration period, Renaissance and 19th c. jewelry. A fine group of 355 rings is shown in two views each. Recommended!

353.297 Clarke, J.R. and Hinton, D.A. Ashmolean Museum.
The Alfred and Minster Lovell Jewels. Oxford, 1979. 12 pp., 2 pls. Paper.
$6.50
Major Saxon jewels, their history and probable use.

558.511 Cote, C. Hotel Drouot.
Catalogue des Antiquités Romaines et des Objets d'Art et de Haute Curiosité. Paris, 1936. 23.5 x 20.5. 22 pp. Paper. $12.50
This auction catalogue lists Roman silver spoons, Greek and Roman gems, Dark Age jewelry and other objects. Photocopies of the original plates can be supplied for an additional $5.00. Scarce.

340.284 Dolfus, M.
Catalogue des fibules de bronze de Haute-Normandie. Paris, 1973. 262 pp., num. illus. $45.00

568.521 Hotel Drouot.
Collection de son excellence Le Bey Paul Adamidi Frasheri. Paris, 1971. 24 x 19. ca. 29 pp., 16 illus. Paper. $8.50
Early jewelry, icons and enamels from the collection of the former ruler of Albania.

644.612 Duczko, W.
The Filigree and Granulation Work of the Viking Period. (Birka, V). Uppsala, 1985. 118 pp., num. illus., num. figs. $32.50
Dissertation investigating 86 pieces of jewelry of the Middle Viking Period. A discussion of the antecedents, of the techniques and of the place of the objects in larger European context are included.

354.298 Dumas, F. Bibliothèque Nationale.
Le Tombeau de Childeric, Père de Clovis. Paris, 1982. 14 x 24. 22 pp., num. illus. Paper. $5.00
Illustrates fifth c. garnet inlaid jewelry.

500.455 Evans, J.
Magical Jewels of the Middle Ages and Renaissance. New York, 1976. 13.5 x 21.5. 264 pp., 3 pls., indexes. Reprint of the 1922 ed. Paper. $9.50
Basic book on early Western lapidaries; includes extensive quotes from the original manuscripts.

306.266 Falke, O.v.
Sammlung Marc Rosenberg. Berlin, 1929. 21 x 28. 68 pp., 27 pls. Paper. $77.50
Illustrated auction catalogue of the sale which dispersed, in 350 lots, the personal collection of this scholar of jewelry. Scarce.

627.576 Gagochidzé, J.
L'Ornament de la Femme Géorgienne. Khelovneba, 1981. 16.5 x 13. 221 pp., 91 color illus., 5 figs. Paper. $14.50
Jewelry from Georgia, (USSR), from the IVth Millenium to the 19th c. AD. The plates are poorly printed but show interesting jewelry: many beads and necklace elements, some ancient rings and cameos. Text in French, Russian and Georgian.

307.267 Galasso, E.
Oreficeria medioevale in Campania. (Miniature e arte minori in Campania, 4). Benevento, 1969. 30 x 21. 153 pp., 12 color pls., 25 pls. Paper. $18.50
Byzantine jewelry from South Italy.

341.285 Garam, E., (et al.).
Avar Finds in the Hungarian National Museum. Budapest, 1975. 368 pp., 37 pls., 152 figs. $48.50

217.180 Garside, A., (Ed.). Walters Art Gallery.
Jewelry, Ancient to Modern. Baltimore, 1979. 32 x 23. 256 pp., num. illus. incl. 116 color. $40.00
Scholarly catalogue, beautifully produced, of jewelry from all periods.

349.293 Gauthier, M.-M. and Francois, G. British Museum.
Medieval Enamels, Masterpieces from the Keir Collection. London, 1981. 22 x 31. 40 pp., 24 color pls., 16 pls. $32.50
Limoges enamels from one of the world's leading collections. Out-of-print.

537.491 Gerlach, M., (Ed.).
Primitive and Folk Jewelry. New York, 1971. 28 x 21. 218 pp., 109 pls. with 1900 illus. Paper. $11.50
Quality reprint of the 1906 edition of **Völkerschmuck**; still an excellent quick reference for ancient, ethnic and unusual jewelry with more than 1900 items illustrated.

516.470 Grand Palais.
Le Trésor de Saint-Marc de Vénise. Paris, 1984. 23 x 26. 337 pp., num pls., incl. color. Paper. $37.50
Superbly produced catalogue of a superb exhibition of major Antique hardstone vessels and related objects. Many additional treasures from the French national collections are added. Recommended! English version also available.

635.583 Hahnloser, H. and Brugger, S.
Corpus der Hartsteinschliffe des XII. - XV. Jahrhunderts. Berlin, 1985. 21 x 27.5. 256 pp., 32 color pls., 464 pls., 29 figs. $145.00
A corpus of early European hardstone vessels, secular and religious. Includes sections on technique, materials, objects now lost but known from the literature, guilds, etc. Profusely illustrated.

629.578 Hansmann, L. and Kriss-Rettenbeck, L.
Amulett und Talisman: Erscheinungsform und Geschichte. Munich, 1984. 20 x 21. 340 pp., 844 illus., 32 color pls. $42.50
New, enlarged, edition of the 1966 study of, mostly, European amulets and talismans. The superstitions that gave rise to their use are clarified; hundreds of amuletic pieces of jewelry are shown and interpreted.

273.231 Hellenkemper, H., (Ed.). Musées d'Histoire.
Trésors romains-Trésors barbares: Industrie d'art à la fin de l'Antiquité et au début du Moyen Age. Brussels, 1979. 13 x 20. 163 pp., 48 pls. incl. 16 color. Paper. $12.50
Jewelry and related precious objects are carefully described, dated and illustrated. Includes section on technology.

292.252 Hinton, D.
Medieval Jewellery from the eleventh to the fifteenth century. Aylesbury, 1982. 15 x 21. 48 pp., 46 illus. Paper. $9.50
Well illustrated book showing mostly British medieval rings and some other jewelry.

352.296 Hinton, D. Ashmolean Museum.
A Catalogue of the Anglo-Saxon Ornamental Metalwork 700-1100. Oxford, 1974. xxi, 81 pp., 20 pls., num. figs. $34.50
Catalogues 40 objects, including some important jewels.

343.287 Kilbride-Jones, H.E.
Zoomorphic Penannular Brooches. London, 1980. 27 x 21.5. 154 pp., 52 illus. $37.50
Corpus of a distinctive series of Celtic brooches, derived from North British prototypes, and dating from the 2nd c. to the mid 5th c. All are catalogued with find-spot, present location and other relevant data.

338.281 Koetzsche, D. Kunstgewerbemuseum.
Der Weltenschatz. Berlin, 1973. 18 x 23.5. 87 pp., 8 color pls., 75 illus. $18.50
Goldsmiths' work from the 11th-15th c.; many close-ups of technical details.

344.288 Kovacs, E.
Romanesque Goldsmiths' Art. Budapest, n.d. 18 x 16. 58 pp., 8 color pls., 11 figs. $26.50
Handsomely illustrates Eastern European early jewelry.

491.448 Kovacs, E.
Limoges Champlevé Enamels in Hungary. Budapest, 1968. 18.5 x 16.5. 53 pp., 8 color pls., 6 figs. $22.50
Illustrates and describes the Hungarian national collections of Mediaeval enamels.

345.289 Kuehn, H.
Germanische Kunst der Völkerwanderung . . . von Kunstwerken aus europäischen Museen. Munich, 1965. 17 x 12. 15 pp., 32 pls. Paper. $7.50
Illustrates Migration Period jewelry.

560.513 Lemaitre, J.-L., (Ed.). Musée du Pays d'Ussel.
Sceaux des Archives communales d'Ussel. Paris, 1982. 19 x 19. 63 pp., 21 illus., 1 color pl. Paper. $14.50
Shows detailed photographs of the wax seals in the Archives, all date from the 13th - 18th c.

346.290 Lightbrown, R.W.
Secular Goldsmiths' Work in Medieval France: A History. London, 1978. 27 x 21.5. 230 pp., 7 color pls., 73 pls. $37.50

663.629 MacGregor, M.
Early Celtic Art in North Britain: A study of decorative metalwork from the third century B.C. to the third century A.D. Leicester, 1976. 25.5 x 15.5. 2 Vols.: 240 pp., 16 pls., 7 figs., 22 maps; and 420 pp., 327 figs. $57.50
Vol. I contains an analysis, identifies several "schools", comparative material and maps. Vol. II contains 353 standardized entries, technical notes and details of discovery. Most are illustrated.

278.236 Malle, L. Museo Civico di Torino.
Smalti - Avori del Museo D'Arte Antica. Turin, 1969. 24 x 17. 354 pp., 5 color pls., 239 illus. $32.50
An extensive catalogue containing European enamels from the 13th to the 19th c. bound together with a second one detailing ivory objects, reliquaries and jewelry from the late Roman to the early 19th c. Both are generously illustrated.

350.294 Meany, A.L.
Anglo-Saxon Amulets and Curing Stones. (BAR, 96). Oxford, 1981. 21 x 29. 364 pp., num. illus., 8 maps. Paper. $28.50
Fascinating account of belief in curative powers of stones and amulets in the early Middle Ages.

141.101 Menghin, W. Museo Nazionale del Borgello.
Gioielli Franchii della collezione Carrand. Florence, 1981. 22 pp., 1 color pl., 171 illus. Paper. $18.50
New publication of a good collection of early Mediaeval jewelry from Italy.

351.295 Milojcic, V.
Zu den spätkaiserzeitlichen und merowingischen Silberlöfflen. Berlin, 1970. 43 pp., 6 pls., 10 figs. Paper. $18.50
Listing of 138 silver spoons from known sites all over Europe.

339.282 Muller, J. Musées d'Histoire.
Orfèvreries Mosanes XIIe-XIIIe Siècles. Brussels, 1977. 13 x 19. 8 pp., 40 pls. Paper. $7.50
Early Flemish goldsmithing and enameling. Many close-ups of technical details.

502.457 Muller, H.
Jet Jewellery and Ornaments. Aylesbury, 1984. 21 x 15. 32 pp., 40 illus. Paper.
$6.50
Chronicles the history and uses of jet from the Bronze Age to the present, emphasis of the illustrations is on 19th c. jewelry. Includes a chapter on tools, techniques and imitations.

531.485 Nicholls, R.
The Wellcome Gems: A Fitzwilliam Museum Catalogue. Cambridge, 1983. 15 x 21. 57 pp., num. illus. Paper. $12.50
Supplementary catalogue of 250 Ancient and Later gems to the soon to be published **Classical Gems: Ancient and Modern Intaglios and Cameos in the Fitzwilliam Museum, Cambridge.**, most are illustrated.

286.245 Oberlin, OH. Allen Memorial Art Museum.
Melvin Gutman Collection of Ancient and Medieval Gold. (**Bulletin**, vol. XVIII, 1961). 298 pp., 2 color pls. Paper. $14.00
Catalogues and describes 180 pieces of jewelry and illustrates all, many in close-up detail.

677.640 Philippe, J.
Réliquaires Mediévaux de l'Orient Chrétien en Verre et en Cristal de Roche conservés en Belgique. Liege, 1975. 24 x 16. 45 pp., 21 figs. Paper. $16.50
Obscure publication shows important Mediaeval and Islamic rockcrystal and cut glass vessels preserved in church treasures. Parallels from other treasures are listed and illustrated.

355.299 Rademacher, F.
Frankische Goldscheibenfibeln aus dem Rheinischen Landesmuseum in Bonn. Munich, 1940. 26 x 20. 82 pp., 32 pls., 6 figs., map. $68.50
Carefully illustrated catalogue of fibulae from the extensive collection in Bonn. Out-of-print.

555.509 Ross, M.C.
Catalogue of the Byzantine and Early Mediaeval Antiquities in the Dumbarton Oaks Collection. I: Metalwork, Ceramics, Glass, Glyptics, Painting. Washington, D.C., 1962. 29 x 22. xv, 115 pp., 65 pls. $38.50
Illustrates, and carefully publishes, Byzantine and early Mediaeval silver objects, the engraved gems and engraved glass vessels and other small objects from the Dumbarton Oaks Collection.

342.286 Sanidkidze, T. and Abrahamsvili, G. Musée d'Art et d'Histoire.
Orfèvrerie géorgienne du VII au XIX Siècle. Geneva, 1979. 17 x 24. n.p., 75 color pls. Paper. $18.00
Handsome exhibition catalogue with English, French and German text.

613. 562 Schlumberger, G., (et al.).
Sigillographie de l'Orient Latin. Paris, 1943. 29 x 23. xix, 281 pp., 22 pls. Paper.
$68.50
Catalogues and shows ca. 450 seals, mostly lead or wax, from the Kingdom of Jerusalem, the Kingdom of Cyprus and from Constantinople. Both ecclesiastic and temporal seals are shown and translated. Scarce!

581.533 Siviero, R.
Jewelry and Amber of Italy: A Collection in the National Museum of Naples.
New York, 1959. 34.5 x 25. 153 pp., 8 color pls., 274 pls., 115 figs. $185.00
Important, well illustrated book showing the Etruscan and Roman jewelry in the Naples' Museum from the excavations in Pompei and Herculaneum.

314.274 Sotheby's, London.
Catalogue of the Avar Treasure. London, 1981. 25 x 37. 30 pp., num. illus., color and B. & W., maps. $26.50
Oversize, beautifully illustrated sales catalogue of 122 gold and silver belt fittings of the Avar Period, ca 700 AD., together with two Byzantine silver plates.

547.501 Sotheby's, London.
The Thomas F. Flannery Jr. Collection: Medieval and Later Works of Art.. London, 1983. 27 x 19. 291 pp., ca 400 illus., many in color. $36.00
Hardbound, single owner, auction sale catalogue, showing large collection of finger rings, medieval and Renaissance jewels, gems and enamels, now dispersed. Very well illustrated with numerous color photographs.

632.581 Tempelmann-Maczynska, M.
Die Perlen der römischen Kaiserzeit und der frühen Phase der Völkerwanderungszeit im mitteleuropäischen Barbaricum. (Römisch-Germanische Forschungen, 47). Mainz, 1985. xii, 339 pp., 14 color pls. with 707 illus., 66 pls. with 207 illus., charts. $67.50
Shows Roman and early Migration Period beads, all types are illustrated and described.

643.611 Webster, L., (Ed.). British Museum.
Aspects of Production and Style in Dark Age Metalwork: Selected papers given to the British Museum Seminar on Jewellery AD 500-600. (OP, 34). London, 1982. 29.5 x 21. iv, 50 pp., 20 pls., 2 tables. Paper. $18.50

661.627 Wentzel, H.
Beiträge zur Kunst des Mittelalters. Festschrift für Hans Wentzel zum 60. Geburtsdag. Berlin, 1975. 16.5 x 23.5. viii, 268 pp., 150 pls. Paper. $55.00
"Festschrift" containing numerous specialized articles on Byzantine and Mediaeval glyptics, jewelry, ivories and allied fields. Recommended.

347.291 Wilson, D.M. British Museum.
Anglo-Saxon Ornamental Metalwork 700-1100. (Catalogue of Antiquities of the later Anglo-Saxon Period, vol. I). London, 1964. 22 x 28.5. 248 pp., 44 pls., 54 figs. $34.50
Presents jewelry and ornaments from the British Museum Collections.

Sasanian Jewelry - Silver Vessels

357.301 Amiet, P.
Orfèvrerie Sassanide au Musée du Louvre. (**Syria**, vol. XLVII, 1970). 13 pp., 2 pls., 3 figs. Paper. $5.50

687.686 Bothmer, D. von Metropolitan Museum of Art.
A Greek and Roman Treasury. (**Bulletin**, vol. XLII, 1984) New York, 1984. 28 x 21.5. 72 pp., 131 illus. incl. num. color. Paper. $9.50
Beautifully illustrated issue of the **Bulletin** shows and carefully describes the 131 gold and silver vessels and related objects newly installed in the Greek and Roman Department of The Museum.

624.573 Galerie Charpentier.
Trésor d'Argenterie Romaine. Paris, 1958. 27 x 21. 18 pp., 7 pls. Paper. $14.50
Scarce catalogue that dispersed a 3rd c. Roman silver treasure at auction. Nine silver vessels are illustrated, several with details of the decorations. Noteworthy is a shell-shaped bowl.

356.300 Grabar, O. The University of Michigan Museum of Art.
Sasanian Silver. Ann Arbor, 1967. 158 pp., 83 illus. Paper. $14.00
Thorough discussion of Sasanian art combined with an illustrated catalogue of 83 objects.

213.176 Harper, P.O. Asia House Gallery.
The Royal Hunter: Art of the Sasanian Empire. New York, 1978. 175 pp., num. illus., incl. color. $32.50
Exhibition catalogue illustrating many aspects of Sasanian life. With important sections on precious metals and engraved gems.

358.302 Harper, P.O. and Meyers, P. Metropolitan Museum of Art.
Silver Vessels of the Sasanian Period. I: Royal Imagery. New York, 1981. 272 pp., 7 color pls., 128 pls., 2 maps. $48.50
Presents a detailed examination of the history, iconography and mode of manufacture of the vessels in The Museum.

686.665 Harper, P.O. Metropolitan Museum of Art.
Ancient Near Eastern Art. (**Bulletin**, vol. XLI, 1984.). New York, 1984. 28 x 21.5. 56 pp., 80 illus. incl. 40 color. Paper. $9.50
Special issue of the **Bulletin** to commemorate the opening of the new Near Eastern Galleries; shows silver vessels and precious jewelry produced over a six thousand year period.

Islamic Gems and Jewelry

359.303 Al-Jadir, S.
Arab and Islamic Silver. London, 1981. 26 x 30. 216 pp., num. pls. incl. color.
$45.00
Handsomely produced survey of silver jewelry from North Africa to South-East Asia.

360.304 Allan, J.W.
Persian Metal Technology 700-1300 AD. London, 1979. 16 x 24. 179 pp., 14 pls., 3 figs., 9 maps. $37.50
Valuable study of early Islamic metallurgy with fascinating quotes from early texts. With glossaries of technical terms.

361.305 Allan, J.W.
Islamic Metalwork, The Nuhad Es-Said Collection. London, 1982. 24 x 33. 128 pp., 47 color pls., 41 pls., 3 figs., map. $105.00
Superb collection of 12th and 13th c. inlaid bronzes and small precious objects; clarifies the symbolism of the decorations.

362.306 Allan, J.W. The Metropolitan Museum of Art.
Nishapur: Metalwork of the Early Islamic Period. New York, 1982. 22 x 28.5. 120 pp., num. illus. $36.00
First group of Islamic metal objects from an excavated context in Iran ever to be published. Very well illustrated.

649.617 Bahnassi, A.
Fabrication des Epées de Damas. (Syria, vol. LIII, 1976.). 28 x 22. 13 pp. Paper.
$6.00
Research into modes of manufacture of "Damascus work", drawn chiefly from Mediaeval and later Arab authors.

363.307 Casanova, P.
Dénéraux en verre Arabes. Paris, 1924. 5 pp., 1 fig. $4.50
Inscribed glass weights from El-Fustat, (Cairo).

568.521 Hotel Drouot.
Collection de son excellence Le Bey Paul Adamidi Frasheri. Paris, 1971. 24 x 19. ca. 29 pp., 16 illus. Paper. $8.50
Early jewelry, icons and enamels from the collection of the former ruler of Albania.

179.141 Förschner, G. Historisches Museum.
Glaspasten, Geschnittene Steine, Arabische Münzgewichte. Melsungen, 1982. 17 x 22. 111 pp., 7 color pls., num. illus. Paper. $18.50
Large and varied collection of interesting material in new publication.

9.155 Fremersdorf, F. Museo Sacro.
Antikes, Islamisches und Mittelalterliches Glas sowie kleinere Arbeiten aus Stein, Gagat und verwandten Stoffen in den Vatikanischen Sammlungen Roms. Vatican City, 1975. 23.5 x 41. 133 pp., 2 color pls., 92 pls. $250.00
Large format catalogue; contains lengthy sections on beads, gems and hardstone carvings-in-the-round in the Vatican Museums.

208.171 Gignoux, P. and Kalus, L.
Les formules des sceaux sasanides et islamiques: continuité ou mutation.
(**Studia Iranica**, vol. 11, 1982). $47.50
Interesting comparison between Sasanian and early Islamic seal inscriptions.

702.681 Goldman-Schwartz, A. The Israel Museum.
The Jews of Kurdistan: Everyday Life and Arts and Crafts. Jerusalem, 1982. 21 x 24. 272 pp., 35 color pls., num illus. $42.50
Shows jewelry, costumes, amulets and related small objects of daily life from the once thriving Jewish community in Kurdistan. Text in Hebrew.

508.463 Goldstein, S., (et al.).
Cameo glass: Masterpieces from 2000 Years of Glassmaking. Corning, N.Y., 1982. 27.5 x 20. 140 pp., 158 illus. incl. many color. Paper. $18.50
Glass vessels and gems, Roman, Islamic, Oriental and Neo-Classical, all created by wheel cutting and other glyptic skills. well catalogued and illustrated, with a glossary and bibliography.

516.470 Grand Palais.
Le Trésor de Saint-Marc de Vénise. Paris, 1974. 23 x 26. 337 pp., num. pls., incl. color. Paper. $37.50
Superbly produced catalogue of a superb exhibition of major Antique hardstone vessels and related objects. Many additional treasures from the French national collections are added. Recommended! English version also available.

542.496 Guerard, M. Musée National des Arts Africains.
Art Islamique au Maghreb. Paris, 1976. 11.5 x 23.5. 17 pp., 18 illus. Paper.
$5.50
Introduction to North African Islamic art, including jewelry.

660.626 Hauptmann von Gladiss, A. and Kröger, J.
Islamische Kunst: Loseblattkatalog unpublizierter Werke aus deutschen Museen. 2: Metall, Stein, Stuck, Holz, Elfenbein, Stoffe. Mainz, 1984. 29.5 x 21. xii, 146 pp., 146 pls., with 323 illus. Loose leaf portfolio. $65.00
Islamic art objects from public collections in Germany; each object is carefully catalogued and fully illustrated on a separate page.

364.308 Jenkins, M. and Keene, M.
Islamic Jewelry in the Metropolitan Museum of Art. New York, 1982. 19.5 x 27.5. 160 pp., 30 color pls., 101 illus., 13 figs , map $35.00
Most welcome survey of hitherto poorly published jewelry! Serious attempt to study development, establish dates, emphasize technology.

523.477 Jouin, J.
Iconographie de la Marie Citadine dans l'Islam Nord-Africain. (**Revue des Études Islamiques**, 1931). Paris, 1932. 24 x 19. 31 pp., 23 pls. Paper. $9.50
Marriage costumes with full sets of sumptuous ethnic jewelry.

367.311 Kalus, L. Bibliothèque National.
Catalogue des Cachets, Bulles et Talismans Islamiques. Paris, 1981. 21 x 30.5. 109 pp., 16 pls. $57.50
First publication of a large national collection of neglected area of glyptics.

575.527 Keene, M.
The Lapidary Arts in Islam. (**Expedition**, vol. 24, 1981). 15 pp., 23 illus. Paper.
$5.50
Cutting techniques as gleaned from the gems and beads of the Mediaeval Islamic period.

587.539 Launois, A.
Catalogue des Étalons Monétaires et Autres Pièces Musulmanes en Verre de la Collection Jean Maspero. Paris, 1960. 28 x 21. 77 pp., 7 pls., 11 figs. Paper.
$18.00
Illustrates 167 dated glass weights and related objects; important for comparison with Islamic gems of the same period.

365.309 Melikian-Chirvani, A.S.
Islamic Metalwork from the Iranian World, 8th -18th Centuries. London, 1982. 23 x 28.5. 445 pp., 1 color pl., num. illus. $135.00
Richly illustrated compendium describes mostly vessels decorated with gold and silver inlays and other jewelry-related techniques.

549.503 Melikian-Chirvani, A.S.
Bronzes et Cuivres Iraniens du Louvre. I: L'École du Fàrs au XIVe Siècle. (**Asiatique**, 1969.). Paris, 1970. 23 x 14.5. 15 pp., 10 pls. Paper. $8.50
Finely chiseled and inlaid vessels from 14th c. Iran are carefully catalogued, inscriptions read and translated, and pictoral detail shown in enlarged photographs.

566. 519 Melikian-Chirvani, A.S.
Le Bassin du Sultan Qara Arslan Ibn Il-Gazi. (**Revue des Études Islamiques**, vol. XXVI, 1968.). Paris, 1968. 23.5 x 19. 13 pp., 4 pls. Paper. $5.50
A signed and dated basin of 13th c. Armenia/Northern Mesopotamia, with other examples of similar nielloed and enameled workmanship.

366.310 Migeon, G.
Orfèvrerie d'Argent de Style Oriental trouvée en Bulgarie. (**Syria**, 1922). 4 pp., 2 pls. Paper. $5.50
Shows Islamic jewelry from a datable context in Bulgaria.

616.565 Morton, A.H. British Museum.
A Catalogue of Early Islamic Glass Stamps in the British Museum. London, 1985. 28.5 x 22. 176 pp., 24 pls. $70.00
A catalogue of 556 glass stamps dating from the 8th C. to 900 AD. Includes a long discussion of metrology, uses and issuing authorities.

701.680 Mueller-Lancet, A. The Israel Museum.
La Vie Juive au Maroc / Jewish Life in Morocco. Jerusalem, 1983. 25 x 21. 268 pp., 467 illus., incl. 50 color. $48.50
Handsome catalogue shows the small objects of daily life, the costumes - and the jewelry worn with these - of the Jewish community in Morocco. The costumes and jewelry differ from those used by their Arab neighbors. Text in Hebrew.

539.493 National Palace Museum.
Masterpieces of Chinese Seals in the National Palace Museum. Taipei, 1974. 27.5 x 22. 111 pp., 100 color pls. Slipcase. $36.00
One hundred Chinese seals are shown, in color, in three views: top, sealing surface and impression. A history of Chinese seals is included.

596.548 Nègre, A. Bibliothèque Nationale.
Trésors de l'Islam au Cabinet des Médailles. Paris, 1981. 24 x 14. ca 17 pp., 25 illus. Paper. $5.50

677.640 Philippe, J.
Réliquaires Mediévaux de l'Orient Chrétien en Verre et en Cristal de Roche conservés en Belgique. Leige, 1975. 24 x 16. 45 pp., 21 figs. Paper. $16.50
Obscure publication shows important Mediaeval and Islamic rockcrystal and cut glass vessels preserved in church treasures. Parallels from other treasures are listed and illustrated.

368.312 Ross, H.C.
Bedouin Jewellery in Saudi Arabia. London, 1981. 22.5 x 30. 128 pp., 40 color pls., 23 pls., 3 maps. $24.00
Provides an outline of the life style that produced the jewelry, describes techniques and materials.

490.447 Schienerl, P.W.
Tierdarstellungen im Islam: Am Beispiel des Schmuck- und Amulettwesens. Göttingen, 1984. 14 x 20.5. 131 pp., 87 illus. Paper. $14.50
Eight chapters dealing with various aspects of amuletic jewelry, its roots and survival into the present century.

655.623 Schienerl, P.W. and McDevitt, E.
Ethnographic Museum, Cairo: A Guide to the Collection of Amulets. Cairo, 1985. 150 pp., num. illus. Paper. $28.50

369.313 Schletzer, D. and R.
Old Silver Jewellery of the Turcomen, A Contribution to the research on symbols in the culture of the nomads of Inner Asia. Berlin, 1983. 22.5 x 30. 304 pp., 136 color illus., 25 pls., 136 illus., 220 figs., maps. $125.00
Handsome book on the iconography, history and technology of Turcomen jewelry; identifies its role in their society.

337.280 Topkapı Sarayı Muezesi.
Topkapi Sarayimuezesi Muhurler Seksiyonu Rehberi / Guidebook of the seals section of the Topkapi Saray Museum. Istanbul, 1959. 58 pp., 7 pls. Paper.
$22.50
Scarce book showing the various seals used by the Ottoman sultans and other officials.

515.469 Zahlhaas, G.
Fingerringe und Gemmen: Sammlung Dr. E. Pressmar. Munich, 1985. 69 pp., 161 illus. Paper. $14.50
First publication of a private collection of 100 finger rings, all are illustrated and classified as to origin and date. The collection is strongest in the more commonly encountered types, Roman, Byzantine and Islamic, some others.

Ethnic Jewelry

685.664 Abrahamian, V.A., (Ed.).
Armenian Jewelry Art: From the Ancient Period to the Present Day. Leningrad, 1985. 222 pp., 154 color pls. $24.50
Early Near Eastern and Armenian jewelry from the third millenium B.C. to the present is shown on 54 color plates. Text in English, Armenian and Russian.

359.303 Al-Jakir, S.
Arab and Islamic Silver. London, 1981. 26 x 30. 216 pp., num. pls. incl. color. $45.00
Handsomely produced survey of silver jewelry from North Africa to South-East Asia.

370.314 Banco de la Republica.
El Museo del Oro. Bogota, 1948. 20 x 27. n.p., (ca.40), 102 color pls., 2 maps. $85.00
Extremely scarce copy of the commemorative edition of 1948, illustrates and describes 100 pieces of Pre-columbian gold.

680.659 Behrmann, I., (Ed.). Museum für Kunst und Gewerbe Hamburg.
Völkstuemlicher Schmuck. Hamburg, 1985. 312 pp., 16 color pls., 1016 illus. $32.50
Basic book on North German folk jewelry.

371.315 Brijbhusan, J.
Masterpieces of Indian Jewellery. Bombay, 1979. 54 pp., 88 pls. $27.50
History of the development of jewelry in India, profusely illustrated and well presented.

522.476 Bucherer-Dietschi, P.
Schmuck- und Silberschmiedearbeiten in Afghanistan und Zentralasien; Schmuck in Sammlungen. Liestal, 1981. 14.5 x 20.5. 79 pp., ca. 50 illus. Paper. $14.50
Twelve chapters dealing with different aspects of Afghani jewelry, its technique and the costumes it is worn with. Attractively illustrated with careful sketches.

668.633 Chadour, A.B. and Joppien, R. Kunstgewerbemuseum.
Schmuck, Bestandskatalog des Kunstgewerbemuseums. Cologne, 1985. 2 vols, with num. illus., incl. color. $45.00
Major new museum catalogue with a lengthy introduction and 910 entries, especially strong in Ancient, Migration Period, Renaissance and 19th c. jewelry. A fine group of 355 rings is shown in two views each. Recommended!

239. 201 Chandra, R.G.
Indo-Greek Jewellery. New Delhi, 1979. 136 pp., 25 pls. $32.50
Most interesting study on unfamiliar aspects of ancient Greek jewelry, includes chapter on technology.

373.317 Galerie Charpentier.
Collection de bijoux et de monnaies. Paris, 1956. 24 x 30.5. 1 color pl., 41 pls. Felted Paper. $18.50
Large collection of African, Pre-columbian and fake "ancient" jewelry, includes some genuine pieces of Roman jewelry.

374.318 Delivorrias, A.
Greek Traditional Jewelry. Athens, 1980. 21.5 x 29.5. 92 illus., incl. 68 color. Paper. $16.50
Attractively illustrated survey of "peasant jewelry".

556.510 Farabee, W.C.
Ancient American Gold. (**The Museum Journal**, 1920). 17 x 25.5. 37 pp., 22 figs. Paper. $5.50
Lengthy article carefully illustrates an exhibition of Pre-Columbian gold jewelry and artefacts held in 1919 in Philadelphia. Also gives a history of the conquest of the gold yielding areas, taken from contemporary sources.

670.430 Farabee, W.C.
Recent Discovery of Ancient Wampum Belts.. (**The Museum Journal**, 1922.). 17 x 25.5. 9 pp., 3 illus. Paper. $8.50
Two wampum belts, dated to 1674 and 1699, made by the Huron and Abnaquis Indians, given to French missionaries to be dedicated in the Chartres Cathedral and kept there ever since.

543.497 Firouz, I.A.
Silver Ornaments of the Turkoman. Tehran, 1978. 24 x 17. 56 pp., 48 color pls., 78 figs. Paper. $65.00
Scarce book, published in Tehran, shows the jewelry of the Turkoman, explains its manufacture and technique, shows the costumes on which it was worn.

552.506 Fisher, A.
Africa Adorned. New York, 1984. 36 x 27. 304 pp., 457 illus., 414 in color. $95.00
Oversized book, richly illustrated with African jewelry and ornaments, its history, uses and geographical distribution. Out-of-print.

627.576 Gagochidzé, J.
L'Ornament de la Femme Géorgienne. Khelovneba, 1981. 16.5 x 13. 221 pp., 91 color illus., 5 figs. Paper. $14.50
Jewelry from Georgia, (USSR), from the IVth Millenium to the 19th c. AD. The plates are poorly printed but show interesting jewelry: many beads and necklace elements, some ancient rings and cameos. Text in French, Russian and Georgian.

537.491 Gerlach, M., (Ed.).
Primitive and Folk Jewelry. New York, 1971. 28 x 21. 218 pp., 109 pls. with 1900 illus. Paper. $11.50
Quality reprint of the 1906 edition of **Völkerschmuck**; still an excellent quick reference for ancient, ethnic and unusual jewelry with more than 1900 items illustrated.

702.681 Goldman-Schwartz, A. The Israel Museum.
The Jews of Kurdistan: Everyday Life and Arts and Crafts. Jerusalem, 1982. 21 x 24. 272 pp., 35 color pls., num. illus. $42.50
Shows jewelry, costumes, amulets and related small objects of daily life from the once thriving Jewish community in Kurdistan. Text in Hebrew.

4.407 Grancière, A. de la
Les Parures Préhistoriques et Antiques en grains d'enfilage et les colliers talismans Celto-Armoricains. Paris, 1897. 17 x 26. 176 pp., 2 color pls., 20 pls.
$55.00
Interesting book describes prehistoric beads and amulets as well as their survival in some ethnic jewelry of the 19th century. Half leather binding.

688.667 Grand Rapids Public Museum.
Beads: Their Use By Upper Great Lakes Indians. Grand Rapids, 1977. 28 x 21.5. 81 pp., 250 illus. incl. num. color. Paper. $11.50
Shows the beads, in color, and their applications by the early Indians.

375.319 Hejj-Detari, A.
Hungarian Jewellery of the Past. Budapest, n.d. 18 x 16.5. 60 pp., 8 color pls., 40 illus., 20 figs. $18.00
Antique and ethnic jewelry from Eastern Europe, well illustrated.

376.320 Janata, A.
Schmuck in Afghanistan. Graz, 1981. 212 pp., 24 color pls., 48 pls., 2 figs., map.
$60.00
Generously illustrated compendium of Afghani ethnic jewelry with a discussion of usage and techniques.

523.477 Jouin, J.
Iconographie de la Marie Citadine dans L'Islam Nord-Africain. (Revue des Études Islamiques, 1931). Paris, 1932. 24 x 19. 31 pp., 23 pls. Paper. $9.50
Marriage costumes with full sets of sumptuous ethnic jewelry.

524.478 Kalter, J.
Aus Steppe und Oase, Bilder turkestanischer Kulturen. London, 1983. 20 x 22.5. 167 pp., 188 illus., incl. num. color. Paper. $12.50
Handsome publication shows, in color and B. & W., the objects of daily use, with special emphasis on jewelry and the costumes on which it was worn, of the Turkestan region.

708.687 Kelley, C.W. The Dayton Art Institute.
Chinese Gold & Silver in American Collections. Tang Dynasty, A.D. 618 - 907. Dayton, 1984. 28 x 21.5. 112 pp., 76 illus., incl. color, map. Paper. $16.50
Handsome catalogue illustrates ancient Chinese jewelry and metal vessels.

344.288 Kovacs, E.
Romanesque Goldsmiths' Art. Budapest, n.d. 18 x 16. 58 pp., 8 color pls., 11 figs. $26.50
Handsomely illustrates Eastern European early jewelry.

372.316 Latif, M. Musées Royaux d'Art et d'Histoire.
Bijoux Moghols/Mogol Juwelen/Mughal Jewels. Brussels, 1982. 24 x 21. 212 pp., num. color and B. & W. illus. Paper. $47.50
Fascinating catalogue, in three languages, showing the history and technology of Indian jewelry.

527.481 Lefèvre-Pontalis, M.P. Musée Guimet.
Notes sur des Amulettes Siamoises. Paris, 1926. 19 x 12.5. 49 pp., 29 pls. Paper. $13.50
Study of 107 metal amulets, all are illustrated, some from several angles, with a thorough discussion of their background and iconography.

525.479 Lewis, P. and E.
Peoples of the Golden Triangle, Six Tribes in Thailand. London, 1984. 23 x 25. 300 pp., 754 illus., incl. 712 color. $38.50
Shows rich and varied ethnic jewelry, the garments on which it was worn and illustrates the life styles that created the jewelry.

526.480 Meerwarth, A.
Les Kathakalis du Malabar. (**Asiatique**, 1926). Paris, 1926. 14 x 23. 91 pp., 16 pls., num. figs. Paper. $12.50
Rich indigenous costumes and jewelry are illustrated; customs described of Indian people.

701.680 Mueller-Lancet, A. The Israel Museum.
La Vie Juive au Maroc / Jewish Life in Morocco. Jerusalem, 1983. 25 x 21. 268 pp., 467 illus., incl. 50 color. $48.50
Handsome catalogue shows the small objects of daily life, the costumes - and the jewelry worn with these - of the Jewish community in Morocco. The costumes and jewelry differ from those used by their Arab neighbors. Text in Hebrew.

377.321 Olson, E. The Newark Museum.
Catalogue of the Tibetan Collection and other Lamaist material . . . Textiles-Rugs-Needlework-Costumes-Jewelry. Newark, 1975. 18 x 24. 76 pp., 39 pls. Paper. $11.50
Shows Tibetan jewelry and ornaments and the garments on which they were worn. Includes descriptive catalogue entries.

538.492 Pressmar, E.
Indische Ringe. Frankfurt, 1981. 24.5 x 17. 105 pp., 55 figs. $21.50
Show, classifies and discusses Indian rings, mostly 18th c. and later.

378.322 Prokot, I. and J.
Schmuck aus Zentralasien. Munich, 1980. 26 x 23. 156 pp., 41 color pls., 227 illus. $35.00
Attractive survey of ethnic jewelry from Central Asia.

379.323 Ritz, G.M.
Alter Bäuerlicher Schmuck. Munich, 1978. 25.5 x 28.5. 221 pp., 16 color pls., 18 figs. $48.50
Exhaustive compendium of European peasant jewelry, with many close-up photographs.

528.482 Rodgers, S. Barbier-Mueller Museum.
Power and Gold: Jewelry from Indonesia, Malaysia, and the Philippines. Geneva, 1985. 27 x 23. 369 pp., 252 illus., incl. num. color pls., maps. Paper. $36.00
First recent publication of jewelry from the outer islands, its history and iconography. Very well illustrated and described.

669.425 Ross, K.
Shell Ornaments of Malaita. (Expedition, vol. 23, 1981.). 28 x 21.5. 6 pp., 8 illus. Paper. $7.50
Bead necklaces and ceremonial shells; their ritualistic use in the Solomon Island group.

490.447 Schienerl, P.W.
Tierdarstellungen im Islam: Am Beispiel des Schmuck- und Amulettwesens. Goettingen, 1984. 14 x 20.5. 131 pp., 87 illus. Paper. $14.50
Eight chapters dealing with various aspects of amuletic jewelry, its roots and survival into the present century.

655.623 Schienerl, P.W. and McDevitt, E.
Ethnographic Museum, Cairo: A Guide to the Collection of Amulets. Cairo, 1985. 150 pp., num. illus. Paper. $28.50

369.313 Schletzer, D. and R.
Old Silver Jewellery of the Turcomen, A Contribution to the research on symbols in the culture of the nomads of Inner Asia. Berlin, 1983. 22.5 x 30. 304 pp., 136 color illus., 25 pls., 136 illus., 220 figs., maps. $125.00
Handsome book on the iconography, history and technology of Turcomen jewelry; identifies its role in their society.

380.324 Schuler-Schoemig, I.v.
Werke indianischer Goldschmiedekunst im Museum für Völkerkunde Berlin. Berlin, n.d. 15 x 21. 44 pp., 4 color pls., 32 pls., 4 figs. $12.50

271.229 Shachar, I. The Israel Museum.
Jewish Tradition In Art: The Feuchtwanger Collection of Judaica. Jerusalem, 1981. 27.5 x 22. 341 pp., 16 color pls., num. illus. Paper. $45.00
Extensive catalogue of amuletic jewelry, seals and related objects illustrating the every day concerns of Jewish communities from Europe to Persia.

381.235 Stillman, Y.K.
Palestinian Costume and Jewelry. Albuquerque, 1979. 22 x 28. 138 pp., 22 color pls., num. figs. $36.00
Survey of ethnic jewelry and the garments on which it was worn.

573.526 Stuckert, R.
Turkmenenschmuck. Liestal, 1981. 15 x 11. 10 pls. Loose leaf portfolio. $5.50
Small portfolio containing 10 cards, each one illustrates and describes one piece of Turcoman jewelry.

382.326 Sugier, C.
Bijoux Tunisiens, Formes et Symboles. Tunis, 1977. 20 x 20. 70 pp., 50 color pls. $22.50
An intelligent survey of North African jewelry, well illustrated.

626.575 Sychova, N.
Traditional Jewellery from Soviet Central Asia and Kazakhstan - 19th and 20th Centuries from the collection of the Museum of Oriental Art Moscow. Moscow, 1984. 23.5 x 22.5. 179 pp., 123 color pls. Slipcase. $33.50
Handsomely illustrated book on the ethnic jewelry from Central Asia; carefully describes uses, native names, lore. Many close-up photographs of jewelry details.

645.613 Thomsen, M., (Ed.).
Java und Bali: Buddhas, Götter, Helden, Dämonen. Mainz, 1980. 23.5 x 21.5. 292 pp., 24 color pls., 275 illus. $18.50
Exhibition catalogue shows hitherto poorly published Javanese and Balinese jewelry and other objects.

337.280 Topkapi Sarayi Muezesi.
Topkapi Sarayimuezesi Muhurler Seksiyonu Rehberi / Guidebook of the seals section of the Topkapi Saray Museum. Istanbul, 1959. 58 pp., 7 pls. Paper.
$22.50
Scarce book showing the various seals used by the Ottoman sultans and other officials.

233.194 Tual, A.
Pour un typologie des bijoux de femmes en Iran. (Studia Iranica, vol. 9, 1980).
$38.50

10.327 Wesley Jernigan, E.
Jewelry of the Prehistoric Southwest. Albuquerque, 1978. 21 x 26. 260 pp., 17 color pls., 101 figs. $32.50
In-depth presentation of early American bead and jewelry styles.

571.524 de Zeltner, F.
La Bijouterie Indigène en Afrique Occidentale. 28.5 x 18. 5 pp., 10 pls. Paper.
$3.50
West-African knotting of ropes and plants as a utilitarian and decorative design element.

Amber

583.535 Barge, H.
Les Parures du Néolithique Ancien au début de l'Age des Métaux en Languedoc. Paris, 1982. 29 x 21. 396 pp., 131 figs., 6 pls. Paper. $45.00
Establishes methodology for the earliest beads and related small objects from France. Shows many hundreds of beads and pendants in, mostly, stone, amber, bone and shell. Some metal beads were also found.

15.332 Brown, D. and Henig, M. Ashmolean Museum.
Figured Amber in the Ashmolean Museum. (BAR, 4, 1977.). Oxford, 1977. 29 x 20.5. 14 pp., 6 pls., 1 fig. Paper. $6.50
Roman amber carvings only.

16.333 Reineking-v. Bock, G.
Bernstein, das Gold der Ostsee. Munich, 1981. 28.5 x 25.5. 188 pp., 21 color pls., 292 illus. $38.50
Well produced book about the history and uses of amber.

17.334 Rice, P.C.
Amber, The Golden Gem of the Ages. New York, 1980. 26 x 18. 289 pp., 16 color pls., num. illus. $28.50
Comprehensive look at amber, its use in science and art.

581.533 Siviero, R.
Jewelry and Amber of Italy: A Collection in the National Museum of Naples. New York, 1959. 34.5 x 25. 153 pp., 8 color pls., 274 pls., 115 figs. $185.00
Important, well illustrated book showing the Etruscan and Roman jewelry in the Naples' Museum from the excavations in Pompei and Herculaneum.

18.335 Stenico, A.
Ambre Scolpite. (Arte e civilta romana nell' Italia settentrionale, n.n.). Bologna, 1965. 21 x 14. 8 pp. Paper. $6.50

13.330 Strong, D.E. British Museum.
Catalogue of the Carved Amber in the Department of Greek and Roman Antiquities. London, 1966. 28.5 x 22. 104 pp., 1 color pl., 43 pls., 2 maps. $32.50
Thorough discussion of many aspects of ancient amber objects.

14.331 Weitschat, W. Naturwissenschaftliches Museum.
Leben im Bernstein. Osnabrück, 1979. 24 x 17. 48 pp., 40 figs. Paper. $12.50
Describes ancient methods of amber collection, its inclusions and history.

19.336 Yon, M.
Les Bijoux d'Ambre de la Nécropole d'Alésia, (Corse). (MEFRA, vol. LXXXIX, 1977). 24 x 16.5. 29 pp., 9 illus. Paper. $11.50
Greek and Etruscan amber carvings of the 6th-5th century BC.

Beads

1.412 Arnaud, D., (et al.).
Ilsu-Ibnisu Orfèvre de l'E. Babbar de Larsa. (Syria, vol. LVI, 1979). 64 pp., 4 pls., 82 figs. Paper. $22.50
Important find of beads, weights, tools and jewelry from the mid 18th Century BC.; many illustrations of beads and jewelry.

583.535 Barge, H.
Les Parures du Néolithique Ancien au début de l'Age des Métaux en Languedoc. Paris, 1982. 29 x 21. 396 pp., 131 figs., 6 pls. Paper. $45.00
Establishes methodology for the earliest beads and related small objects from France. Shows many hundreds of beads and pendants in, mostly, stone, amber, bone and shell. Some metal beads were also found.

512.467 Bateson, J.D.
Enamel-working in Iron Age, Roman and Sub-Roman Britain: The Products and Techniques. (BAR, 93, 1981). Oxford, 1981. 167 pp., 15 pls. Paper. $22.50
Comprehensive survey of the enameled objects from Britain from 200 BC - 700 AD. Millefiori enamels and their techniques are studied in detail.

682.661 Beck, H.
Classification and Nomenclature of Beads and Pendants. Lancaster, n.d. 19 x 25.5. 76 pp., 87 figs. Paper. $15.00
Excellent reprint of one of the first books to scientifically study beads and small amulets. Includes numerous detailed drawings of individual beads of all types and dates.

2.283 Callmer, J.
Trade beads and bead trade in Scandinavia ca. 800-1000 AD. (Acta Arch. Lund., vol. IV). Lund, 1977. 229 pp., 4 color pls., 22 pls., 16 figs. Paper. $48.50
Clear illustrations show many types of beads previously known from Near Eastern sites and other evidence of extensive bead trade.

483.440 Cristofani, M. and Martelli, M.
L'Oro degli Etruschi. Novara, 1983. 23 x 31. 343 pp., 310 color illus., 17 figs. Slipcase. $110.00
Superbly illustrated publication shows the full range and splendor of Etruscan gold and bead jewelry, some set with gems, of all periods. Includes a separate section on technique. Likely to become a standard reference!

670.430 Farabee, W.C.
Recent Discovery of Ancient Wampum Belts. (The Museum Journal, 1922.). 17 x 25.5. 9 pp., 3 illus. Paper. $8.50
Two wampum belts, dated to 1674 and 1699, made by the Huron and Abnaquis Indians, given to French missionaries to be dedicated in the Chartres Cathedral and kept there ever since.

9.155 Fremersdorf, F. Museo Sacro.
Antikes, Islamisches und Mittelalterliches Glas sowie kleinere Arbeiten aus Stein, Gagat und verwandten Stoffen in den Vatikanischen Sammlungen Roms. Vatican City, 1975. 32.5 x 41. 133 pp., 2 color pls., 92 pls. $250.00
Large format catalogue; contains lengthy sections on beads, gems and hardstone carvings-in-the-round in the Vatican Museums.

627.576 Gagochidzé, J.
L'Ornament de la Femme Géorgienne. Khelovneba, 1981. 16.5 x 13. 221 pp., 91 color illus., 5 figs. Paper. $14.50
Jewelry from Georgia, (USSR), from the IVth Millenium to the 19th c. AD. The plates are poorly printed but show interesting jewelry: many beads and necklace elements, some ancient rings and cameos. Text in French, Russian and Georgian.

659.625 Goldstein, S.
Pre-Roman and Early Roman Glass in The Corning Museum of Glass. Corning, 1979. 28 x 20.5. 312 pp., 42 pls., incl. 36 color., 919 illus. $45.00
Significant catalogue of glass beads, amulets, and vessels from the earliest period until ca. 50 BC. Each object is clearly catalogued, described, and often illustrated either in color or black and white.

468.427 Gorelick, L.
The Origin and Development of the Ancient Near Eastern Cylinder Seal. (Expedition, vol. 23, 1981). 14 pp., 15 illus. Paper. $5.50
Plausible speculation on the development of cylinder seals out of early bead shapes and technologies.

574.527 Gorelick, L. and Gwinnett, A.J.
Beadmaking in Iran in the Early Bronze Age. (Expedition, vol. 24. 1981). 14 pp., 29 illus. Paper. $5.50
Fascinating study of the earliest technologies employed to create stone beads; includes many detailed scanning electron microscope photographs showing actual processes used. Equally applicable to the manufacture of early seals.

4.407 Grancière, A. de la
Les Parures Préhistoriques et Antiques en grains d'enfilage et les colliers talismans Celto-Armoricains. Paris, 1897. 17 x 26. 176 pp., 2 color pls., 20 pls. $55.00
Interesting book describes prehistoric beads and amulets as well as their survival in some ethnic jewelry of the 19th century. Half leather binding.

688.667 Grand Rapids Public Museum.
Beads: Their Use By Upper Great Lakes Indians. Grand Rapids, 1977. 28 x 21.5. 81 pp., 250 illus. incl. num. color. Paper. $11.50
Shows the beads, in color, and their applications by the early Indians.

3.239 Guido, M.
The glass Beads of the Prehistoric and Roman Periods in Britain and Ireland.
London, 1978. xxxvi, 250 pp., 4 color pls., 38 figs. $65.00
Beads from Britain, ca. 700 BC - 410 AD are presented in carefully annotated detail; includes classification tables, typology, etc.

5.328 Haevernick, T.E.
Beiträge zur Glasforschung: die wichtigsten Aufsätze von 1938 bis 1981.
Mainz, 1981. 23 x 31.5. xxxvii, 440 pp., 21 color illus., 26 pls., 215 figs., 17 maps. $120.00
Indispensable to any serious glass bead collector; almost 50 years of research is presented in these collected papers. Major articles on beads of all periods, Phoenician head pendants, European Dark Age glass objects, technology and glass jewelry.

582.534 Haevernick, T.E., (et al.).
Glasperlen der vorrömischen Eisenzeit I. (Marburger Studien zur Vor- und Frühgeschichte, 5). Mainz, 1983. 28.5 x 19.5. viii, 178 pp., 1 color pl., 2 pls., 19 figs. 7 maps. $52.50
Very thorough discussion of the distribution patterns of various types of beads; beads as part of jewelry suites; manner of wearing beads.

12.125 Hayes, C.F., (Ed.).
Proceedings of the 1982 Glass Trade Bead Conference. (Research Records, No. 16). Rochester, 1983. 28 x 21.5. 284 pp., num. illus. figs. and maps. Paper. $22.50
Contains 20 articles discussing beads, their manufacture and classification, from Antiquity to 18th century American Indian trade beads.

11.79 Holm, E.
Glasperlen, Mythologie, Schmuck und Spielereien aus fünf Jahrtausenden.
Munich, 1984. 20 x 21. 216 pp., 40 color pls., 200 illus. $28.50
In spite of the all-encompassing title, the book shows mostly 18th and 19th c. beads, beaded objects and garments. Some ancient and ethnic material is also included.

666.431 Legrain, L.
The Boudoir of Queen Shubad. (The Museum Journal, 1929). 17 x 27.5. 34 pp., 12 pls., 4 illus. Paper. $5.50
Precious metal and stone regalia from early Ur, 3500 BC, are shown and discussed. Cylinder seals show the fashions that complemented the metal and bead jewelry.

591.543 De Morgan, J.
Fouilles à Dahchour: Mars-Juin, 1894. Vienna, 1895. 32.5 x 26.5. 166 pp., 40 pls., incl. 7 color., 274 figs. Paper. $185.00
Scarce excavation report of the XI-XII Dynasty jewelry and beads found by De Morgan in 1894. Major finds of datable royal jewelry and other objects; well illustrated.

658.427 Possehl, G.
Cambay Beadmaking. (**Expedition**, vol. 23, 1981.). 8 pp., 12 illus. Paper. $5.50
Modern survival of ancient bead making techniques in India, all stages are illustrated and explained.

6.193 Quillard, B.
Bijoux Carthaginois. I: Les Colliers. Louvain, 1979. 133 p., 20 color pls., 2 tables.
$48.50
Welcome addition to small but growing number of books on ancient necklace components.

669.425 Ross, K.
Shell Ornaments of Malaita. (**Expedition**, vol. 23, 1981.). 28 x 21.5. 6 pp., 8 illus. Paper. $7.50
Bead necklaces and ceremonial shells; their ritualistic use in the Solomon Island group.

7.329 Seefried, M.
Les pendentifs en verre sur noyau des pays de la Méditerrannée Antique. (Collection de L'École Française de Rome, 57). Rome, 1982. 22.5 x 28. xiv, 186 pp., 1 color pl., 20 pls., 4 maps, tables. Paper. $42.50
Well illustrated survey of Phoenician glass head pendants, eye beads and related small glass objects. Establishes typology and datable sequences.

683.662 Smith, M. and Good, M.E.
Early Sixteenth Century Glass Beads in the Spanish Colonial Trade. Lancaster, 1985. 74 pp., 8 pls., incl. 4 color., maps. $16.50
Illustrates European beads made for trade with native Americans. Includes maps showing distribution patterns.

632.581 Tempelmann-Maczynska, M.
Die Perlen der römischen Kaiserzeit und der frühen Phase der Völkerwanderungszeit im mitteleuropäischen Barbaricum. (**Römisch-Germanische Forschungen**, 47). Mainz, 1985. xii, 339 pp., 14 color pls. with 707 illus., 66 pls. with 207 illus., charts. $67.50
Shows Roman and early Migration Period beads, all types are illustrated and described.

577.529 Tosi, M. and Piperno, M.
Lithic Technology behind the Ancient Lapis Lazuli Trade. (**Expedition**, vol. 16, 1973). 9 pp., 14 illus., map. Paper. $6.50
Discusses finds from Shahr-i Sokta, Afghanistan, dating to 3000-2000 BC., which illustrates the techniques and tools used to make beads and seals.

8.69 Tufnell, O. and Ward, W.A.
Relations between Byblos, Egypt and Mesopotamia at the end of the third Millenium BC, a study of the Montet Jar. (**Syria**, vol. XLIII, 1966). Paris, 1966. 77 pp., 6 pls., 10 figs. Paper. $18.50
Large closed find of jewelry, scarabs and beads, all illustrated and dated.

545.499 Van der Sleen, W.G.N.
A Handbook on Beads. York, PA, 1973. 22.5 x 15. 128 pp., 8 pls. illus. 130 figs. Paper. $15.00
In-depth survey of beads, their technology, dating and distribution, with emphasis on beads of ancient and European manufacture.

10.327 Wesley Jernigan, E.
Jewelry of the Prehistoric Southwest. Albuquerque, 1978. 21 x 26. 260 pp., 17 color pls., 101 figs. $32.50
In-depth presentation of early American bead and jewelry styles.

Ancient "Kleinkunst" - Metal Vessels - Objects

580.532 Alborino, V.
Das Silberkästchen von San Nazaro in Mailand. Bonn, 1981. 20.5 x 15. 282 pp., 113 figs. Paper. $22.50
Careful iconographical study of the Late Roman silver reliquary from Milano. A date is established, 375 AD., and the reliquary is fitted into its overall context.

621.570 Amandry, P.
Rapport Préliminaire sur les Statues Chryséléphantines de Delphes. (**BCH**, vol. LXIII, 1939.). Paris, 1939. 25 x 18.5. 33 pp., 23 pls., 13 figs. Paper. $26.50
Important article describing the small finds in precious materials, ivory, gold and silver, made during the excavations of 1938. Most date from the 6th and 5th c. BC.

650.618 Avitabile, G.G.
Chinesische und japanische Cloisonne- und Champleve-Arbeiten von 1400 -1900. Munich, 1981. 21 x 24. 272 pp., 235 illus. incl. 59 color., 2 maps. $45.00
Oriental enameled vessels and tsubas, made during the last 500 years, are discussed, 179 objects are illustrated, many for the first time.

385.339 Barratte, F.
Vaisselle d'argent au Bas-Empire. Rémarques à propos d'un vase du Musée du Louvre. (**Antiquité**, 1976). 28 x 22. Paper. $4.50

386.340 Baratte, F.
Le Trésor d'Argenterie Gallo-Romaine de Notre-Dame-d'Alençon. (Maine-et-Loire). (**Gallia**, Suppl. XL). Paris, 1982. 22 x 28. 93 pp., 39 pls., num. figs. Paper. $28.50
Careful examination of a large hoard of silver plate.

544.498 Baratte, F. Musée du Louvre.
L'Argenterie Romaine. Paris, 1976. 11.5 x 23.5. 17 pp., 16 illus. Paper. $5.50
Survey of Roman silver vessels.

550.504 Baratte, F. and Guyon, J.
Récherches Archéologiques à Sirmium (II). (**MEFRA**, vol. 87, 1975). Paris, 1975. 24.5 x 17. 27 pp., 16 figs. Paper. $4.50
Contains three articles describing the general excavations, the finds of jewelry and of a silver reliquary at Sirmium in a 4th c. context.

387.341 Barnett, R.D.
A Syrian Silver Vase. (**Syria**, vol. XXXIV, 1957.). 6 pp., 2 pls., 1 fig. Paper. $3.50

687.686 Bothmer, D. von Metropolitan Museum of Art.
A Greek and Roman Treasury. (**Bulletin**, vol. XLII). New York, 1984. 28 x 21.5. 72 pp., 131 illus. incl. num. color. Paper. $9.50
Beautifully illustrated issue of the **Bulletin** shows and carefully describes the 131 gold and silver vessels and related objects newly installed in the Greek and Roman Department of The Museum.

300.260 Bréhier, L.
Un Trésor d'Argenterie Ancienne au Musée de Cleveland. (**Syria**, vol. XXVIII, 1951). Paris, 1951. 9 pp., 4 pls., 3 figs. Paper. $5.50
Three Byzantine silver chalices and a 5th-6th c. paten.

15.332 Brown, D. and Henig, M. Ashmolean Museum.
Figured Amber in the Ashmolean Museum. (**BAR**, 4, 1977.). Oxford, 1977. 29 x 20.5. 14 pp., 6 pls., 1 fig. Paper. $6.50
Roman amber carvings only.

348.292 Bruce-Mitford, R., (et al.). British Museum.
The Sutton Hoo Ship-Burial. II: Arms, Armour and Regalia. London, 1978. 651 pp., 24 color pls., 443 figs. $160.00
Scientific examination of all aspects of the famous treasure, including chapters on style, provenance and techniques.

316.589 Bruce-Mitford, R., (et al.). British Museum.
The Sutton Hoo Ship-Burial. III, 1-2: Late Roman and Byzantive Silver, Hanging Bowls, Drinking Vessels, Cauldrons and Other Containers, Textiles, The Lyre, Pottery Bottle and Other Items. London, 1983. 32 x 26. xliv, 479 pp., 16 color pls., 340 figs. and xix, 518 pp., 339 figs. $175.00

173.135 Buehler, H.-P.
Antike Gefässe aus Edelsteinen. Mainz, 1973. 30 x 21. 85 pp., 40 pls., incl. 2 color pls., 1 fig. $65.00
First attempt at a corpus of surviving hardstone vessels, with discussion of shapes, dates.

558.511 Cote, C. Hotel Drouot.
Catalogue des Antiquités Romaines et des Objets d'Art et de Haute Curiosité. Paris, 1936. 23.5. x 20.5. 22 pp. Paper. $12.50
This auction catalogue lists Roman silver spoons, Greek and Roman gems, Dark Age jewelry and other objects. Photocopies of the original plates can be supplied for an additional $5.00. Scarce.

301.261 Cruikshank Dodd, E.
Byzantine Silver Stamps. Washington, D.C., 1962. 29 x 22. 283 pp., 103 pls., 5 fold-out tables, 1 map. $85.00
Comprehensive listing and description of all known Byzantine objects with control stamps, fully illustrated and with a lengthy introduction. Out-of-print.

302.262 Cruikshank Dodd, E.
Byzantine Silver Treasures. Bern, 1973. 24 x 19. 76 pp., 15 pls., 46 figs. Paper.
$20.00
Thorough discussion of the Bern Treasure with additional material drawn from other collections. Well illustrated.

177.139 Dacos, N., (et al.). Museo Mediceo.
Il Tesoro di Lorenzo il Magnifico: Le Gemme. Catalogue della Mostra, Palazzo Medici Riccardi, Firenze, 1972. Florence, 1973. 24 x 17. vi, 167 pp., 15 color pls., 99 illus. Paper. $32.50
Contains descriptions of ancient and Neo-Classical gems and an important 15th century inventory.

178.140 Dacos, N., (et al.). Museo Mediceo.
Il Tesoro di Lorenzo il Magnifico, repertorio delle gemme e dei vasi. Florence, 1980. 17.5 x 25. 302 pp., 23 color pls., 208 illus. $45.00
Contains all of the above plus the 1974 catalogue of the hardstone vases and other carvings, now in a 2nd edition combined in one volume.

303.263 Diehl, C.
Argenteries Syriennes. (Syria, vol. XI, 1930). 7 pp., 3 figs. Paper. $7.50
Describes a hoard of early Christian "apostle spoons".

304.264 Diehl, C.
L'École Artistique d'Antioche et les trésors d'Argenterie Syrienne. 15 pp., 6 pls. some foxing. Paper. $6.50
Discusses Late Antique and Byzantine silver vessels.

615.564 Diehl, C.
Un Nouveau Trésor d'Argenterie Syrienne. (Syria, 1926.). Paris, 1926. 28.5 x 22.5. 17 pp., 13 pls., 1 fig. Paper. $9.50
Twenty three Byzantine silver vessels, discovered together with, but later separated from, "The Chalice of Antioch", are published and illustrated.

625.574 Hotel Drouot.
Antiques - Art Chrétien: Bijoux d'Or, IVe Siècle - Xe Siècle. Paris, 1959, 27 x 21. 33 pp., 9 pls. Paper. $12.50
Auction catalogue showing Byzantine and earlier gold jewelry, 26 finger rings, as well as pottery and other objects.

389.343 Gallo, R.
Il Tesoro di S. Marco e la sua Storia. Venice, 1967. 18 x 25. xvi, 424 pp., 80 pls. $45.00
Presentation of Venetian church treasure which contains Antique harstone and glass vessels and gem-set objects.

390.344 Gehrig, U.
Hildesheimer Silberfund. Berlin, 1980. 17 x 23. 24 pp., 4 color pls., 51 pls. Paper. $11.50
Handsome publication of the famous treasure, see also no. 392-347.

508.463 Goldstein, S., (et al.).
Cameo Glass: Masterpieces from 2000 Years of Glassmaking. Corning, N.Y., 1982. 27.5 x 20. 140 pp., 158 illus. incl. many color. Paper. $18.50
Glass vessels and gems, Roman, Islamic, Oriental and Neo-Classical, all created by wheel cutting and other glyptic skills. Well catalogued and illustrated, with a glossary and bibliography.

356.300 Grabar, O. The University of Michigan Museum of Art.
Sasanian Silver. Ann Arbor, 1967. 158 pp., 83 illus. Paper. $14.00
Thorough discussion of Sasanian art combined with an illustrated catalogue of 83 objects.

516.470 Grand Palais.
Le Trésor de Saint-Marc de Venise. Paris, 1984. 23 x 26. 337 pp., num. pls., incl. color. Paper. $37.50
Superbly produced catalogue of a superb exhibition of major Antique hardstone vessels and related objects. Many additional treasures from the French national collections are added. Recommended! English version also available.

620.569 The Hague Municipal Museum.
Messen en Vorken in Nederland 1500 - 1800 / Knives and Forks in the Netherlands 1500 - 1800. The Hague, 1972. 16 x 16. 24 pp., 24 illus. Paper. $8.50
Early knives and forks, illustrates many elaborate types and styles. Text in Dutch and English.

635.583 Hahnloser, H. and Brugger, S.
Corpus der Hartsteinschliffe des XII. - XV. Jahrhunderts. Berlin, 1985. 21 x 27.5. 256 pp., 32 color pls., 464 pls., 29 figs. $145.00
A corpus of early European hardstone vessels, secular and religious. Includes sections on technique, materials, objects now lost but known from the literature, guilds, etc. Profusely illustrated.

281.240 Harhoiu, R.
The fifth-century AD, treasure from Pietroasa, in the light of recent research. (BAR, S-24). Oxford, 1977. 57 pp., 13 pls. Paper. $11.50
Famous Rumanian find, representing Late Roman industrial relations with "Barbaricum", newly studied and illustrated.

358.302 Harper, P.O. and Meyers, P. Metropolitan Museum of Art.
Silver Vessels of the Sasanian Period. I: Royal Imagery. New York, 1981. 272 pp., 7 color pls., 128 pls., 2 maps. $48.50
Presents a detailed examination of the history, iconography and mode of manufacture of the vessels in the Museum.

686.665 Harper, P.O. Metropolitan Museum of Art.
Ancient Near Eastern Art. (Bulletin, vol. XLI, 1984.). New York, 1984. 28 x 21.5. 56 pp., 80 illus. incl. 40 color. Paper. $9.50
Special issue of the **Bulletin** to commemorate the opening of the new Near Eastern Galleries; shows silver vessels and precious jewelry produced over a six thousand year period.

559.512 Haug, H.
L'Orfèvrerie de Strasbourg dans les Collections Publiques Françaises. Paris, 1978. 24 x 18. 237 illus., 4 tables. Paper. $22.50
Shows, in 221 photographs, silver objects made in the Strasbourg region of France. The flatware, vessels and hallmarks illustrated date mostly from the XVI - XIX century.

660.626 Hauptmann von Gladiss, A. and Kroeger, J.
Islamische Kunst: Loseblattkatalog unpublizierter Werke aus deutschen Museen. 2: Metall, Stein, Stuck, Holz, Elfenbein, Stoffe. Mainz, 1984. 29.5 x 21. xii, 146 pp., 146 pls., with 323 illus. Loose leaf portfolio. $65.00
Islamic art objects from public collections in Germany; each object is carefully catalogued and fully illustrated on a separate page.

391.345 Hayward, J.F.
Virtuoso Goldsmiths and the Triumph of Mannerism 1540-1620. New York, 1976. 25 x 32.5. 751 pp., 24 color pls., 740 illus. $150.00
Sumptuously produced book illustrates Renaissance jewelry and objects from all creating countries, identifies schools, artists.

132.92 Higgins, R.A.
The Aegina Treasure: An Archaeological Mystery. London, 1979. 23.5 x 15.5. 72 pp., 65 illus. Paper. $24.00
Fascinating history of the discovery of the treasure, with careful description of its parts. Now out-of-print.

392.347 Holzer, H.
Der Hildesheimer antike Silberfund. Hildesheim, 1870. 15.5 x 23.5. 107 pp., 13 pls. $65.00
Scarce book published in the same year as the discovery of the treasure, gives detailed information about original condition of the objects before their restoration.

282.241 Johns, C. and Potter, T. British Museum.
The Thetford Treasure: Roman Jewellery and Silver. London, 1983. 22.5 x 28.5. 136 pp., 4 color pls., 16 B. & W. pls., 45 figs. $45.00
Major recent find of Late 4th c. jewelry, incl. 22 gold rings and 33 silver spoons, expertly described and illustrated. With a technical examination of the Treasure and an arthistorical interpretation of its significance.

185.147 Kähler, H., (Ed.).
Alberti Rubeni Dissertatio de Gemme Augustea. (**Monumente Artis Romanae**, IX). Berlin, 1968. 40 pp., 1 color pl., 24 pls. $48.50
Includes a facsimile of the text and illustration by Rubens from ca. 1625. With 24 superbly detailed photographs of this famous cameo. Out-of-print.

394.349 Keim, J. and Klumbach, H.
Der roemische Schatzfund von Straubing. Munich, 1978. viii, 46 pp., 46 pls., 2 figs., map. Paper. $17.50

395.350 Kellner, H.-J. and Zahlhaas, G.
Der römische Schatzfund von Weissenburg. Munich, 1983. 52 pp., 35 illus. Paper. $8.50
Recent find of silver and bronze vessels, statuettes and votive plaques.

708.687 Kelley, C.W. The Dayton Art Institute.
Chinese Gold & Silver in American Collections. Tang Dynasty, A.D. 618 - 907. Dayton, 1984. 28 x 21.5. 112 pp., 76 illus., incl. color, map. Paper. $16.50
Handsome catalogue illustrates ancient Chinese jewelry and metal vessels.

384.338 Kent Hill, D. Walters Art Gallery.
Greek and Roman metalware; a loan exhibition . . . Baltimore, 1976. 16 pp., 78 illus. Paper. $7.50
Exhibition catalogue of 78 bronze and silver vessels dating from 8th c. BC. - 4th c. AD. All are illustrated.

636.584 Kent, J.C.P. and Painter, K.S. British Museum.
Wealth of the Roman World: AD 300 - 700. London, 1977. 24.5 x 19. 190 pp., 269 illus., 12 color pls., 5 maps. Paper. $18.50
Discusses 873 objects, including some coins, all from 300 - 700 AD.

491.448 Kovacs, E.
Limoges Champlevé Enamels in Hungary. Budapest, 1968. 18.5 x 16.5. 53 pp., 8 color pls., 6 figs. $22.50
Illustrates and describes the Hungarian national collections of Mediaeval enamels.

684.663 Kovacs, E. and Lovag, Z.
The Hungarian Crown and Other Regalia. Budapest, 1984. 97 pp., 42 color pls. $22.50
Detailed color plates show all sides of the Byzantine crown with close-ups of the cloisonné and of the gems, also includes color plates of the mantle, sceptre, orb and sword.

129.89 Laffineur, R.
Les vases en métal précieux à l'époque mycenienne. Göteburg, 1977. 21 x 11.5. 171 pp., 47 pls. Paper. $38.50
Discussion of silver and gold vessels with their decorations.

579.531 Laufer, B.
Jade: A Study in Chinese Archaeology and Religion. New York, 1974. 21 x 13.5. 370 pp., 68 pls., 204 figs. Paper. $9.50
Unabridged reprint of the 1912 edition, still one of the best general books introducing archaic and later jade carvings, their meaning and use.

383.337 Laur-Belart, R. Roemermuseum.
Der spätrömische Silberschatz von Kaiseraugst. Augst, 1967. 36 pp., 26 illus. Paper. $18.00
Well illustrated catalogue of a major Late Roman silver treasure, Now out-of-print.

308.268 Lazovic, M., (et al.). Musée d'Art et d'Histoire.
Objects byzantins de la collection du Musée d'Art et d'Histoire. Geneva, 1977. 20 x 25.5. 62 pp., 38 illus. Paper. $12.50
Careful examination of inscribed silver spoons and vessels, with technical analyses.

501.456 Malle, L. Museo Civico di Torino.
Vetri - Vetrate - Giade - Cristalli di Rocca e Pietre Dure. Turin, 1971. 24 x 17. 384 pp., 218 pls., incl. 17 color. $36.00
Detailed collection catalogue of the early glass vessels and stained glass panels, also of jade and other hardstone carvings, oriental and occidental, in the Museo Civico.

278.236 Malle, L. Museo Civico di Torino.
Smalti - Avori del Museo D'Arte Antica. Turin, 1969. 24 x 17. 354 pp., 5 color pls., 239 illus. $32.50
An extensive catalogue containing European enamels from the 13th to the 19th c. bound together with a second one detailing ivory objects, reliquaries and jewelry from the late Roman to the early 19th c. Both are generously illustrated.

609.558 Markoe, G.
Phoenician Bronze and Silver Bowls from Cyprus and the Mediterranean. Berkeley, 1985. 508 pp., num. pls., and illus. Paper. $45.00
A fully illustrated corpus of all extant decorated bronze and silver repousse bowls from the Mediterranean region.

646.614 Markoe, G., (Ed.).
Ancient Bronzes Ceramics and Seals: The Nasli M. Heeramaneck Collection of Ancient Near Eastern, Central Asiatic, and European Art. Los Angeles, 1981. 25 x 23.5. 271 pp., 360 illus., incl. 13 color. Paper. $18.50
A catalogue showing 1349 objects ranging from cylinder seals to small Luristan bronzes. Much unusual material from various Steppe Cultures and an extensive series of early stampseals is also included.

569.522 Martin, M.
Römische Schatzfunde aus Augst und Kaiseraugst. August, 1977. 21 x 15. 47 pp., 23 figs. Paper. $7.50

398.353 Matz, F.
Die Lauersforter Phalerae. (**BWP**, 92.). Berlin, 1932. 22 x 30. 41 pp., 5 pls., 14 figs. Paper. $28.50
Large find of Roman military insignia.

549.503 Melikian-Chirvani, A.S.
Bronzes et Cuivres Iraniens du Louvre. I: L'École du Fàrs au XIVe Siècle. (**Asiatique**, 1969.). Paris, 1970. 23 x 14.5. 15 pp., 10 pls. Paper. $8.50
Finely chiseled and inlaid vessels from 14th c. Iran are carefully catalogued, inscriptions read and translated, and pictoral detail shown in enlarge photographs.

566.519 Melikian-Chirvani, A.S.
Le Bassin du Sultan Qara Arslan Ibn Il-Gazi. (**Revue des Études Islamiques**, vol. XXVI, 1968.). Paris, 1968. 23.5 x 19. 13 pp., 4 pls. Paper. $5.50
A signed and dated basin of 13th c. Armenia/Northern Mesopotamia, with other examples of similar nielloed and enameled workmanship.

351.295 Milojcic, V.
Zu den spätkaiserzeitlichen und merowingischen Silberlöfflen. Berlin, 1970. 43 pp., 6 pls., 10 figs. Paper. $18.50
Listing of 138 silver spoons from known sites all over Europe.

675.638 Namur.
Orfèvreries du Trésor de la cathédrale de Namur. Brussels, 1969. 79 pp., num. illus. $9.50
History of the treasure in Namur, rich in early hardstone vessels and other regalia.

539.493 National Palace Museum.
Masterpieces of Chinese Seals in the National Palace Museum. Taipei, 1974. 27.5 x 22. 111 pp., 100 color pls. Slipcase. $36.00
One hundred Chinese seals are shown, in color, in three views: top, sealing surface and impression. A history of Chinese seals is included.

639.606 Negahban, E.O.
Metal Vessels from Marlik. (PBF, vol. X.3, 1983.). 120 pp., 52 pls. $55.00

264.223 Ninou, K., (Ed.). Archaeological Museum.
Treasures of Ancient Macedonia. Thessalonika, n.d. 110 pp., 25 color pls., 37 pls. Paper. $34.50
First exhibition catalogue of recent finds from the tomb of Philip II of Macedon, with many equally impressive objects added.

309.269 Painter, K.S. British Museum.
The Water Newton Early Christian Silver. London, 1977. 48 pp., 35 illus., 11 figs. Paper. $19.50
First publication of a major recent find of Late Antique silver objects.

396.351 Painter, K.S. British Museum.
The Mildenhall Treasure: Roman Silver from East Anglia. 79 pp., 36 illus., 14 figs. paper. $9.50
Well illustrated catalogue of an important 4th c. treasure.

653.621 Pechstein, K. Kunstgewerbemuseum.
Goldschmiedewerke der Renaissance. Berlin, 1971. 23 x 18.5. n.p., 8 color pls., num. illus. Paper. $28.50
Catalogue of 165 Renaissance objects, vessels, jewelry and small sculpture, all are illustrated.

677.640 Philippe, J.
Réliquaires Mediévaux de l'Orient Chrétien en Verre et en Cristal de Roche conservés en Belgique. Liege, 1975. 24 x 16. 45 pp., 21 figs. Paper. $16.50
Obscure publication shows important Mediaeval and Islamic rockcrystal and cut glass vessels preserved in church treasures. Parallels from other treasures are listed and illustrated.

638.605 Radwan, I.
Die Kupfer- und Bronzegefässe Ägyptens. (PBF, vol. X.2, 1983.). 180 pp., 90 pls. $75.00

399.354 Riha, E. and Stern, W.B.
Die römischen Löffel aus Augst und Kaiseraugst. Augst, 1982. 80 pp., 32 pls., map. Paper. $26.50
Wide ranging survey of Roman spoons from a dated context. See also our no. 351.295.

555.509 Ross, M.C.
Catalogue of the Byzantine and Early Mediaeval Antiquities in the Dumbarton Oaks Collection. I: Metalwork, Ceramics, Glass, Glyptics, Painting. Washington, D.C., 1962. 29 x 22. xv, 115 pp., 65 pls. $38.50
Illustrates, and carefully publishes, Byzantine and early Mediaeval silver objects, the engraved gems and engraved glass vessels and other small objects from the Dumbarton Oaks Collection.

451.405 Rossi, F.
Italian Jeweled Arts. London, 1957. 24 x 30.5. 233 pp., 93 color pls., 42 pls. 42 figs. $77.50
Describes and lavishly illustrates chalices, reliquaries, jewelry, vases, candelabra and altarpieces, all dating from the twelfth to the seventeenth century.

484.441 Rowe, D.F. The Martin D'Arcy Gallery of Art.
Enamels: the XII to the XVI century. Chicago, 1970. 19 x 26. 41 pp., 65 illus. 1 color pl. Paper. $9.50
Careful publication of 41 early enamels, all illustrated.

671.634 Scheffler, W.
Gemalte Goldschmiedearbeiten: Kostbare Gefässe auf den Dreikoenigs-bildern in den Niederlanden und in Deutschland 1400-1530. Berlin, 1985. xiv, 293 pp., 249 illus. $115.00
A systematic study of a hitherto neglected field; it treats 17 Flemish and 23 German paintings by well known artists and studies their representations of precious metal objects.

262.221 Segall, B.
Tradition und Neuschöpfung in der frühalexandrinischen Kleinkunst. (BWP, 119/120). Berlin, 1966. 63 pp., 22 figs. Paper. $52.50
Study of development of Hellenistic preciosa in various media.

263.222 Segall, B.
Zur Griechischen Goldschmiedekunst des vierten Jahrhunderts v. Chr. Wiesbaden, 1966. 24 x 31. viii, 51 pp., 47 pls., 3 figs. $48.50
Thorough examination of Classical Greek jewelry, superbly illustrated.

397.352 Shelton, K.J. British Museum.
The Esquiline Treasure. London, 1981. 104 pp., 48 pls., 30 figs. $95.00
In-depth analysis of this large and famous Roman hoard of silver plate, its history and relation to other treasures.

547.501 Sotheby's.
The Thomas F. Flannery Jr. Collection: Medieval and Later Works of Art.. London, 1983. 27 x 19. 291 pp., ca 400 illus., many in color. $36.00
Hardbound, single owner, auction sale catalogue, showing large collection of finger rings, Mediaeval and Renaissance jewels, gems and enamels, now dispersed. Very well illustrated with numerous color photographs.

13.330 Strong, D.E. British Museum.
Catalogue of the Carved Amber in the Department of Greek and Roman Antiquities. London, 1966. 28.5 x 22. 104 pp., 1 color pl., 43 pls., 2 maps. $32.50
Thorough discussion of many aspects of ancient amber objects.

400.355 Strong, D.E.
Greek and Roman Gold and Silver Plate. Ithaca, 1966. 16 x 24. 235 pp., 68 pls., 40 figs. $40.00
Basic book on shapes and styles of ancient metal vessels.

401.356 Svoboda, B. and Concev, D.
Neue Denkmäler antiker Toreutik. Prague, 1956. 21 x 31. 173 pp., 32 pls., 46 figs. $48.00
Contains: **Zur Geschichte des Rhytons**, and **Der Goldschatz von Panagjuriste**. Rare book describing gold and silver vessels from Eastern European site.

334.278 Tassinari, S.
La Vaisselle de bronze, romaine et provincale au Musée des Antiquités Nationales. (**Gallia**, Suppl. XXIX). Paris, 1975. 22 x 28. 84 pp., 40 pls. Paper. $11.50
Typology of metal vessels, ladles and strainers from Gaul.

402.357 Toynbee, J.M.C.
A Silver Casket and Strainer from the Walbrook Mithraeum in the City of London. (EPRO, 4, 1963). iv, 15 pp., 15 pls. Paper. $14.50

403.358 Vermeule, C.C.
A Silver Cup of the Augustan or Julio-Claudian Period. 5 pp., 4 pls., 9 figs. Paper. $4.50
First publication of an important repoussé cup.

388.342 Vermeule, C.C. Museum of Fine Arts.
Greek and Roman sculpture in gold and silver. Boston, 1974. ix, 43 pp., num. illus. Paper. $9.50
Catalogues and illustrates 111 figurines in precious metal, including known forgeries.

661.627 Wentzel, H.
Beiträge zur Kunst des Mittelalters. Festschrift für Hans Wentzel zum 60. Geburtsdag. Berlin, 1975. 16.5 x 23.5. viii, 268 pp., 150 pls. Paper. $55.00
"Festschrift" containing numerous specialized articles on Byzantine and Mediaeval glyptics, jewelry, ivories and allied fields. Recommended.

Renaissance and Later Jewelry

429.383 Abeler, J.
Kronen, Herschaftszeichen der Welt. Wuppertal, 1980. 15 x 21. 160 pp., 56 color pls., num. illus. $18.50
Well illustrated introduction to regalia from many cultures and periods.

650.618 Avitabile, G.G.
Chinesische und japanische Cloisonné- und Champlevé-Arbeiten von 1400 -1900. Munich, 1981. 21 x 24. 272 pp., 235 illus. incl. 59 color., 2 maps. $45.00
Oriental enameled vessels and tsubas, made during the last 500 years, are discussed, 179 objects are illustrated, many for the first time.

161.121 Babelon, E. Bibliothèque Nationale.
Les Pierres Gravées, Guide du Visiteur. Paris, 1930. 14 x 19. 155 pp., 32 pls.
$57.50
Illustrates 158 important gems from the French national collection.

404.359 Badcock, W.
A new Touchstone for Gold and Silver Wares. New York, 1971. 15 x 22. ca 300 pp., num. figs. $22.50
Photolithographic facsimile of the second London ed. of 1679, with a most useful new introduction by W. O'Sullivan, clarifying legal and technical aspects of 17th c. trade.

532.486 Born, G.M.
Chinese Jade: An Annotated Bibliography. Chicago, 1982. 15.5 x 24. 431 pp., 1 color pl. $25.00

109.642 Bott, G.
Sepp Schmölzer: Kunst im Schmuck. Klagenfurt, 1970. 31 x 23.5. 136 pp., 341 illus. $22.50
A modern German goldsmith shows his jewelry.

676.639
10 Artistes 200 Bijoux - 10 Artiesten 200 Juwelen. Brussels, 1976. 43 pp., illus.
$15.50
Modern Belgian goldsmiths show their recent work. Well illustrated.

450.404 Carroll, D.L. The Newark Museum.
European and American Jewelry of the Nineteenth Century. (The Museum, vol. 19, 1967). 24 pp., 22 illus. Paper. $6.50
Well illustrated survey!

498.453 Cellini, B.
The Treatises of Benvenuto Cellini on Goldsmithing and Sculpture. New York, 1967. 17 x 23.5. xv, 167 pp., num. illus. Paper. $9.50
Fascinating writings of Cellini; descriptions of his experiments with gold, enamel, silver and sculpture, his political insights and aesthetic beliefs. Recommended.

434.388 Chadour, A.B.
Antonio Gentili und der Altarsats von St. Peter. Münster, 1980. 330 pp., 132 pls. Paper. $45.00
Privately printed Ph.D. dissertation about the gems, materials used and iconography of the famous altar pieces in Rome and the artist who created them.

668.633 Chadour, A.B. and Joppien, R. Kunstgewerbemuseum.
Schmuck, Bestandskatalog des Kunstgewerbemuseums. Cologne, 1985. 2 vols. with num. illus., incl. color. $45.00
Major new museum catalogue with a lengthy introduction and 910 entries, especially strong in Ancient, Migration Period, Renaissance and 19th c. jewelry. A fine group of 355 rings is shown in two views each. Recommended!

431.385 Clasen, C.-W. Rheinische Landesmuseum.
Rheinische Goldschmiedekunst der Renaissance- und Barockzeit. Bonn, 1975. 14 x 21. 195 pp., 199 pls. Paper. $18.00
The catalogue of the gold- and silversmith's work in the Bonn museum.

612.561 Clifford, D.
Anne Clifford's Antique Jewellery: The Story of a Collection. London, 1985. 80 pp., 44 color pls. $36.00
A collection of, mostly, 18th and 19th c. paste- and gem-set jewelry.

432.386 Museen der Stadt Koeln.
Russische Schatzkunst aus dem Moskauer Kreml und der Leningrader Eremitage. Mainz, 1982. 21 x 23.5. 120 pp., 60 color pls. 98 illus. $18.00
17th c. and later objects in precious metals.

177.139 Dacos, N., (et al.). Museo Mediceo.
Il Tesoro di Lorenzo il Magnifico: Le Gemme. Catalogue della Mostra, Palazzo Medici Riccardi, Firenze, 1972. Florence, 1973. 24 x 17. vi, 167 pp., 15 color pls., 99 illus. Paper. $32.50
Contains descriptions of ancient and Neo-Classical gems and an important 15th century inventory.

178.140 Dacos, N., (et al.). Museo Mediceo.
Il Tesoro di Lorenzo il Magnifico, repertorio delle gemme e dei vasi. Florence, 1980. 17.5 x 25. 302 pp., 23 color pls., 208 illus. $45.00
Contains all of the above plus the 1974 catalogue of the hardstone vases and other carvings, now in a 2nd edition combined in one volume.

654.622 Danon, M.
Amulettes Sabbatiennes. (Asiatique, 1910.). 22.5 x 14. 10 pp., 3 illus. Paper. $6.50
The seal and amulets used by the 17th c. Kabbalistic leader Shabtai Zvi.

433.387 Denaro, V.
The Goldsmiths of Malta and their marks. Florence, 1972. 22 x 32. 248 pp., 61 illus. $58.50
Fascinating study of Medieval and Later jewelry; literary sources supplement information gleaned from the jewelry itself.

568.521 Hotel Drouot.
Collection de son excellence Le Bey Paul Adamidi Frasheri. Paris, 1971. 24 x 19. ca. 29 pp., 16 illus. Paper. $8.50
Early jewelry, icons, and enamels from the collection of the former ruler of Albania.

499.454 Egger, G.
Buergerlicher Schmuck: 15. - 20. Jahrhundert. Munich, 1984. 25 x 28. 224 pp., 52 color pls., 410 illus. $65.00
Interesting book shows the ordinary jewelry that common people used to wear. Emphasis is on the Italian Renaissance, Dutch 17th c. and the German speaking countries of the 19th c.

500.455 Evans, J.
Magical Jewels of the Middle Ages and Renaissance. New York, 1976. 13.5 x 21.5. 264 pp., 3 pls., indexes. Reprint of the 1922 ed. Paper. $9.50
Basic book on early Western lapidaries; includes extensive quotes from the original manuscripts.

618.657 Evans, J.
A History of Jewellery 1100 - 1870. Boston, 1970. 25.5 x 19. 224 pp., 204 pls. incl. 12 color., 35 figs. $165.00
A thorough survey of European antique jewelry by one of its leading experts. A basic text!

435.389 Falk, F.
Edelsteinschliff und Fassungsformen im späten Mittelalter und im 16. Jahrhundert. Ulm, 1975. 150 pp., 82 figs. $50.00
In-depth study of early Renaissance gem-cutting and mounting styles.

306.266 Falke, O. von
Sammlung Marc Rosenberg. Berlin, 1929. 21 x 28. 68 pp., 27 pls. Paper. $77.50
Illustrated auction catalogue of the sale which dispersed, in 350 lots, the personal collection of this scholar of jewelry. Scarce.

179.141 Förschner, G. Historisches Museum.
Glaspasten, Geschnittene Steine, Arabische Münzgewichte. Melsungen, 1982. 17 x 22. 111 pp., 7 color pls., num. illus. Paper. $18.50
Large and varied collection of interesting material in new publication.

280.238 Fontenay, E.
Les Bijoux Anciens et Modernes. Paris, 1887. 19.5 x 27.5. 520 pp., 700 illus. $160.00
Early, but still relevant, work on the history and technology of jewelry. Rare!

610.559 Gabardi, M.
I Gioielli Degli Anni Quaranta in Europa / Les Bijoux des Années Quarante en Europe / The Jewels of 1940's in Europe. Milan, 1984. 24.5 x 31. 141 pp., num. illus. incl. color. $42.50

307.267 Galasso, E.
Oreficeria medioevale in Campania. (Miniature e arte minori in Campania, 4).
Benevento, 1969. 30 x 21. 153 pp., 12 color pls., 25 pls. Paper. $18.50
Byzantine jewelry from South Italy.

389.343 Gallo, R.
Il Tesoro di S. Marco e la sua Storia. Venice, 1967. 18 x 25. xvi, 424 pp., 80 pls.
$45.00
Presentation of Venetian church treasure which contains Antique hardstone and glass vessels and gem-set objects.

217.180 Garside, A., (Ed.). Walters Art Gallery.
Jewelry, Ancient to Modern. Baltimore, 1979. 32 x 23. 256 pp., num. illus. incl. 116 color. $40.00
Scholarly catalogue, beautifully produced, of jewelry from all periods.

608.557 Gebhart, H.
Gemmen und Kameen. Berlin, 1925. 24 x 16. viii, 232 pp., 255 illus. $165.00
Excellent overview with a strong section on Post-Byzantine gems, the later artists and their signatures as they appear on gems. With 254 illustrations of individual stones.

537.491 Gerlach, M., (Ed.).
Primitive and Folk Jewelry. New York, 1971. 28 x 21. 218 pp., 109 pls. with 1900 illus. Paper. $11.50
Quality reprint of the 1906 edition of **Völkerschmuck**; still an excellent quick reference for ancient, ethnic and unusual jewelry with more than 1900 items illustrated.

681.660 Nuremberg. Germanisches National Museum.
Wenzel Jamnitzer und die Nuernberger Goldschmiedekunst 1500 - 1700. Nuremberg, 1985. 531 pp., num. color pls., num. illus. $28.50
Recent catalogue shows, in 800 catalogue entries, the work of the South German school of jewelry between 1500 - 1700.

508.463 Goldstein, S., (et al.).
Cameo Glass: Masterpieces from 2000 Years of Glassmaking. Corning, N.Y., 1982. 27.5 x 20. 140 pp., 158 illus. incl. many color. Paper. $18.50
Glass vessels and gems, Roman, Islamic, Oriental and Neo-Classical, all created by wheel cutting and other glyptic skills. Well catalogued and illustrated, with a glossary and bibliography.

534.488 Gonzales-Palacios, A., (et al.).
The Art of Mosaics: Selections from the Gilbert Collection. Los Angeles, 1982. 26 x 23. 224 pp., num. illus., incl. color. $36.00
An expanded version of our no. 447.401. It includes many new mosaics, an important essay on the history and technique of Roman mosaics, and a new section on Florentine "pietre dure" work. Numerous illustrations.

180.142 Gramatopol, M.
Les pierres gravées du Cabinet Numismatique de l'Académie Roumaine. (**Collection Latomus**, 138). Brussels, 1974. 130 pp., 47 pls. Paper. $32.50
Catalogues and illustrates 965 gems, mostly Roman and Later.

516.470 Grand Palais.
Le Trésor de Saint-Marc de Vénise. Paris, 1984. 23 x 26. 337 pp., num. pls., incl. color. Paper. $37.50
Superbly produced catalogue of a superb exhibition of major Antique hardstone vessels and related objects. Many additional treasures from the French national collections are added. Recommended! English version also available.

437.391 Hackenbroch, Y.
Exhibition of Renaissance Jewels selected from the Collection of Martin J. Desmoni. San Francisco, 1958. 22.5 x 30.5. 4 color pls., 16 B. & W. pls., 4 figs. Paper. $45.00
Privately printed exhibition catalogue of a large collection of Renaissance jewels and objects.

438.392 Hackenbroch, Y.
Renaissance Jewellery. Munich, 1979. 424 pp., 35 color pls., 927 B. & W. illus. $135.00
An impressive compendium of Renaissance jewelry. History, artists, and the development of iconography are discussed for each of the various schools that produced the jewelry.

563.516 Hackenbroch, Y. Metropolitan Museum of Art.
Commessi. (Bulletin, vol. XXIV, 1966). New York, 1966. 25 x 20.5. 12 pp., 29 illus. Paper. $12.50
Important article on commessi, the combination of carved gems with enamel and goldsmiths' work. The article describes all known examples. Scarce!

620.569 The Hague Municipal Museum.
Messen en Vorken in Nederland 1500 - 1800 / Knives and forks in the Netherlands 1500 - 1800. The Hague, 1972. 16 x 16. 24 pp., 24 illus. Paper. $8.50
Early knives and forks, illustrates many elaborate types and styles. Text in Dutch and English.

629.578 Hansmann, L. and Kriss-Rettenbeck, L.
Amulett und Talisman: Erscheinungsform und Geschichte. Munich, 1984. 20 x 21. 340 pp., 844 illus., 32 color pls. $42.50
New, enlarged, edition of the 1966 study of, mostly, European amulets and talismans. The superstitions that gave rise to their use are clarified; hundreds of amuletic pieces of jewelry are shown and interpreted.

598.550 von Hase, U.
Schmuck in Deutschland und Österreich 1895 - 1914. Munich, 1985. 430 pp., 64 color pls., 1000 illus., 120 figs. $78.50
Catalogues more than 900 pieces of jewelry made by 270 artists, shows their individual hallmarks.

391.345 Hayward, J.F.
Virtuoso Goldsmiths and the Triumph of Mannerism 1540-1620. New York, 1976. 25 x 32.5. 751 pp., 24 color pls., 740 illus. $150.00
Sumptuously produced book illustrates Renaissance jewelry and objects from all creating countries, identifies schools, artists.

375.319 Hejj-Detari, A.
Hungarian Jewellery of the Past. Budapest, n.d. 18 x 16.5. 60 pp., 8 color pls., 40 illus., 20 figs. $18.00
Antique and ethnic jewelry from Eastern Europe, well illustrated.

439.393 Heuser, H.J.
Oberrheinische Goldschmiedekunst im Hochmittelalter. Berlin, 1974. 21 x 28. 2 vols.: 249 pp., color pl., map.; and 1 color pl., 207 pls. $135.00

440.394 Holme, C., (Ed.).
Modern Design in Jewellery and Fans. (The Studio, 1902). London, 1902. 21 x 28.5. 41 pp., 16 color pls., 103 pls. $145.00
Scarce special issue of **The Studio**. Writing when the Art Nouveau Style was in full bloom, it discusses artists, workshops and developing trends. With many illustrations of Art Nouveau jewelry.

442.396 Kagan, J. Hermitage Museum.
Western European Cameos in the Hermitage Collection. Leningrad, 1973. 14 x 18. 96 pp., 103 color pls. $32.50
Attractive presentation of 13th c. and later cameos. Out-of-print.

640.607 Kahlert, H., (et al.).
Armbanduhren: 100 Jahre Entwicklungsgeschichte. Munich, 1984. 312 pp., 10 color pls., 1000 illus., num. figs. $48.50
Survey of stylish wrist watches; very well illustrated.

338.281 Koetzsche, D. Kunstgewerbemuseum.
Der Welfenschatz. Berlin, 1973. 18 x 23.5. 87 pp., 8 color pls., 75 illus. $18.50
Goldsmiths' work from the 11th-15th c.; many close-ups of technical details.

441.395 Kris, E.
Renaissance-Kleinkunst in Italien, Gefässe, Gemmen, Schmuckstücke und Skulpturen in Bergkristall und Edelstein. Leipzig, n.d. 23 x 28.5. 12 pp., 200 pls.
$245.00
Very scarce copy of this basic book on Italian Renaissance glyptics and hardstone objects in the round.

560.513 Lemaitre, J.-L., (Ed.). Musée du Pays d'Ussel.
Sceaux des Archives communales d'Ussel. Paris, 1982. 19 x 19. 63 pp., 21 illus., 1 color pl. Paper. $14.50
Shows detailed photographs of the wax seals in the Archives, all date from the 13th - 18th c.

430.384 Lesley, P. Baltimore Museum of Art.
Renaissance jewels and jeweled objects from the Melvin Gutman collection. Baltimore, 1968. 23 x 28.5. 194 pp., 5 color pls., num. illus. $28.50
Catalogues and illustrates 70 major pieces. Out-of-print.

156.116 Lippold, G.
Gemmen und Kameen des Altertums und der Neuzeit. Stuttgart, 1921. 23 x 30. xii, 190 pp., 167 pls. $185.00
Clearly illustrates and briefly identifies 1695 engraved gems. Scarce!

443.397
Catalogue des Joyaux Colliers de Perles, Joailleries, Perles & Brillants ... ayant composé l'écrin de la Princesse Lobanoff de Rostoff. Lausanne, 1920. 25 x 33. 75 pp., 29 pls. Paper. $240.00
Extremely scarce auction catalogue of a major collection of antique Russian jewelry, mostly pearls, important diamonds, colored stones.

501.456 Malle, L. Museo Civico di Torino.
Vetri - Vetrate - Giade - Cristalli di Rocca e Pietre Dure. Turin, 1971. 24 x 17. 384 pp., 218 pls., incl. 17 color. $36.00
Detailed collection catalogue of the early glass vessels and stained glass panels, also of jade and other hardstone carvings, oriental and occidental, in the Museo Civico.

278.236 Malle, L. Museo Civico di Torino.
Smalti - Avori del Museo D'Arte Antica. Turin, 1969. 24 x 17. 354 pp., 5 color pls., 239 illus. $32.50
An extensive catalogue containing European enamels from the 13th to the 19th c. bound together with a second one detailing ivory objects, reliquaries and jewelry from the late Roman to the early 19th c. Both are generously illustrated.

651.619 Marquardt, B.
Schmuck: Klassizismus und Biedermeier 1780 - 1850. Munich, 1983. 21.5 x 26. 332 pp., 712 illus., incl. 300 + color. $48.50
Antique jewelry of the 18th and 19th c. The costumes that dictated jewelry design are shown, the social background illuminated. 577 pieces are illustrated.

141.101 Menghin, W. Museo Nazionale del Borgello.
Gioielli Franchii della collezione Carrand. Florence, 1981. 22 pp., 1 color pl., 171 illus. Paper. $18.50
New publication of a good collection of early Mediaeval jewelry from Italy.

448.402 Muller, P.E.
Jewels in Spain 1500-1800. New York, 1972. 26 x 28.5. 195 pp., 16 color pls., 265 illus. $42.50
A documented account of the jewels, jewelers and their patrons from the reign of Ferdinand and Isabella through that of Charles IV.

502.457 Muller, H.
Jet Jewellery and Ornaments. Aylesbury, 1984. 21 x 15. 32 pp., 40 illus. Paper. $6.50
Chronicles the history and uses of jet from the Bronze Age to the present, emphasis of the illustrations is on 19th c. jewelry. Includes a chapter on tools, techniques and imitations.

551.505 Munn, G.
Castellani and Guiliano: Revivalist Jewellers of the 19th Century. New York, 1984. 25 x 26. 207 pp., 200 pls. 42 in color. $67.50
Most interesting and readable account of the leading 19th century jewelers, their sources of inspiration, clients and development. Illustrated with many pieces from private collections. Recommended!

584.536 Munn, G.
Castellani and Giuliano. Revivalist Jewellers of the Nineteenth Century.
London, 1984. 21 x 16. 28 pp., 14 color illus., 7 illus. Paper. $11.50
Privately printed catalogue of a loan exhibition to coincide with the publication of the book by the same title, (above), shows jewelry and supplies information not in the larger book.

449.403 Muthmann, F.
L'Argenterie hispano-sud-américaine à l'époque coloniale. Mainz, 1973. 20 x 27. 180 pp., 40 pls., 25 figs. Paper. $32.50
Handsome complement to our no. 448.402.

675.638 Namur.
Orfèvreries du Trésor de la cathédrale de Namur. Brussels, 1969. 79 pp., num. illus. $9.50
History of the treasure in Namur, rich in early hardstone vessels and other regalia.

422.376 Newman, H.
An illustrated Dictionary of Jewelry. London, 1981. 336 pp., 16 color pls., 685 illus. $29.50
Useful quick reference with 2500 entries.

554.508 Oman, C.C. Victoria and Albert Museum.
Catalogue of Rings. London, 1930. 24.5 x 18.5. xvi, 154 pp., 39 pls., index. Paper. $325.00
Classic catalogue of 992 rings with ca. 500 rings from ancient Egypt to the 19th c. illustrated. Original paper wrappers. Recommended!

653.621 Pechstein, K. Kunstgewerbemuseum.
Goldschmiedewerke der Renaissance. Berlin, 1971. 23 x 18.5. n.p., 8 color pls., num. illus. Paper. $28.50
Catalogue of 165 Renaissance objects, vessels, jewelry and small sculpture, all are illustrated.

503.458 Petochi, D., (et al.).
Mosaici Minuti Romani dei secoli XVIII e XIX. Rome, 1981. 25.5 x 27. 251 pp., 118 color pls., 5 figs. Includes a separate 24 page English summary. $75.00
Beautifully produced and well researched book on all aspects of Italian mosaics, profusely illustrated with datable examples.

423.377 Rawlings, R.D.
The Manufacture of Cut Steel Studs and Beads. (Journal of The Historical Metallurgy Society, vol. 12, 1978). 10 pp., 14 figs. Paper. $6.50
Technology of popular 18th and 19th century decorative element.

164.124 Reinach, S.
Pierres Gravées. Paris, 1895. 20 x 29. 195 pp., 138 pls. Paper. $245.00
Illustrates, on 137 engraved plates, 2,150 engraved gems from famous European collections; incorporates early research by Eckel, Gori, Levesque de Gravelle, Mariette, Millin and Stosch.

190.152 Righetti, R.
Gemme e cammei delle collezioni comunali. (Cataloghi dei musei comunali di Roma, 4). Rome, 1955. 115 pp., 20 pls. Paper. $13.50
Catalogues 276 gems, Roman and Neo-Classical, from three museums.

191.153 Righetti, R.
Opere di Glittica dei Museo Sacro e Profano. Vatican City, 1955. 52 pp., 17 pls. Paper. $16.50
Collectioin strong in Byzantine gems, some Roman and Neo-Classical.

451.405 Rossi, F.
Italian Jeweled Arts. London, 1957. 24 x 30.5. 233 pp., 93 color pls., 42 pls. 42 figs. $77.50
Describes and lavishly illustrates chalices, reliquaries, jewelry, vases, candelabra and altarpieces, all dating from the twelfth to the seventeenth century.

484.441 Rowe, D.F. The Martin D'Arcy Gallery of Art.
Enamels: the XII to the XVI century. Chicago, 1970. 19 x 26. 41 pp., 65 illus. 1 color pl. Paper. $9.50
Careful publication of 41 early enamels, all illustrated.

485.442 Rowe, D.F. The Martin D'Arcy Gallery of Art.
The Art of Jewelry 1450-1650. Chicago, 1975. 19 x 26. 72 pp., 88 illus. Paper. $9.50
Publishes 52 pieces of Renaissance jewelry, some set with engraved gems, all from private collections.

342.286 Sanidkidze, T. and Abrahamsvili, G. Musée d'Art et d'Histoire.
Orfèvrerie georgienne du VIIe au XIXe Siècle. Genèva, 1979. 17 x 24. n.p., 75 color pls. Paper. $18.00
Handsome exhibition catalogue with English, French and German text.

163.123 Scarisbrick, D.
The Wellington Gems. London, 1977. 23 x 15.5. 72 pp. Paper. $18.50
Together with: Scarisbrick, D., **Further Wellington Gems and Historic Rings.** London, 1978. 22 pp., 4 pls. Two privately printed handlists of a large and varied collection of ancient and later gems.

504.459 Scarisbrick, D.
Il Valore dei Gioielli e degli Orologi da Collezione / Antique Jewellery and Watch Values. Turin, 1984. 31 x 21. 287 pp., 336 illus., incl. 16 color pls. $65.00
A guide to recent auction prices of antique jewelry and watches, with a chapter on engraved gems. Also includes a fascinating section on the history of collecting and collectors from the Renaissance to the present.

671.634 Scheffler, W.
Gemalte Goldschmiedearbeiten: Kostbare Gefässe auf den Dreikoenigsbildern in den Niederlanden und in Deutschland 1400-1530. Berlin, 1985. xiv, 293 pp., 249 illus. $115.00
A systematic study of a hitherto neglected field; it treats 17 Flemish and 23 German paintings by well known artists and studies their representations of precious metal objects.

271.229 Shachar, I. The Israel Museum.
Jewish Tradition In Art: The Feuchtwanger Collection of Judaica. Jerusalem, 1981. 27.5 x 22. 341 pp., 16 color pls., num. illus. Paper. $45.00
Extensive catalogue of amuletic jewelry, seals and related objects illustrating the every day concerns of Jewish communities from Europe to Persia.

447.401 Sherman, A.C. Los Angeles County Museum of Art.
The Gilbert Mosaic Collection. Los Angeles, 1971. 30 x 30. 64 pp., num. color. pls. $24.50
Large collection of 19th Century mosaics, beautifully illustrated.

630.579 von Solodkoff, A.
Russische Goldschmiedekunst 17. - 19. Jahrhundert. Silber, Email, Niello. Golddosen, Schmuck. Munich, 1981. 25 x 28. 234 pp., 70 color pls., 175 illus.
$55.00

446.400 Somers Cocks, A. Victoria and Albert Museum.
Princely Magnificence: Court Jewels of the Renaissance, 1500-1630. London, 1980. 140 pp., num. color and B. & W. illus. Paper. $55.00
Technical, social and arthistorical background of surviving jewels and their representations in paintings.

505.460 Somers Cocks, A. and Truman, C.
Renaissance jewels, gold boxes and objets de vertu. (Catalogue of the Thyssen-Bornemisza Collection). London, 1984. 384 pp., 150 color pls., 200 illus.
$115.00
Important general discussion of Renaissance and later history of jewelry, as well as a careful catalogue of a major collection.

547.501 Sotheby's.
The Thomas F. Flannery Jr. Collection: Medieval and Later Works of Art.. London, 1983. 27 x 19. 291 pp., ca 400 illus., many in color. $36.00
Hardbound, single owner, auction sale catalogue, showing large collection of finger rings, medieval and Renaissance jewels, gems and enamels, now dispersed. Very well illustrated with numerous color photographs.

454.127 Story-Maskelyne, N.M.H.
Catalogue of the Marlborough Gems, being a collection of Works in Cameo and Intaglio, formed by George, 3rd Duke of Marlborough. London, 1899. 17 x 25.5. xix, 122 pp., 14 pls. Full leather binding. $450.00
Extremely scarce sale catalogue of the Marlborough Collection with a lenghty introduction by Story-Maskelyne; our copy includes prices realized written in the margins. A superbly bound copy in full red morocco with gold stamping and gilt top edge.

436.390 Sturm, F.X. and Winter-Jenson, A. Musée d'Art et d'Histoire.
Bijoux Art Nouveau.. Geneva, 1982. 17 x 24. 31 pp., 30 illus. Paper. $8.50
Well illustrated introduction to Art Nouveau jewelry.

444.398 Tait, H. and Gere, C. British Museum.
The Jeweller's Art. London, 1978. 23 pp., 16 color pls., 32 pls. Paper. $16.00
First publication of a recent large gift of 17th-19th c. jewelry. Out-of-print.

445.399 Tait, H., (Ed.). British Museum.
The Art of the Jeweller: A Catalogue of the Hull Grundy Gift to the British Museum of Jewellery, Engraved Gems and Goldsmiths' work. London, 1983. 27.5 x 22. 2 vols.: 208 pp.; and 372 pp., 116 color pls., 1400 B. & W. illus. 2 Vols., Cased. $245.00
Limited edition describing and illustrating nearly 1200 pieces of jewelry and engraved gems from the late 17th to the mid 20th Century. Recommended!

337.280 Topkapi Sarayi Muezesi.
Topkapi Sarayimuezesi Muhurler Seksiyonu Rehberi / Guidebook of the seals section of the Topkapi Saray Museum. Istanbul, 1959. 58 pp., 7 pls. Paper.
$22.50
Scarce book showing the various seals used by the Ottoman sultans and other officials.

162.122 Vermeule, C.C. The University Museum.
Cameo and Intaglio, Engraved Gems from the Sommerville Collection. Philadelphia, 1957. 15 x 21.5. 35 pp., 2 pls. Paper. $12.50
Exhibition catalogue of 650 gems of all periods.

452.406 Williamson, G.C.
Portrait Miniatures. London, 1910. 32 pp., 41 color pls., 15 pls. Original Paper Covers. $120.00
Scarce copy of **The Studio**, gives information about most of the important miniaturists of the time with data about their works.

298.258 Woeiriot, P.
Livre d'Anneaux d'Orfèvrerie. Oxford, 1978. Intr. by D. Scarisbrick. vii, 40 pls.
$15.00
Facsimile reprint of the Lyons ed. of 1561. Sumptuous engravings illustrating 16th c. rings.

481.438 Zazoff, P. and Zazoff, H.
Gemmensammler und Gemmenforscher. Munich, 1983. 24.5 x 16.5. 285 pp., 48 pls., 55 figs. $95.00
Companion volume to our no. 480.437. Fascinating and quite readable account of the history of gem collecting, early collectors and authors. Illustrated with numerous facsimile engravings of title pages, gems and portraits.

506.461 Zucker, B.
Gems and Jewels: A Connoisseur's Guide. New York, 1984. 28 x 23. 248 pp., 256 color illus., figs. $50.00
Most interesting survey of the history, origins and use of colored gemstones throughout history. Recommended!

Technology - Ancient Texts - Varia

497.452 Agricola, G.
De Re Metallica. New York, 1950. 28 x 17.5. 638 pp., 289 illus. Translated by H.C. Hoover and L.H. Hoover. $27.50
First published in 1556, this reprint contains all the original woodcuts; it describes and illustrates medieval mining and metallurgy technology and remained the standard work for more than 200 years. Text in English.

360.304 Allan, J.W.
Persian Metal technology 700-1300 AD. London, 1979. 16 x 24. 179 pp., 14 pls., 3 figs., 9 maps $37.50
Valuable study of early Islamic metallurgy with fascinating quotes from early texts. With glossaries of technical terms.

404.359 Badcock, W.
A new Touchstone for Gold and Silver Wares. New York, 1971. 15 x 22. ca 300 pp., num. figs. $22.50
Photolithographic facsimile of the second London ed. of 1679, with a most useful new introduction by W. O'Sullivan, clarifying legal and technical aspects of 17th c. trade.

649.617 Bahnassi, A.
Fabrication des Epées de Damas. (**Syria**, vol. LIII, 1976.). 28 x 22. 13 pp. Paper. $6.00
Research into modes of manufacture of "Damascus work", drawn chiefly from Mediaeval and later Arab authors.

512.467 Bateson, J.D.
Enamel-working in Iron Age, Roman and Sub-Roman Britain: The Products and Techniques. (**BAR**, 93, 1981). Oxford, 1981. 167 pp., 15 pls. Paper. $22.50
Comprehensive survey of the enameled objects from Britain from 200 BC - 700 AD. Millefiori enamels and their techniques are studied in detail.

532.486 Born, G.M.
Chinese Jade: An Annotated Bibliography. Chicago, 1982. 15.5. x 24. 431 pp., 1 color pl. $25.00

498.453 Cellini, B.
The Treatises of Benvenuto Cellini on Goldsmithing and Sculpture. New York, 1967. 17 x 23.5. xv, 167 pp., num. illus. Paper. $9.50
Fascinating writings of Cellini; descriptions of his experiments with gold, enamel, silver and sculpture, his political insights and aesthetic beliefs. Recommended.

239.201 Chandra, R.G.
Indo-Greek Jewellery. New Delhi, 1979. 136 pp., 25 pls. $32.50
Most interesting study on unfamiliar aspects of ancient Greek jewelry, includes chapter on technology.

405.360 Contenau, G.
L'Incrustation sur Métal et l'Orfèvrerie Cloisonnée en Mésopotamie. (Syria, vol. XXXIII, 1965). 5 pp., Paper. $4.50

406.361 Craddock, P.T., (Ed.)
Scientific Studies in Early Mining and Extractive Metallurgy. (BM, OP, 20). London, 1980. 173 pp., num. illus. Paper. $13.50

483.440 Cristofani, M. and Martelli, M.
L'Oro degli Etruschi. Novara, 1983. 23 x 31. 343 pp., 310 color illus., 17 figs. Slipcase. $110.00
Superbly illustrated publication shows the full range and splendor of Etruscan gold and bead jewelry, some set with gems, of all periods. Includes a separate section on technique. Likely to become a standard reference!

407.362 Dayton, J.
Minerals, Metals, Glazing and Man, or who was Sesostris I. London, 1978. 496 pp., 32 color pls., 393 illus. $85.00
Often controversial but fascinating book, discussing ancient technology and its effect on ancient history.

644.612 Duczko, W.
The Filigree and Granulation Work of the Viking Period. (Birka V). Uppsala, 1985. 118 pp., num. illus., num. figs. $32.50
Dissertation investigating 86 pieces of jewelry of the Middle Viking Period. A discussion of the antecedents, of the techniques and of the place of the objects in larger European context are included.

500.455 Evans, J.
Magical Jewels of the Middle Ages and Renaissance. New York, 1976. 13.5 x 21.5. 264 pp., 3 pls., indexes. Reprint of the 1922 ed. Paper. $9.50
Basic book on early Western lapidaries; includes extensive quotes from the original manuscripts.

408.363 Forbes, R.J.
Studies in ancient technology. VIII: Metallurgy in Antiquity. part 1: Early Metallurgy, the smith and his tools, gold, silver and lead, zinc and brass. Leiden, 1971. x, 295 pp., 45 figs., tables, maps. $58.50
Other volumes also available, please write for details.

409.364 Friess, G.
Edelsteine im Mittelalter; Wandel und Kontinuitaet in Ihrer Bedeutung durch zwoelf Jahrhunderte. (in Aberglauben, Medizin, Theologie und Goldschmiedkunst). Hildesheim, 1980. 206 pp.
Title information just received, price not certain yet, order now accepted, will quote before shipment.

414.369 Galerie Koller.
Collection d'Orfèvrerie Antique Moyen-Orient, Antiquité Classique, Époque Byzantine. Zurich, 1982. 21 x 29.5. 67 pp., 23 color illus., 70 illus. Paper. $27.50
Scarce catalogue of a fascinating recent auction of, mostly fake, "ancient" jewelry and gems.

464.424 Gorelick, L. and Williams-Forte, E.
Ancient Seals and the Bible. Malibu, 1983. 21 x 27.5. 63 pp., 12 pls., 20 figs. Paper. $18.50
Six lengthy articles by six different authors dealing with Hebrew seals, seal manufacture, seal lore and iconography.

465.425 Gorelick, L. and Gwinnett, A.J.
Close work without Magnifying Lenses? (**Expedition**, vol. 23, 1981). 8 pp., 10 illus. Paper. $7.50
Fascinating account of gem cutters lack of need for magnifying glasses; myopia, increased through hereditary factors, may have sufficed. See also our no. 467.427.

466.426 Gorelick, L. and Gwinnett, A.J.
Ancient Seals and Modern Science. (**Expedition**, vol 20, 1978). 9 pp., 12 illus. Paper. $5.50
Using the scanning electron microscope as an aid in the study of ancient seals.

467.427 Gorelick, L. and Gwinnett, A.J.
Close work without Magnifying Lenses? (**Expedition**, vol. 23, 1981). 2 pp., 2 illus. Paper. $5.50
Follow-up article to our no. 465.425, above. This issue of **Expedition** contains five related articles.

468.427 Gorelick, L.
The Origin and Development of the Ancient Near Eastern Cylinder Seal. (**Expedition**, vol. 23, 1981). 14 pp., 15 illus. Paper. $5.50
Plausible speculation on the development of cylinder seals out of early bead shapes and technologies.

574.527 Gorelick, L. and Gwinnett, A.J.
Beadmaking in Iran in the Early Bronze Age. (**Expedition**, vol. 24, 1981). 14 pp., 29 illus. Paper. $5.50
Fascinating study of the earliest technologies employed to create stone beads; includes many detailed scanning electron microscope photographs showing actual processes used. Equally applicable to the manufacture of early seals.

656.624 Gorelick, L. and Gwinnett, A.J.
Ancient Egyptian Stone-Drilling. (**Expedition**, vol. 25, 1983.). 7 pp., 9 illus. Paper. $5.50
Interesting speculation on abrasives used by the Egyptians, the tool marks that testify to their use, and their possible use as an aid in the detection of forgeries.

473.431 Graham, K.
Scientific Notes on the Finds from Ur. (**The Museum Journal**, 1929). 17 x 27.5. 12 pp., 8 illus. Paper. $5.50
Technical information about the cleaning of the silver objects and jewelry found in Ur. This issue of **The Museum Journal** contains two additional articles of related interest.

267.226 Guarducci, M.
La Cosidetta Fibula Prenestina Antiquari, Eruditi e Falsari nella Roma dell'Ottocento. (**Atti della Accademia Nazionale dei Lincei**, vol. XXIV, 1980.). 162 pp., 5 color pls., 6 pls., 9 figs. Paper. $38.50
Most fascinating study proving the famous Etruscan fibula to be a forgery!

585.537 Guebelin, E.
Internal World of Gemstones. 23.5 x 28. 236 pp., 360 illus, mostly color.
$95.00
Fascinating research into the origin of inclusions in gemstones, a valuable aid in the study of ancient trade routes. See also our no. 647.615

469.428 Gwinnett, A.J. and Gorelick, L.
Ancient Lapidary. (**Expedition**, vol. 22, 1979). 15 pp., 30 illus. Paper. $5.50
Most interesting article describes, and illustrates with scanning micrographs, ancient drilling techniques and materials.

247.206 Hackens, T., (Ed.).
Studies in Ancient Jewelry. (**Aurifex**, I.). Louvain, 1980. 154 pp., num. color pls., num. illus. $48.50
Contains six lengthy articles on ancient jewelry and technology, incl. four articles on various aspects of Greek toreutics.

248.207 Hackens, T. and Winkes, R., (Eds.).
Gold Jewelry: Craft, Style and Meaning from Mycenae to Constantinopolis. (**Aurifex**, V.). Louvain, 1983. 17.5 x 26. 227 pp., num. illus., incl. 21 color.
$36.00
Descriptive catalogue of 46 items, with 40 page section on Greek jewelry and photographs showing technical details.

410.365 Hager, B.
Der Stempelschmied. Basel, 1974. 16 x 24. 24 pp., 21 illus. Paper. $14.50
Step-by-step account of a professional die cutter at work, with clear illustrations of tools and techniques.

635.583 Hahnloser, H. and Brugger, S.
Corpus der Hartsteinschliffe des XII. - XV. Jahrhunderts. Berlin, 1985. 21 x 27.5. 256 pp., 32 color pls., 464 pls., 29 figs. $145.00
A corpus of early European hardstone vessels, secular and religious. Includes sections on technique, materials, objects now lost but known from the literature, guilds, etc. Profusely illustrated.

629.578 Hansmann, L. and Kriss-Rettenbeck, L.
Amulett und Talisman: Erscheinungsform und Geschichte. Munich, 1984. 20 x 21. 340 pp., 844 illus., 32 color pls. $42.50
New, enlarged, edition of the 1966 study of, mostly, European amulets and talismans. The superstitions that gave rise to their use are clarified; hundreds of amuletic pieces of jewelry are shown and interpreted.

358.302 Harper, P.O. and Meyers, P. Metropolitan Museum of Art.
Silver Vessels of the Sasanian period. I: Royal Imagery. New York, 1981. 272 pp., 7 color pls., 128 pls., 2 maps. $48.50
Presents a detailed examination of the history, iconography and mode of manufacture of the vessels in the Museum.

665.631 Hartmann, A.
Prähistorische Goldfunde aus Europa: Spektralanalytische Untersuchungen und deren Auswertung. (Studien zu den Anfängen der Metallurgie, vol. III.). Berlin, 1970. 129 pp., 3 pls., 59 illus. $87.50

333.277 Hartmann, A.
Prähistorische Goldfunde aus Europa II: Spektralanalytische Untersuchengen und deren Auswertung. (Studien zu den Anfängen der Metallurgie, vol. V.). Berlin, 1983. 21 x 30. 112 pp., 115 pls., 5 maps. $125.00
Shows pre-historic jewelry and trade routes, mostly in Iberia, France, and Denmark.

411.366 Healy, J.F.
Mining and Metallurgy in the Greek and Roman World. London, 1978. 316 pp., 73 pls., 28 figs., 2 maps. $32.50
All aspects of early mining technology are explored: authors, physical evidence, extant metal remains. Usage of metal in Greek and Roman life is discussed. Detailed maps of metal producing areas are included.

517.471 Hebing, C.
Vergolden und Bronzieren: Untergrund · Arbeitstechniken · Werkstoffe. Ein Handbuch für die Praxis. Munich, 1983. 17 x 24. 120 pp., 13 color pls., 67 pls. Paper. $21.50
Everything one would want to know about gold- and bronze plating.

273.231 Hellenkemper, H., (Ed.). Musées d'Histoire.
Trésors romains-Trésors barbares: Industrie d'art à la fin de l'Antiquité et au début du Moyen Age. Brussels, 1979. 13 x 20. 163 pp., 48 pls. incl. 16 color. Paper. $12.50
Jewelry and related precious objects are carefully described, dated and illustrated. Includes section on technology.

678.641 Hendy, M.F.
Studies in the Byzantine Monetary Economy C. 300 - 1450. Cambridge, 1985. 773 pp., 36 pls., 39 maps, tables. $150.00
Extremely thorough study of the economy of the Byzantine Empire, with a wealth of information about trade, both internal and with its neighbors, ratios of gold and silver, values of other commodities, professional associations. Recommended.

124.84 Hoffmann, H. and von Claer, V. Museum für Kunst und Gewerbe Hamburg.
Antiker Gold- und Silberschmuck; Katalog mit Untersuchung der Objekte auf technischer Grundlage. Mainz, 1968. 23.5. x 19. x, 246 pp., num. illus. $38.50
Catalogues and illustrates 137 pieces of ancient jewelry. Includes a thorough section on technology with many close-up photographs.

238.200 Hoffmann, H. and Davidson, P.F. The Brooklyn Museum.
Greek Gold, Jewelry from the Age of Alexander. Brooklyn, 1965. xi, 311 pp., 8 color pls., 138 illus. Paper. $40.00
Significant catalogue surveying both the technology and the iconography of Early Hellenistic jewelry.

412.367 Hugger, P. and Mutz, A.
Der Ziseleur. Basel, 1976. 16 x 24. 32 pp., 20 illus. Paper. $14.50
Step-by-step account of chasing and repousse work with clear illustrations of tools and techniques employed.

393.348 Ippel, A.
Guss- und Treibarbeit in Silber. (**BWP**, 97.). Berlin, 1937. 58 pp., 5 pls., 31 figs. Paper. $28.50
Inquiry into the technology of raised decorations on ancient silver vessels.

413.368 Jazdewski, K., (Ed.).
Glossarium Archaeologicum. Warsaw, 1965. $35.00
Fasc. 24, 25, 26. **Fibula, (Construction I-II)**, and **Two Piece Fibula**. Three portfolios detailing construction and stylistical points in 23 languages.

664.630 Junghans, S., (et al.).
Metallanalysen kupferzeitlicher und frühbronzezeitlicher Bodenfunde aus Europa. (**Studien zu den Anfängen der Metallurgie**, vol. I.). Berlin, 1960. 220 pp., 37 pls. $67.50

672.635 Junghans, S., (et al.).
Kupfer und Bronze in der frühen Metallzeit Europas. (**Studien zu den Anfängen der Metallurgie**, vol. II.). Berlin, 1968. 490 pp., 65 pls., 17 tables., 81 maps.
$225.00
The text is based on 12,000 analyses of early metal objects, all carefully catalogued. Includes 81 maps showing distribution patterns all over Europe.

673.636 Junghans, S., (et al.).
Kupfer und Bronze in der frühen Metallzeit Europas. (**Studien zu den Anfängen der Metallurgie**, vol. II.). Berlin, 1974. 408 pp. $140.00
Sequel to the above, with a catalogue of 10,000 additional analyses.

575.527 Keene, M.
The Lapidary Arts in Islam. (**Expedition**, vol. 24. 1981). 15 pp., 23 illus. Paper.
$5.50
Cutting techniques as gleaned from the gems and beads of the Mediaeval Islamic period.

535.489 Kunz, G.F.
The Curious Lore of Precious Stones. New York, 1971. 21.5 x 14. xiv. 406 pp., 5 color pls., 87 illus. Reprint of the 1913 ed. Paper. $7.00
A veritable mine of information - some controversial - facts, lore, etc., about all aspects of gems, amulets, religious use of gems, planetary "influences" on stones, crystal balls, more.

662.628 Lagercrantz, O.
Papyrus Graecus Holmiensis (P. Holm.): Recepte Fuer Silber, Steine und Purpur. Uppsala, 1913. 25.5 x16.5. 247 pp., 1 pl. Paper. $32.50
Fascinating late 3rd-Early 4th c. papyrus from Thebes (?), containing numerous recipes for metal alloys, dyes and precious stones, Text in Greek and German.

579.531 Laufer, B.
Jade: A Study in Chinese Archaeology and Religion. New York, 1974. 21 x 13.5. 370 pp., 68 pls., 204 figs. Paper. $9.50
Unabridged reprint of the 1912 edition, still one of the best general books introducing archaic and later jade carvings, their meaning and use.

557.510 Legrain, L.
Nippur's Gold Treasure. (The Museum Journal, 1920). 17 x 25.5. 7 pp., 1 fig. Paper. $5.50
Translation and background of an inscribed cuneiform tablet which contains a catalogue of 125 jewels and seals dating from the 14th c. BC.

560.513 Lemaitre, J.-L., (Ed.). Musée du pays d'Ussel.
Sceaux des Archives communales d'Ussel. Paris, 1982. 19 x 19. 63 pp., 21 illus., 1 color pl. Paper. $14.50
Shows detailed photographs of the wax seals in the Archives, all date from the 13th - 18th c.

415.370 Lipinsky, A.
Oro, Argento, Gemme e Smalti. Florence, 1975. 514 pp., num. illus, B. & W. and color. $95.00
Extensive study of technology in use from 3000 BC - 1500 AD

475.427 Loding, D.
Lapidaries in the Ur III Period, Written Sources Concerning Stoneworkers, (ca. 2000 B.C.). (Expedition, vol. 23, 1981). 9 pp., 9 illus. Paper. $5.50
Textual information about ancient Near Eastern lapidaries. This issue of **Expedition** contains five related articles.

167.129 Maaskant-Kleibrink, M. Royal Coin Cabinet.
Catalogue of the Engraved Gems in the Royal Coin Cabinet. The Hague, 1978. 2 vols.: 380 pp., 37 figs.; and 189 pls. $225.00
Major research into the technology of glyptic arts applied to a collection of 1172 gems, particularly strong in Roman gems. All are illustrated, with many technical details enlarged.

416.371 McDonald, D. and Hunt, L.B.
A History of Platinum and its Allied Metals. London, 1983. 450 pp., 20 color pls., 215 illus. $42.50
Most interesting book about all aspects of platinum and related metals: history, mining, fabrication and applications.

633.582 Merrill, G.
Handbook and Descriptive Catalogue of the Collections of Gems and Precious Stones in the United States National Museum. (**Bulletin**, 118). Washington, 1922. 24.5 x 15. viii, 225 pp., 14 pls., incl. 2 color pls., 26 figs. Paper. $48.50
The collection of gems and minerals in the Smithonian Institution, Washington. Characteristics of each mineral are given, provenances noted, illustrations supplied where helpful. Includes appendices on lore, gem cutting, etc.

502.457 Muller, H.
Jet Jewellery and Ornaments. Aylesbury, 1984. 21 x 15. 32 pp., 40 illus. Paper. $6.50
Chronicles the history and uses of jet from the Bronze Age to the present, emphasis of the illustrations is on 19th c. jewelry. Includes a chapter on tools, techniques and imitations.

422.376 Newman, H.
An illustrated Dictionary of Jewelry. London, 1981. 336 pp., 16 color pls., 685 illus. $29.50
Useful quick reference with 2500 entrees.

417.372 Oddy, W.A. and Zwalf, W., (Eds.).
Aspects of Tibetan Metallurgy. (**BM**, OP, 15). London, 1981. 21 x 30. 137 pp., 121 illus. Paper. $35.00
Alloys, traditional techniques and tools employed are investigated and carefully tabulated.

418.373 Ogden, J.M.
Platinum Group metal inclusions in Ancient Gold Artifacts. (**Journal of the Historical Metallurgy Society**, vol. 11, 1977). 19 pp., 11 figs., 4 tables. Paper. $7.50

419.374 Ogden, J.M.
Jewellery of the Ancient World: The Materials and Techniques. London, 1982. 25 x 26. 32 color pls., ca. 200 illus. $62.50
Eagerly awaited study of ancient jewelry, with emphasis on technology, detection of forgeries and gradual development of craftsmanship Recommended.

493.656 Onassoglu, A.
Die "Talismanischen" Siegel. (**CMS**, Beiheft II.). Berlin, 1985. 308 pp., 38 pls., 20 figs., fold-out table. $105.00
Attempt to classify the gems of the MM III - LM IB according to their general iconography; includes a chapter on cutting technique.

420.375 Pliny, G.
Natural History. (**Loeb Ed.**, vols. XXXIII-XXXV). Cambridge, 1968. 11 x 17. 421 pp. $14.00
One of two volumes giving Pliny's observations about gems, jewelry and related matters. Text in Latin with English translation on facing pages. Other volumes available upon request @ $14.00.

421.346 Pliny, G.
Natural History. (Loeb Ed., vols. XXXVI- XXXVII). Cambridge, 1971. 11 x 17. 344 pp. $14.00
One of two volumes giving Pliny's observations about gems, jewelry and related matters. See also no. 420.375 (previous listing).

658.427 Possehl, G.
Cambay Beadmaking. (Expedition, vol. 23, 1981.). 8 pp., 12 illus. Paper. $5.50
Modern survival of ancient bead making techniques in India, all stages are illustrated and explained.

423.377 Rawlings, R.D.
The Manufacture of Cut Steel Studs and Beads. (Journal of The Historical Metallurgy Society, vol. 12, 1978). 10 pp., 14 figs. Paper. $6.50
Technology of popular 18th and 19th century decorative element.

425.379 Roesslin, E., The Younger.
Ars Medica, On Minerals and Mineral Products; Chapters on Minerals from his "Kruetterbuech". New York, 1978. Belkin, J.S. and Caley, E.R., (Eds.). 418 pp. $165.00
Critical text, English translation and detailed commentary of this fascinating early 16th century Herbal, much information on gemstones, mineralogy and late medieval chemistry.

424.378 Rosenberg, M.
Geschichte der Goldschmiedekunst auf technischer Grundlage: I: Einfeührung, II: Granulation, III: Zellenschmelz, IV: Zellenschmelz, V; Niello bis zum Jahre 1000 n. Chr., VI: Niello seit dem Jahre 1000 n. Chr. 24.5 x 34.5. 658 pp., 7 color pls., 830 figs. $275.00
Reprint of the 1 - 2 edition of 1910 - 1915. The six volumes of the previous editions are now bound together, but still contain all of the original text and illustrations of this seminal work. Recommended!

518.472 Rothenberg, B. and Blanco-Freijeiro, A.
Studies in Ancient Mining and Metallurgy in South-West Spain. London, 1981. 22 x 28.5. 320 pp., 298 illus., maps. $38.50
Major survey, by the Institute for Archaeo-Metallurgical Studies, of mining technology from the Early Chalcolithic to Late Roman periods in the Huelva Province of South-West Spain.

487.444 Ruxer, M.S. and Kubczak, J.
Naszyjnik Grecki w Okresach Hellenistycznym i Rzymskim / Greek Necklace of the Hellenistic and Roman Ages. Warsaw, 1972. 17 x 24. 271 pp., 6 color pls., 74 pls., 32 figs. Paper. $110.00
Describes the differences in conception and construction between the necklaces of the Greek and Roman periods; illustrated with many examples from obscure or lost collections. Rare!

426.380 Sadek, A.I.
The Amethyst Mining Inscriptions of Wadi El-Hudi. I: text. London, 1981. 128 pp. Paper. $42.50
Middle Kingdom mining and its technology is elucidated by inscriptions recorded in this ancient mining center.

707.686 Sadek, A.I.
The Amethyst Mining Inscriptions of Wadi el-Hudi, vol. II. Warminster, 1985. 21.5 x 30. 100 pp., and pls. Paper. $18.50
First publication of three important new inscriptions, together with photographs of all other texts given in volume one, our no. 426.380, above.

504.459 Scarisbrick, D.
Il Valore dei Gioielli e degli Orologi da Collezione / Antique Jewellery and Watch Values. Turin, 1984. 31 x 21. 287 pp., 336 illus., incl. 16 color pls. $65.00
A guide to recent auction prices of antique jewelry and watches, with a chapter on engraved gems. Also includes a fascinating section on the history of collecting and collectors from the Renaissance to the present.

427.381 Sinkankas, J.
Emerald and other Beryls. Radnor, 1981. 18.5 x 24. 665 pp., 24 color pls., num. figs., maps. $44.50
Exhaustive portrait of all aspects of Beryls, including history, lore, physical properties, usage.

519.473 Tardy.
Les Poinçons de Garantie Internationaux pour l'Or, le Platine et le Palladium. Paris, 1981. 13 x 16.5. 418 pp. Paper. $19.50
Indispensible quick reference for hallmarks in precious metal, the new 11th edition is illustrated with thousands of enlarged hallmarks arranged by country.

520.474 Tardy.
International Hallmarks on Silver. Paris, 1981. 13 x 16.5. 550 pp., 12 pls. Paper. $22.50
Companion to above, English text.

577.529 Tosi, M., and Piperno, M.
Lithic Technology behind the Ancient Lapis Lazuli Trade. (Expedition, vol. 16, 1973). 9 pp., 14 illus., map. Paper. $6.50
Discusses finds from Shahr-i Sokta, Afghanistan, dating to 3000-2000 BC., which illustrates the techniques and tools used to make beads and seals.

674.637 Van Dievoet, W.
De geschiedenis en de officiele merken van de keurkamers voor de waarborg van goud en zilver in Belgie van 1794 tot nu. Brussels, 1980. 307 pp., illus.
$18.50
The official hall marks in gold and silver and their history in Belgium from 1794 to the present.

643.611 Webster, L., (Ed.). British Museum.
Aspects of Production and Style in Dark Age Metalwork: Selected papers given to the British Museum Seminar on Jewellery AD 500-600. (OP, 34). London, 1982. 29.5 x 21. iv, 50 pp., 20 pls., 2 tables. Paper. $18.50

647.615 Weibel, M. and Guebelin, E.
Edelsteine und ihre Mineraleinschluesse. Zurich, 1984. 21.5 x 24.5. 112 pp., 106 illus., incl. 83 color. $36.00
See also our no. 585.537.

428,382 Wolters, J.
Die Granulation: Geschichte und Technik einer alten Goldschmiedekunst. Munich, 1983. 332 pp., 28 color pls., 371 pls., 47 figs., maps. $115.00
Major research into every aspect of granulation from 2600 BC to the present day, more than 1200 examples are studied. Recommended!

689.668 Wolters, J.
Der Gold- und Silberschmied: Werkstoffe und Materialien. Stuttgart, 1984. 23 x 16. 312 pp., 247 illus., 42 tables. $28.50
A thorough handbook for the modern gold- and silversmith, describes workshop practices, tools, alloys, metals and other materials used in a well-equipped jeweller's studio.

657.427 Younger, J.G.
Creating A Sealstone. (**Expedition**, vol. 23, 1981.). 8 pp., 23 illus. Paper.
$5.50
Study showing the tools and techniques used to create Minoan and Mycenaean seals; evidence includes unfinished seals and tool marks.

481.438 Zazoff, P. and Zazoff, H.
Gemmensammler und Gemmenforscher. Munich, 1983. 24.5 x 16.5. 285 pp., 48 pls., 55 figs. $95.00
Companion volume to our no. 480.437. Fascinating and quite readable account of the history of gem collecting, early collectors and authors. Illustrated with numerous facsimile engravings of title pages, gems and portraits.

506.461 Zucker, B.
Gems and Jewels: A Connoisseur's Guide. New York, 1984. 28 x 23. 248 pp., 256 color illus., figs. $50.00
Most interesting survey of the history, origins and use of colored gemstones throughout history. Recommended!

INDEX OF AUTHORS

Abeler, J. 80, 120
Abrahamian, V.A. 57
Abrahamsvili, G. 99
Acquaro, E. 14
Agricola, G. 139
Akishev, K. 57
Al-Jadir, S. 102
Alborino, V. 85
Aldred, C. 55
Alexander, K. 62
Allan, J.W. 102
Amandry, P. 21, 62
Amiet, P. 3, 14, 57, 101
Andrews, C.A.R. 55
Arnaud, D. 57
Arthaud, G. 4
Audouze, F. 90
Avent, R. 94
Avigad, N. 14
Avitabile, G.G. 118

Babelon, E. 26
Badcock, W. 128
Bader, T. 90
Bahnassi, A. 102
Baratte, F. 72, 118
Barge, H. 90
Barnett, R.D. 4, 118
Barrelet, M.-T. 4
Bateson, J.D. 72
Battaglia, G.B. 21
Battke, H. 80
Beck, H. 113
Beckmann, B. 72
Beckmann, C. 72
Behrmann, I. 106
Beran, T. 4
Berge, L. 62
Berry, B.Y. 38
Betts, J.H. 21
Betzler, P. 90
Bielefeld, E. 21
Biggs, R.D. 7
Billiet, J. 4
Bittel, K. 4
Bivar, A.D.H. 46
Blanco-Freijeiro, A. 147
Blankenberg-Van Delden, C. 19

Blinkenberg, C. 57
Boardman, J. 14, 27
Boehmer, R.M. 4
Bordreuil, P. 14
Borisov, A.Y. 46
Born, G.M. 128
Bossier, A. 4
Bott, G. 128
Bouras, L. 85
Brandes, M.A. 4
Brandt, E. 21, 26
Breglia, L. 63
Bréhier, L. 85
Brentjes, B. 5
Brijbhusan, J. 106
Brown, D. 112
Brown, K.R. 73
Bruce-Mitford, R. 94, 95
Brugger, S. 97
Brunner, C.J. 46
Bruns, G. 38
Buchanan, B. 5
Bucherer-Dietschi, P. 106
Budd, D. 86
Buehler, H.-P. 38
Buhl, M.-L. 5

Callmer, J. 95
Caner, E. 58
Carancini, G.L. 90
Carroll, D.L. 128
Casanova, P. 102
Caskey, J.L. 21
Catling, H.W. 21
Cellini, B. 128
Chadour, A.B. 51, 63
Chandon de Briailles. 49
Chandra, R.G. 58, 63
Chieco Bianchi, A.M. 69
Chiesa, G.S. 38
Cintas, P. 15
Clarke, J.R. 95
Clasen, C.-W. 129
Clifford, D. 129
Coarelli, F. 63
Coche de la Ferté, É. 63, 73
Collon, D. 5
Concev, D. 68

Contenau, G 6, 58
Cosack, E. 74
Cote, C. 28
Courtois, J.C. 90
Craddock, P.T. 140
Cristofani, M. 34
Cruikshank Dodd, E. 86
Culican, W. 58
Cumont, F. 38
Curiel, R. 47

Dacos, N. 39
Danon, M. 129
Davidson, P.F. 63, 65
Dayagi-Mendels, M. 16
Dayton, J. 140
De Clercq-Fobe, D. 58
De Juliis, M. 28
De Mecquenem, R. 10
De Morgan, J. 55
De Ricci, S. 82
De Ridder, A. 15
De Serres, J.-P. 17
De Zeltner, F. 111
Delange-Bazin, E. 55
Delaporte, L. 6
Delatte, A. 39
Delivorrias, A. 107
Deloche, M. 81
Denaro, V. 129
Dennison, W.A. 74
Densmore Curtis, C. 15
Deonna, W. 39
Deppert-Lippitz, B. 64
Derchain, P. 39
Deshayes, J. 6
Diehl, C. 86
Digard, F. 6
Dimitrova-Milcheva, A. 39
Dolfus, M. 95
Duczko, W. 95
Dumas, F. 95
Dusenberry, E.B. 64
Dusenbury, E. 86
Duvail, A. 90

Ebersolt, J. 86
Effenterre, H. and M. 21
Egger, G. 51
Eichler, F. 39

Eleure, C. 91
Ergil, T. 64
Evans, J. 51, 130

Falk, F. 130
Farabee, W.C. 107
Firouz, I.A. 107
Fisher, A. 107
Foerschner, G. 40
Fontenay, E. 74
Forber, B.A. 34
Forbes, R.J. 140
François, G. 96
Frankfort, H. 6
Fremersdorf, F. 40
Friess, G. 140
Frye, R.N. 46
Furlani, G. 6
Furmanek, V. 91
Furtwaengler, A. 15

Gabardi, M. 130
Gagochidze, J. 64
Galasso, E. 87
Galerie Charpentier 85, 107
Galerie Koller 140
Gallo, R. 52
Garam, E. 96
Garside, A. 55
Gauthier, M.-M. 96
Gebhart, H. 28
Gedl, M. 91
Gehrig, U. 120
Genouillac, H. 7
Gere, C. 137
Gerlach, M. 55
Ghirshman, R. 59
Gibson, M. 7
Gignoux, P. 46, 47
Goebl, R. 48
Goldman-Schwartz, A. 103
Goldstein, S. 40, 114
Gonzales-Palacios, A. 131
Good, M.E. 116
Gorelick, L. 7, 141
Grabar, O. 101
Graham, K. 59
Gramatopol, M. 40
Grancière, A. de la 108
Greifenhagen, A. 64

Guarducci, M. 70
Guebelin, E. 142, 148
Guérard, M. 103
Gueterbock, H.G. 8
Guido, M. 75
Gurney, O.R. 10
Guyon, J. 72
Guzzo, P.G. 34
Gwinnett, A.J. 7, 8, 141
Gyselen, R. 47

Hackenbroch, Y. 52, 132
Hackens, T. 65
Haevernick, T.E. 91, 115
Hafner, G. 40
Hager, B. 142
Hahnloser, H. 97
Hamburger, A. 41
Hansmann, L. 97
Hardmeyer, B. 91
Harhoiu, R. 75
Harper, P.O. 48, 59, 101
Hartmann, A. 91
Haug, H. 121
Hauptmann von Gladiss, A. 103
Hayes, C.F. 115
Hayward, J.F. 122
Healy, J.F. 143
Hebing, C. 143
Hejj-Detari, A. 108
Hellenkemper, H. 76
Hendy, M.F. 87
Henig, M. 41, 112
Hestrin, R. 16
Heurgon, J. 70
Heuser, H.J. 133
Heuzey, L. 8
Higgins, R.A. 22, 65
Hinton, D. 81, 95, 97
Hoffmann, H. 22, 65
Holm, E. 115
Holme, C. 133
Holzer, H. 122
Homes-Fredericq, D. 8
Hornung, E. 19
Horster, G. 28
Hotel Drouot. 17, 28, 39, 70, 74
Houston-Smith, R. 8
Hrozny, B. 8
Hugger, P. 144

Huot, J.-L. 59
Hunt, L.B. 145

Ippel, A. 144

Jacob-Rost, L. 11
Janata, A. 108
Jazdewski, K. 144
Jenkins, M. 103
Johns, C. 76
Jones, W. 81
Joppien, R. 63
Jouin, J. 103
Junghans, S. 91, 92

Kaehler, H. 41
Kagan, J. 52
Kahlert, H. 133
Kalter, J. 108
Kalus, L. 47, 103
Karageorghis, G. 8
Karg, N. 8
Keene, M. 103, 104
Keim, J. 122
Kelley, C.W. 108
Kellner, H.-J. 122
Kenna, V.E.G. 16, 22, 23, 24
Kent Hill, D. 123
Kent, J.C.P. 123
Klumbach, H. 122
Kibaltchich, T.W. 41
Kilbride-Jones, H.E. 97
Kilian-Dirlmeier, I. 92
Kilian, K. 67
Koetzsche, D. 97
Kovacs, E. 87, 97
Kris, E. 39, 53
Kris-Rettenbeck, L. 97
Kroeger, J. 103
Krug, A. 41
Kubach, W. 92
Kubczak, J. 67
Kuehn, H. 98
Kuehne, H. 8
Kunz, G.F. 82

Laffineur, R. 23, 65, 66
Lagercrantz, O. 145
Lambert, M. 9
Latif, M. 109

Laufer, B. 123
Launois, A. 104
Laur-Belart, R. 123
Laux, F. 92
Lazovic, M. 88
Le Blant, E. 38
Le Brun, A. 9
Lefèvre-Pontalis, M.P. 109
Legrain, L. 9
Lemaire, A. 9
Lemaitre, J.-L. 53
Lerat, L. 76
Lerner, J. 48
Lesley, P. 53
Lévy, E. 66
Lewis, P. and E. 109
Lightbrown, R.W. 98
Lipinsky, A. 145
Lippold, G. 29
Loding, D. 9
Lovag, Z. 87
Lukonin, V.G. 46

Maaskant-Kleibrink, M. 29
MacGregor, M. 92
Malle, L. 98, 123
Manns, F. 88
Margain, J. 16
Markoe, G. 10, 59
Marquardt, B. 134
Marshall, F. 23
Martelli, M. 34
Martin, M. 76, 77
Martin, S. 76
Martini, W. 35
Masson, E. 10
Masson, O. 29
Matouk, F.S. 19
Matous, L. 10
Matousova-Rajmova, M. 10
Matousova, M. 10
Matthiae, P. 10
Matz, F. 124
Maxwell-Hyslop, K.R. 60
McDevitt, E. 105
McDonald, D. 145
Meany, A.L. 98
Meerwarth, A. 109
Melikian-Chirvani, A.S. 104
Menghin, W. 98

Merrill, G. 146
Mesnil du Buisson. 38
Metzger, C. 66
Meyers, P. 101
Michon, E. 77
Migeon, G. 104
Miller, S.G. 66
Millet, G. 88
Milojcic, V. 98
Moorey, R.S. 5, 10
Morton, A.H. 104
Muller, H. 99
Muller, J. 98
Muller, P.E. 134
Müller-Lancet, A. 104
Munn, G. 134, 135
Muscarella, O.W. 66
Muthmann, F. 135
Mutz, A. 144

Naumann, F. 77
Navarro, R. 92
Negahban, E.O. 125
Negbi, O. 60
Nègre, A. 105
Nesbitt, J. 50
Neverov, O. 29
Newberry, P.E. 19
Newman, H. 135
Niccacci, A. 19
Nicholls, R. 17
Niemeier, W.-D. 23
Ninou, K. 66
Nougayrol, J. 10
Novatna, M. 92
Noveck, M. 11

Oddy, W.A. 145
Ogden, J.M. 55, 146
Oliver, A. 63
Olson, E. 109
Oman, C.C. 82
Onassoglu, A. 23
Ondrejova, I. 77

Painter, K.S. 88, 123, 125
Parrot, A. 11
Pearce, S. 92
Pechstein, K. 125
Perry, R. 60

Persson, A.W. 23
Petochi, D. 135
Petrie, Sir, W.M.F. 20
Pfeiler, B. 77
Philipp, H. 42, 67
Philippe, J. 53
Pierides, A. 67
Pini, I. 24
Piperno, M. 12
Pisano, G.Q. 60
Platon, N. 24
Platz-Horster, G. 42
Pliny, G. 146, 147
Popovich, L. 40
Porada, E. 11, 47
Possehl, G. 116
Pottier, M.H. 47
Potter, T. 76
Pressmar, E. 82
Prokot, I. and J. 109

Quillard, B. 60

Raddatz, K. 67
Rademacher, F. 99
Radwan, I. 125
Ravn, O.E. 11
Rawlings, R.D. 135
Reinach, S. 29
Reineking-von Bock, G. 112
Rice, P.C. 112
Richter, G.M.A. 24, 30
Richter, I. 93
Righetti, R. 43
Riha, E. 78, 125
Rihovsky, J. 93
Ritz, G.M. 109
Rodgers, S. 110
Roesslin, E., The Younger. 147
Rosenberg, M. 147
Ross, H.C. 105
Ross, K. 110
Ross, M.C. 50
Rossi, F. 126
Rothenberg, B. 147
Rowe, D.F. 54, 126
Rudolph, W. and E. 78
Rutten, M. 11, 12
Ruxer, M.S. 67

Sadek, A.I. 148
Sakellarakis, J.A. 24
Sakellariou, A. 24
Sanidkidze, T. 99
Sapouna-Sakellaris, E. 67
Sarianidi, V. 61
Scandone, G.M. 17
Scarisbrick, D. 27, 30, 83, 136
Scarpignato, M. 35
Schaeffer-Forrer, C.F.A. 12
Scheffler, W. 126
Scherf, V. 26
Schienerl, P.W. 105
Schletzer, D. and R. 105
Schlumberger, G. 50
Schluter, M. 26
Schuler-Schoemig, I.von 110
Schumacher-Matthaeus, G. 93
Seefried, M. 116
Segall, B. 67
Shachar, I. 110
Shelton, K.J. 126
Sherman, A.C. 137
Sinkankas, J. 148
Siviero, R. 71
Six, J. 12
Smith, M. 116
Soler Garcia, J.M. 93
Somers Cocks, A. 54, 137
Sotheby's, London 54, 83, 89
Speleers, L. 12, 48
Staehelin, E. 19
Stenico, A. 43, 112
Stern, W.B. 125
Stillman, Y.K. 110
Story-Maskelyne, N.M.H. 30
Strong, D.E. 112, 127
Stuckert, R. 110
Sturm, F.X. 137
Sugier, C. 110
Svoboda, B. 68
Sychova, N. 111

Tait, H. 24, 54, 137
Tardy 148
Tassinari, S. 93
Taylor, G. 83
Taylor, J.J. 93
Teissier, B. 12
Tempelmann-Maczynska, M. 79

Thaplyal, K.K. 12
Thomsen, M. 111
Tillot, M. 17
Tosi, M. 12
Toynbee, J.M.C. 127
Truman, C. 54
Tual, A. 61
Tufnell, O. 17, 20
Tunca, Ö. 12

Van der Sleen, W.G.N. 117
Van Dievoet, W. 148
Veillard, J.-Y. 43
Vercoutter, J. 18
Vermeule, C.C. 30, 127
Vickers, M. 68
Vikan, G. 50
Vilimkova, M. 56
Vodoz, I. 20
Vollenweider, M.-L. 13, 18, 27, 31
von Beste 20
von Bothmer, D. 101
von Claer, V. 22
von Falke, O. 87
von der Osten, H.H. 13
von Hase, U. 132
von Solodkoff, A. 137

Ward, A. 83
Ward, W. 13, 17, 20
Weber, O. 13
Webster, L. 100
Weibel, M. 149
Weitschat, W. 112
Wels-Weyrauch, U. 93
Wentzel, H. 50
Werner, J. 79
Wesley Jernigan, E. 111
Williams, C.R. 56
Williams-Forte, E. 7
Williamson, G.C. 138
Wilson, D.M. 100
Winkes, R. 65
Winlock, H.E. 56
Winter, Jenson, A. 137
Woeiriot, P. 84
Wolters, J. 149

Xenaki-Sakellariou, A. 25

Yalouris, N. 68
Yon, M. 112
Younger, J.G. 25
Yule, P, 25

Zahlhaas, G. 45, 122
Zahn, R. 45
Zazoff, H. 138
Zazoff, P. 18
Zucker, B. 138
Zwalf, W. 145
Zwierlein-Diehl, E. 21, 25, 32

INDEX of MUSEUMS and INSTITUTIONS

(Page numbers refer to first occurrence of title issued by institution).

Ann Arbor. The University of Michigan Museum of Art. 101
Athens. Benaki Museum. 62, 85
Augst. Römermuseum. 76, 77, 78, 123

Baltimore. Museum of Art. 53
Baltimore. Walters Art Gallery. 55
Berlin. Aegyptisches Museum. 42
Berlin. Kunstgewerbemuseum. 97, 125
Berlin. Museum für Völkerkunde. 110
Berlin. Staatliche Museen preussischer Kulturbesitz. 21, 64
Berlin-East. Staatliche Museen zu Berlin. 11
Bloomington. Indiana University Art Museum. 38, 78
Bogota. Banco de la Republica. 106
Bonn. Rheinisches Landesmuseum. 42, 129
Boston. Museum of Fine Arts. 30, 127
Brooklyn. The Brooklyn Museum. 11, 19, 63, 65
Brussels. Musées Royaux d'Art et d'Histoire. 76, 98
Brussels. Musées Royaux du Cinquantenaire. 12
Budapest. Hungarian National Museum. 96

Cagliari. Museo Nazionale di Cagliari. 14, 17, 60
Cairo. Ethnographic Museum. 105
Cambridge. Fitzwilliam Museum. 17
Carthage. Musée Lavigerie. 3
Chicago. The Martin d'Arcy Gallery of Art. 54, 126
Cologne. Kunstgewerbe museum. 63
Cologne. Römisch-Germanisches Museum. 41, 63, 79
Cologne. Museum der Stadt Köln. 129
Copenhagen. Danish National Museum. 11
Corning. The Corning Museum of Glass. 40, 114

Dayton. The Dayton Art Institute. 108
Dijon. Musées d'Alise-Sainte-Reine. 76

Florence. Museo Mediceo. 39
Florence. Museo Nazionale del Borgello. 98
Frankfurt. Historisches Museum. 40

Geneva. Barbier-Müller Museum. 109
Geneva. Musée d'Art et d'Histoire. 13, 18, 20, 31, 88, 99
Grand Rapids. Grand Rapids Public Museum. 108

The Hague. The Hague Municipal Museum. 121
The Hague. Royal Coin Cabinet. 29
Hamburg. Museum für Kunst und Gewerbe. 22, 106
Hanover. Kestner Museum. 20, 37

Istanbul. Istanbul Archaeological Museum. 64
Istanbul. Topkapi Sarayi Museum. 105

Jerusalem. Museum of the Flagellation. 88
Jerusalem. The Israel Museum. 16, 103, 104, 110

Kassel. Staatliche Kunstsammlungen. 77

Leningrad. Hermitage Museum. 29, 46, 52
London. British Museum. 5, 23, 24, 46, 54, 55, 76, 88, 94, 95, 96, 100, 104, 112, 123, 125, 126, 137, 146
London. Burlington Fine Arts Club. 27
London. Victoria and Albert Museum. 82, 137
Los Angeles. Los Angeles County Museum of Art. 137

Madrid. Museo Arquelogico Nacional. 14
Mainz. Roemisch-Germanisches Zentral Museum. 73
München. Staatliche Münzsammlung, München. 21, 26

Naples. Museo Nazionale di Napoli. 34, 63
Newark. The Newark Museum. 64, 86, 109, 128
New Haven. Yale University Art Gallery. 5
New York. Asia House Gallery. 48
New York. Historical Society. 56
New York. The Metropolitan Museum of Art. 24, 30, 46, 52, 56, 59, 73, 101, 102, 103
Nicosia. Cyprus Museum. 67
Nuremberg. Germanisches National Museum. 131

Oberlin. Allen Memorial Art Museum. 77
Osnabrück. Naturwissenschaftliches Museum. 112
Oxford. Ashmolean Museum. 5, 10, 27, 68, 95, 97, 112

Paris. Bibliothèque Nationale. 21, 26, 39, 47, 95, 103, 105
Paris. Grand Palais. 40
Paris. Musée du Louvre. 55, 66, 118
Paris. Musée Guimet. 109
Paris. Musée National des Arts Africains. 103
Philadelphia. The University Museum. 30
Prague. Karls University. 10
Princeton. Art Museum. 34
Providence. Rhode Island School of Design. 65

Rennes. Musée de Rennes. 43
Rome. Musei Comunali di Roma. 43
Rome. Museo Gregoriano-Etrusco. 71
Rome. Museo Nazionale Romano. 72

Sofia. National Archaeological Museum. 39

Taipei. National Palace Museum. 10
Thessalonike. Thessalonike Archaelogical Museum. 66
Tübingen. Eberhard-Karls-Universität. 8
Turin. Museo Civico di Torino. 98, 123
Turin. Palazzo Chiablese. 60

Ussel. Musée du Pays d'Ussel. 53

Vatican City. Museo Sacro e Profano. 40, 43
Vienna. Kunsthistorisches Museum. 25, 32, 39

Washington, D.C. Dumbarton Oaks Collection. 50
Washington, D.C. Smithsonian Institution. 146